Catching Readers Before They Fall

Catching Readers Before They Fall

Supporting Readers Who Struggle, K–4

Pat Johnson and Katie Keier

Stenhouse Publishers
Portland, Maine

Stenhouse Publishers
www.stenhouse.com

Credits
Page 13: "Wash in the Street" from STREET TALK by Ann Turner. Text copyright © 1986 by Ann Turner. Reprinted by permission of Houghton Mifflin Harcourt Publishing Company. All rights reserved.
Page 120: Figure 7.1 © Fairfax County Public Schools. Used by permission.
Page 147: "When It Is Snowing," from *Color Poems* by Siv Cedering. Published by Calliopea Press. © Siv Cedering. Used by permission of Hans Van de Bovenkamp.
Page 161: "Forget-me-not" from *Poetry Matters: Writing a Poem from the Inside Out* by Ralph Fletcher. Copyright © 2002. Reprinted with permission of HarperCollins.
Page 176: From the July 2008 issue of *Ranger Rick* ® Magazine, with the permission of the publisher, the National Wildlife Federation ®.
Page 196: *Gilbert the Pig Goes on a Diet* by Michele Dufresne, © 2002 Pioneer Valley Books. Used by permission.
Pages 245 and 246: "How do snakes open their mouths so wide?" and "How come the moon seems to follow you when you move?" Reprinted by permission of Highlights for Children, Inc. Copyrighted material.

Library of Congress Cataloging-in-Publication Data
Johnson, Pat, 1950–
    Catching readers before they fall : supporting readers who struggle, K–4 / Pat Johnson, Katie Keier.
        p. cm.
    Includes bibliographical references and index.
    ISBN 978-1-57110-781-7 (alk. paper)
    1. Reading disability. 2. Reading comprehension. 3. Oral reading. 4. Slow learning children—Books and reading. I. Keier, Katie, 1970- II. Title.
    LB1525.76.J64 2009
    372.43—dc22
                                                                        2009045978

Cover, interior design, and typesetting by Martha Drury
Manufactured in the United States of America

PRINTED ON 30% PCW
RECYCLED PAPER

15 14 13 12 11 10   9 8 7 6 5 4 3 2

For my dad, James Matthews, whose kind spirit and generous nature taught me the importance of reaching out to those who struggle

PJ

To my parents, who taught me never to give up, to pursue my dreams, and that anything is possible

KK

CONTENTS

ACKNOWLEDGMENTS

Writing this book has been quite a learning journey for us. We are lucky to be surrounded by so many talented and reflective educators who always challenge us to deepen our thinking. And we are forever grateful for the love and support of family and friends. Without all of them, this book never would have happened.

We want to thank the many dedicated teachers who allowed us to use their names and experiences as we told their stories in this book. We thank them for sharing lessons with us, supporting our efforts, cheering us on, and giving us time to talk through various issues and conflicts that came up during the writing. Those marvelous teachers include: Barbara Anzalone, Tricia Brown, Kent Buckley-Ess, Carrie Cantillana, Rachel Coelho, Kara Conques, Tania Dedham, Gina Elliott, Kathleen Fay, Pat Fege, Carol Felderman, Susan Fullerton, Christy Hermann, Ann Mabry, Jodi Maher, Lisa Merkel, Steve Miner, Kassia Omohundro-Wedekind, Tess Pardini, Carleen Payne, Heather Petruzzini, Ada Prabhavat, Mary Schulman, Jessica Shumway, Marcela Vargas, Suzanne Whaley, and Marcela Zuniga.

Our teaching has been enriched because we have had the privilege of teaching children who openly share their cultures, traditions, and celebrations, as well as their struggles, as they become a part of our lives each school year. We thank them, especially the students of Bailey's Elementary School in Falls Church, Virginia, for making it possible for us to have such rewarding careers.

Writers need honest, critical feedback from colleagues they admire and respect as fellow teachers and fellow writers. For this we thank Kathleen Fay, Mary Schulman, Carleen Payne, Jennifer Allen, and Erin Trainer. Kath, we could always count on you to catch us when we thought we could read teachers' minds. You also saved us from embarrassing ourselves when we would get "that tone"; you helped make this a better book. Mary, you graciously praised our work and at the same time asked just the right questions to push our thinking. Carleen, with scissors and tape in hand, you saw the whole picture, no matter the chapter topic, and kept a watchful eye on our organization and attention to detail. We also thank Jennifer Allen for taking time out of her busy schedule of teaching, coaching, and writing to give us valuable feedback that helped us find our joint writing voice. To Erin Trainer, we thank you for helping us clarify our audience and connect the threads of our thinking through the chapters.

Our work rests on the strong foundations built by great literacy thinkers. Thanks to all those whose wise words fill our bookshelves and nightstands—Marie Clay, Carol Lyons, Lev Vygotsky, Peter Johnston, Frank Smith, Irene Fountas, Gay Su Pinnell, Linda Dorn, Carla Soffos, Ellin Keene, Sue

Zimmermann, Debbie Miller, Maria Nichols, Stephanie Harvey, Anne Goudvis, Franki Sibberson, Karen Szymusiak, Katie Wood Ray, Ralph Fletcher, Lucy Calkins, Shelley Harwayne, Nancie Atwell, Don Graves, Dick Allington, Regie Routman, Cris Tovani, Randy and Katherine Bomer, Jerome Harste, Vivian Vasquez, Sonia Nieto, Paulo Freire, and countless others.

We are indebted to our extraordinary editor, Philippa Stratton, whose feedback was always clear and concise, and who supported us in a kind and gentle manner. You believed we had something worthwhile to say even early on when the focus kept shifting. Thanks also to the other members of Stenhouse Publishers whose expertise helped shape this book: Chris Downey, Chandra Lowe, Erin Trainer, Anne Sauve, Jay Kilburn, and Martha Drury. We thank you for your dedication to providing quality professional literature for teachers and by teachers.

Our thanks wouldn't be complete without giving a nod to Panera bakeries, where we sat for hours, eating and writing, drinking iced tea and writing, gobbling cookies and writing, and writing some more.

From Pat:

I have been privileged to work in a county with an abundance of high-quality teachers, coaches, Reading Recovery trainers, language arts specialists, and administrators. Thanks to all those amazing educators with whom I have worked in Fairfax County Public Schools. Special thanks to my lifetime friends, colleagues, and fellow authors, Mary and Carleen, for all the good times at conferences, in schools, at reading teacher meetings, and just hanging out. No teacher could ask for two better mentors and friends.

Thanks to my niece, Kathleen Fay, who never looks back in education, but keeps all of us looking toward the future, striving to discover what else we can do to make literacy happen for every single child.

A boatload of thanks goes to my siblings and their spouses—Barb and Jim, Andy and Jeanie, Mary, Susan and John, Joanne and Sam—for always offering the perfect balance of love and support. I consider myself so lucky to be part of this enormous extended family. What fun to keep adding a new member every few months!

Katie, thanks for eagerly jumping aboard when I asked if you wanted to take this writing ride with me. It was such an honor to watch you teach and to work so closely with you and your wonderful students over these past few years. I am grateful for your boundless dedication to the teaching profession. Thanks for pushing me forward technology-wise and for all the great conversations about literacy.

To my daughters, Heather and Jodie, and their wonderful husbands—thanks for keeping me grounded, for loving me no matter what, and especially for giving me such amazing grandchildren. And thanks to Rick, my husband and best friend, for making me feel incredibly special. I love you every single day and then some.

From Katie:

Pat, what an honor it was to be asked by you to coauthor this book. Working with you I am continually challenged to think deeply about teaching reading to children. Thank you for your trust in me and for your ongoing support through this project. What a fabulous experience it has been!

Tania, thank you for introducing me to "Aunt Pat" many years ago. This book (and so many other things for me professionally) never would have happened without you persuading and encouraging me to move to the big city. You are always there for me as a listening ear and a lifelong friend.

Writing this book would not have been possible without the love and support of the many friends and family who believed in me and cheered me on throughout the process. I am grateful to my colleagues and administrators at all the schools where I have been fortunate to teach, and especially those at Bailey's Elementary—a professional learning community unlike any other. How fortunate I am to teach and learn with such an amazing group of educators. To Rosary Lalik and the literacy studies cohort at Virginia Tech, thank you for transforming my teaching life and inspiring me in so many endeavors. To all the families and children I have taught, you each have a special place in my heart. Thank you for all you have taught me.

When it seemed like every waking moment was spent on writing, I could always count on Ann for those much-needed early morning bike rides and breakfasts at Luna. Thank you for the support, book titles, laughs, listening, and happy diversions you provided. Kassia, thank you for always asking how it was going and for your wonderful sense of humor. You put a smile on my face every time we talked. Carol, from one writer to another, I could count on you to understand the ups and downs of this experience. Thank you for your listening ear and assurance that all was well. Julie, thank you for my happy place you provide so often and graciously. The King Resort was the perfect space for writing and your encouragement lifted my spirits every time we chatted. Rachel, thank you for letting me share your story of your first year teaching. You are a natural! Christy, thank you for your help in so many ways, for sharing many great ideas, and for your wonderful outlook on teaching. Christy, Carol, and Kassia—our Monday meeting of the minds was just what I needed to keep going this summer. Your dedication, thoughtfulness, and passion for teaching is so inspiring. I am lucky to be able to teach—and play—with you.

Thank you, Mom, Denny, and Kevin for understanding all those times when I had to write rather than visit. I am so grateful for a family that supports, loves, and encourages me. Thank you, Dad, for your support and confidence in me as a fellow educator.

And to Joseph, my partner and best friend, thank you for being there for me—no matter what. Your love and encouragement means the world to me. I couldn't have done this without you. It's now done! What's our next adventure?

CHAPTER 1

Expanding Our Paradigm of Reading

How many of us have lamented, "If I only knew then what I know now about teaching reading, I would have done such a better job of teaching so-and-so to read." There is no going back, of course, but thank goodness for all the research and understanding that has become available to us in the literacy field in recent years. If you could rewind to see us fifteen or more years ago, you would see some very different teaching going on. Just as we have made great gains in the past decades, so too have all teachers made changes in their thinking throughout their careers. And there's always room for more growth. We found that the more we layered our knowledge about reading process, the better equipped we became for teaching readers who struggle with that process.

We titled this book *Catching Readers Before They Fall* because we do not want any child to have to struggle with the process of learning to read. We strongly believe in the power of quality literacy instruction and effective early intervention that provides *safety nets* for readers who struggle. Although many safety nets (Reading Recovery, Leveled Literacy Intervention, Title I programs, and coaches or specialists who provide extra literacy instruction) already exist in some districts, we would argue that the strongest safety net of all is the classroom teacher.

There is no silver bullet when working with struggling readers. At times the teaching is quite challenging. Each child is a potential new puzzle, and we must remain active learners in order to solve these puzzles. We realize how hard teachers already work day in and day out. We hope to ease that load by sharing our knowledge about reading process and sharing our experiences with teaching struggling readers in the classroom. Our intent is that the information, scenarios, and examples in this book will broaden your vision of what reading process is and how it all comes together as children are learning to read. In turn, this will help you provide a safety net for catching the readers in your classroom before they fall.

Starting from What We Know and Believe

In Debbie Miller's recent book, *Teaching with Intention* (2008), she talks about teachers clarifying their beliefs and letting their practice flow from there. By doing this we teach with intention and purpose, know why we are doing what we do in our classrooms, and have direction and goals clear in our heads before we begin to teach.

We begin this book by presenting our beliefs about teaching reading to primary students, keeping struggling readers constantly in our minds since they are the most challenging of all.

We Believe

❋ By expanding one's knowledge of reading process in all its complexity, any teacher can increase his or her repertoire of teaching reading to children who struggle.

❀ A major problem for children who struggle is that they are not putting a reading process system together in their heads to help them read with understanding and fluency.

❀ Learning about reading process is done best by observing children *while* they read, by talking with colleagues, and by reflecting on our own reading process.

❀ Knowing *how to teach*, that is, using explicit modeling and gradual release of responsibility, is just as important as the literacy knowledge we acquire.

❀ It is important to be aware of our language and a child's response to it in order to teach effectively.

❀ Observation and assessment should drive our instruction as we build on students' known skills and strategies in order to help them integrate new learning.

❀ Classrooms should be incredibly safe places where every student feels respected and valued; where it's okay to make a mistake; and where it's acceptable by all to have strengths and weaknesses that may be different from other students in the classroom community.

We realize this is a long list. Believe us when we say we really did cut it down!

A funny thing happened when we listed our beliefs that build the foundation of this book. Despite several months of daylong conversations about what to include in our book and which examples we would use to illustrate certain points, it was when we sat down to write out our beliefs that we realized—*this is it*! This is what we want our book to say to teachers.

A Few Dos and Don'ts for Reading This Book

Teachers talking and learning together is what energizes and motivates us to do our best work with children. By remaining lifelong learners, we all risk making ourselves vulnerable. At times, grappling with new ideas or living with unanswered questions is what helps us grow and become better teachers of reading. Occasionally we even have to question what we've always believed to be true. As you begin our book, we hope you feel the same. We would like to offer a few dos and don'ts to encourage you to read on:

❀ Do construct your own theory of how children learn to read as you make your way through our text. Keep your theory tentative, since it will change as you acquire new thoughts and gain new insights while teaching your students, struggling readers, or otherwise.

❀ Don't back off because you heard the words "complex theory" or "reading process." Paulo Freire (2005) tells us to have courage and face our fears. "One of the most dreadful mistakes we can possibly make as we study, either as students or as teachers, is to retreat before the first obstacle we face" (52).

❋ Do share your thinking with others as you read this text. When you try explaining what you are learning to someone else, you will *own* the information more concretely.

❋ Don't think that because we said "theory," there won't be plenty of practical information to take to your own classrooms. There will be. One of our goals is to present reading process theory clearly so you can see how it translates to your work with children. In so doing, we hope this also aids you as you communicate with parents about reading.

❋ Do reflect on our examples and see if you can find a similar example with a student in your class. The more connections you make to real children, the easier it will be to grasp theoretical concepts.

❋ Do keep trying to develop *teaching stamina.* The struggling readers in your classroom need you desperately. We know it's difficult and we know you can do it.

How This Text Is Organized

In Chapters 2, 3, and 4, we will lay some foundations. Using both adult and student examples, Chapter 2 presents what it means to develop a reading process system. An important graphic depicting aspects of a reading process system (Figure 2.1) can be found on the inside back cover. Chapter 3 elaborates on the ways we support children building their reading process systems, for example, working within a child's zone of proximal development and teaching with explicit modeling and gradual release of responsibility. In Chapter 4 you will get an explanation of how readers solve words using all the sources of information available to them. You'll also read concrete examples of how to model, prompt, and assess children as they learn to use a balance of these information sources.

The next two chapters, 5 and 6, describe the kind of classroom environment that lends itself well to supporting all students as they build their reading process systems. Special attention is paid to how each context can benefit struggling readers.

Following that, we propose some lesson ideas for supporting children as they take on various strategic actions and behaviors. Chapter 7 focuses on the teaching that we do with beginning struggling readers and the earliest strategies they need to get under way, and Chapters 8 and 9 expand upon the comprehension strategies and how to help children integrate their network of strategies.

Although there are lots of assessment ideas woven throughout the entire text, Chapter 10 highlights some important points about ongoing assessment and explains in detail one teacher's method for organizing and using her assessment data.

Chapter 11 offers answers to commonly asked questions from parents, colleagues, and others involved with the teaching of reading. You'll probably recognize some of these questions. The information you share with others can broaden their vision of reading process and, in the end, will benefit readers who struggle.

A note about pronouns. We will use *we*, meaning Katie Keier and Pat Johnson, throughout this text, because writing together was truly a joint endeavor. Occasionally we will use our names and third-person pronouns for a specific lesson or personal experience that one of us had. Also, when referring to a student or teacher, we will sometimes alternate between *he* and *she* to be as inclusive as possible.

Postcards to Professionals

Though we have chosen to write to teachers of grades K–4, there are certainly others who may benefit from this text. The following postcards include a few ideas about what you can find in our book based on your present position in the education field.

Because Katie works in a highly diverse school, you will see how she and others plan and carry out instruction to meet the needs of these challenging learners. You'll watch them make decisions about assessment, plan shared and guided reading lessons, choose books for reading aloud, support connections to writing, and much more. You'll witness them implementing ideas into their classrooms to maximize students' purposeful talk about texts.

To classroom teachers and special education teachers:

If your job involves facilitating literacy learning alongside teachers, this book can support you in finding the language you seek to explain reading process. By using our book as a teachers-as-readers or study group text, you could facilitate discussions on the topic of supporting struggling readers as they build a reading process system. It is only through conversations that we construct the understandings necessary to teach struggling readers. We encourage you to add your own stories of working with children to our examples. (A Study Guide for this book can be found at www.Stenhouse.com)

To literacy coaches or reading teachers:

This text will help you build on your mentee's knowledge base in a way that will not overwhelm the newcomer. The interactions we have had with teachers will give you some concrete ideas on how to scaffold those who are new to the profession. As you read our interactions with children, feel free to use them as examples to spur on "real talk about real kids."

To any teacher who mentors first-year teachers or student teachers:

Many principals and assistant principals want updated information about literacy. Learning more about reading process will help you continue to be a strong literacy leader. The knowledge you gain in the areas of assessment, comprehension, and reading instruction will give you a lens with which to observe and support the teachers in your school. This text will <u>not</u> give you quick fixes or bandwagons to jump on (you're not that type anyway, right?), but will help you stay focused on the goal of making literacy attainable for all of your school's population.

To administrators:

_____

_____

_____

_____

If you've ever drawn a blank when talking to parents about reading or you struggle to make yourself understood when talking with colleagues, this book may help you find the language to answer some of their questions. And it may even help you with that random literacy question you are confronted with at a cocktail party or neighborhood barbecue!

To all educators:

_____

_____

_____

_____

CHAPTER 2

How Reading Works

I n a school nearby, teachers are using the reading basal series that their school adopted for all the elementary grades. It has a scope and sequence chart for each grade level. For the most part, teachers follow the manuals, here and there adding ideas of their own. Many of the students are learning to read just fine, *but some are struggling and falling behind.*

At another elementary school, the teachers use a literature-based, individualized reading program. The classrooms are filled with books and the children choose books to read daily. Teachers teach lessons on phonics, fluency, and comprehension. Many of the students are learning to read just fine, *but some are struggling and falling behind.*

At a third location, the first- through fifth-grade teachers use a computerized reading program. The children read leveled books and answer comprehension questions on the computer. The computer-generated scores guide the teachers as they move children through the levels. Many of the students are learning to read just fine, *but some are struggling and falling behind.*

At yet another school, several primary teachers and their special education colleagues primarily use the phonics kits that were bought for their classrooms. They supplement these kits by reading aloud daily to the class and by taking the children to the school library to choose books. Many of the students are learning to read just fine, *but some are struggling and falling behind.*

Last, primary teachers at another school use a balanced literacy approach to teach reading. Among other things, they model skills with shared reading of Big Books or poems on charts. They divide children into groups and have small guided reading sessions daily. Many of the students are learning to read just fine, *but some are struggling and falling behind.*

Do any of these classrooms sound familiar to you? Though the schools we've described are fictional, schools like these do exist in actuality all over the country. There seem to be many paths to successful reading. Millions of children are learning to read in all different kinds of programs, with all different kinds of books and materials, with all sorts of different teachers and teaching styles, *but some are not.* It's those struggling readers who are continually falling behind that concern us the most.

Why Aren't All Kids Successful Readers?

The children who are not learning to read are often confused, frustrated, and slowly giving up hope on themselves as readers. They struggle to do what seems to come so easily and naturally to their classmates. Why don't we have the answer for these students? With all of the extensive literacy research and brilliant literacy educators, why do we still have children who are struggling to learn to read?

Part of the problem, as we see it, is twofold. First, struggling readers are not doing the kinds of thinking that proficient readers do in their heads as they read. They have not learned ways to fix errors or even to recognize when they have made an error. In other words, they are not constructing a reading process system in their heads to make meaning from texts and solve problems as their nonstruggling classmates are doing. Second, many teachers have not had the opportunity to learn about how reading works, that is, how a child constructs a reading process system in his or her own head. Oftentimes there is not enough room in the literacy curriculum of undergraduate and graduate programs to properly prepare teachers to teach reading to children who struggle.

Elementary teachers from second grade up often start the school year with students who already read, and therefore, they do not give much thought to how reading actually begins. They attribute the progress of their students to what they do daily during their reading instruction time. Some teachers surmise that if most of their students are successful, it must be a result of the program or materials they are using, as if there is a direct cause-and-effect relationship. "After all," they might conclude, "if most of our kids are learning to read this way, the program must be effective."

If this were actually true, it would mean that in each case the *children* who are not learning to read must be at fault, not the program or the teaching methods. There must be something about their brains—a deficit or disability—keeping them from learning to read. And so, what often happens? Those children are tested, given a label, and some of us no longer feel responsible for them. We try to make ourselves believe, "It's not our fault. There was something wrong with those kids; the tests have proven it!"

Are you satisfied with that scenario? We're not. We are very much opposed to the deficit model that blames the child for his or her reading difficulties. If struggling readers are not learning how to read, then we need to look at ourselves and our teaching, searching harder and longer to discover how to teach them better. All children (except perhaps the 1 percent with severe neurological problems) can learn to read, though not all at the same pace (Clay 2001). Carol Lyons agrees, saying, "Every child is capable of learning given the right opportunities, context, and assistance" (2003, 56).

Our own action research, ongoing professional development, reading of professional texts, and years of experience have led us to believe that the reason many children learn to read, no matter the particular methods and materials, is because *something else* is going on in the heads of these readers alongside the teaching they are being exposed to. That *something else* is that they are developing a way of thinking that enables them to make meaning when they read and helps them when they get stuck. Readers who have developed a thinking system—a reading process system—often do the following:

❋ Keep a constant check on themselves and think about what they are reading

❋ Notice when their reading doesn't sound right, or look right, or make sense

* Stop when something doesn't seem quite right and take action
* Use a variety of strategies, behaviors, and strategic actions to fix up their errors and confusions

And what's most interesting is that these readers seem to be developing this thinking system, or repertoire of strategies, *regardless of the way they are being taught.*

The act of reading involves making meaning out of the printed page. Lucy Calkins (2005) once said at a conference, "Reading is thinking guided by print." The print is nothing more than black marks on a paper. But proficient readers are able to take all those black marks and make sense of them. Proficient readers are not merely calling word after word correctly, but rather are actively working to comprehend what the author has written.

Occasionally even proficient readers get stuck while reading. They come across words they are unable to read automatically, vocabulary words they are not familiar with, or sentences or phrases that are confusing to them. But most readers have developed ways to notice when they are getting confused, and they stop themselves. They try a variety of strategies to help solve the problems they encounter. That is their reading process system at work. What is this thinking system they've constructed to assist them when they get stuck? We go deeper into explaining a reading process system of strategies later in this chapter. But first let's be clear about what is happening, or rather *not* happening, for the struggling reader.

The struggling reader, no matter what grade the child is in, has *not* built an efficient reading process system to make meaning from texts or help him or her solve problems when stuck. Struggling readers often wait for someone else to intervene, or substitute words that don't make sense, or do nothing when they come to a tricky word or a difficult passage. They don't realize that they have or can develop some strategic actions for solving their own problems. These children desperately need teachers who understand that a reading process system must be constructed by each individual. For teachers, that means learning how to teach *in support of* the child as he or she gains more control of strategic actions.

This theory of reading is complex. It is much more than merely learning letters, sounds, and sight vocabulary. Although about 80 percent of children learn to read just fine with a variety of programs, there are still 20 percent who struggle (Clay 2001, Allington 2005). In order to advocate for these struggling readers, we believe that more teachers need to become knowledgeable about the reading process and how to support children as they construct a network of strategies. It is our hope that this book will support you in that learning journey.

Before we offer our definition of what a reading process system is, we would first like you to view your own system at work. Then, we will take a look at some children's systems in action. This will give you experiences for grounding our explanation of a reading process system.

Notice Your Own Reading Process at Work

One of the best ways to gain understanding of reading as a processing system is to notice your own system at work. Read the following poem. Once you comprehend it on a literal level, try going a bit deeper. Think about why the author might have chosen to write this poem. Is she trying to send a message?

Wash in the Street
Ann Turner

I pass 'em
on my way to school
dumped like wash
in the street:
Gus and Bones and Sleepy
Maria

scrunched up on a bench
all their flapdoodle on—
gray, wrinkled socks,
a jacket drabby loose,
hats knit by trembly hands.

Once in a bus station I saw
a woman dressed like an opera,
a red turban on her head.
She sang so loud the pipes
hummed,
washing her purple feet
in the sink.

And people smile
or not
edge by like they're a dog
about to shake out all
its wet.
(1986)

Here is what happened as Pat read the poem. When she first saw the title "Wash in the Street," she thought of two images. One was of laundry draped on a line between apartment buildings in the early 1900s in New York City. The other was of kids washing or playing in the city street in front of an open fire hydrant. How quickly those predictions were revised as soon as she read the first stanza and realized the poem was about homeless people. Having seen many such people in Washington, DC, and New York City, she could agree with the narrator that, indeed, a sleeping homeless person might appear to be a pile of laundry lying next to a building.

Try a similar activity with your staff or grade-level team to help each teacher feel his or her reading process system at work.

- Pick a poem or short vignette. (The Library of Congress's Poetry 180 Web site, www.loc.gov/poetry/180/, gives possibilities for poems to use.)
- Have participants read, paying attention to what they are doing as they read, and talk about their comprehension.
- Then ask them to discuss with partners how they arrived at their understanding. Were there places in the text where they could pinpoint their strategies at work?
- Share ideas.

By the second stanza she was getting a clear picture in her mind because of the many connections she was making to her prior knowledge of the homeless. But she began to wonder, Who is the narrator of this poem? Is this a child or an adult speaking? A child could walk to school, but so could a teacher. Who would be more likely to know the names of the people—Gus and Bones and Sleepy Maria? Or were these just names the narrator gave to those she saw each day? Pat also wondered as to the setting of this poem. Background knowledge told her it was definitely a big city. Los Angeles? New York? Chicago? Miami? Washington, DC?

With the third stanza a few of her questions were answered. "Trembly hands" and "purple feet" indicated a cold city, so she ruled out Los Angeles and Miami. Also the unusual use of the word *opera* made her think that the narrator was a child who wasn't quite sure what an opera was, but maybe had once seen a billboard picture.

The last stanza threw her for just a split second (why is she talking about dogs?), but after rereading it, she understood the analogy. She knows what it's like to step back from a dog that just had a bath. And she could envision how people walk around the homeless person on the street, swinging out in a half circle, not knowing whether to look or not look, smile or frown.

Upon completing this poem Pat reflected for a moment. What else is the poet trying to say? Perhaps Ann Turner is suggesting that as a society we don't treat homeless people with much respect, that we don't think of them as people, but as piles of dirty laundry. Did she present this poem through the eyes of a child for a reason, as if the child is asking, "Why aren't the homeless treated better? They are people too." The innocent observation of a child about how we all walk wide circles around the homeless makes a reader stop and think.

When Pat shared these ideas in a workshop once, a teacher spoke up and said, "I'm not sure I did all that thinking like you did. It seems to me like I just read it and understood it." She's absolutely right. Since you are all proficient readers, you probably understood this poem simultaneously to reading the words. Most of what you did was subconscious. If you did make any connections, visualize, or question anything (as we explained) you did those things so automatically without much attention to what you were doing. *Comprehension is thought.* And thought is much quicker than slowing it down and explaining it all in words as we explained Pat's experience.

But we described Pat's reading process in words for a reason—so that we could deconstruct what happens in the brain as we read and be able to talk about it. Having conversations with colleagues about our own reading process and naming the strategic actions so that we can discuss them is a way of raising the awareness level of teachers of reading. By slowing down Pat's reading process for you, we were able to identify some of the strategies she used as she read this poem. That's exactly the reason Keene and Zimmermann in *Mosaic of Thought* (1997) and Harvey and Goudvis in *Strategies That Work* (2000) name the comprehension strategies—to give teachers a way to talk about the process. This deconstruction of comprehension allows us to think and talk about what we actually do as we make meaning from a text.

The danger of deconstructing comprehension is that it may appear as though there is a set way of comprehending or that it can be broken into distinct pieces. *What happens in the brain as a person reads is much more complex than our description of how Pat understood this poem.* However, finding ways to talk about comprehension is beneficial to all of us who work with the hardest-to-teach children. Many struggling readers think that reading is a matter of calling the words accurately. It is much more than that. Reading is making meaning. Struggling readers do not realize the kind of thinking that is going on as a person reads. How can we help students who are not comprehending as they read if we can't talk about, model, and make visible for them what it is that a proficient reader does?

If struggling readers are *not* building their own network of strategies, that is, a reading process system, then the big question is, "How do I teach a child to construct this reading process system?" The teacher/student examples in this book are intended to help with ways to answer that question. It is difficult to learn this in a day or with one book. We hope to get you started so that you take an interest in acquiring the necessary tools and techniques to support struggling readers. Keep your own students in mind as you read and discuss parts of this book with colleagues.

A Child's System at Work

In the previous section you got to feel and think about what it was like to put your reading process system to work as you read a poem. Now let's turn our attention to children. In order to recognize struggling readers who are *not* building a reading process system, it's beneficial to start observing children who have efficient working systems. What might that look like? Let's take a look at a few children as their reading process systems go to work.

Angie

As second grader Angie read the book *Henry and Mudge, The First Book* (Rylant 1987), she had long stretches of fluent reading. Her reading sounded smooth, she grouped words into phrases, and she paid attention to punctuation. She also laughed at appropriate points and made comments about the story as she turned pages. These facts provide evidence that she comprehended what she read. We know that she was self-monitoring because on several occasions she stopped and fixed up an error she made. One self-correction looked like this:

Text: "I want to live on a different street," he told his parents.
Angie: I want to live on a d . . . dif . . . di . . . I want to live on a dusty street. No . . . d . . . er . . . ent. "I want to live on a different street," he told his parents.

This self-correction illustrates how Angie is willing to make multiple attempts at a word. In other words, she is flexible with her problem solving. First she tried to sound out the beginning letters, then she reread the sentence and tried a word that made sense. She said, "No" when she realized the letters weren't quite right. So she made another attempt at searching the print and she saw parts she recognized. Finally, on another reread of the sentence, she was able to put in the correct word. All of this problem solving happened quickly.

Angie was focused on making meaning as she read this story. When we think about all that Angie was doing—laughing, making connections, self-correcting her errors, reading fluently—we realize that she was using her system of strategies in an *integrated* way. She wasn't just practicing one strategy but rather was using a number of them all at once. Angie predicted words, searched the print, maintained fluency, made connections, and made inferences.

Dawson

Third grader Dawson was enjoying a nonfiction book about snakes. We listened to an individual reading conference that he was having with his teacher, Kara Conques.

Kara: How's your reading going? Are you picking up some good information about snakes?
Dawson: Yeah, I'm reading now about the boa constrictor. (*Shows the teacher the picture of the boa.*)
Kara: (*In a teasing voice, recites a line from a Shel Silverstein poem.*) "Oh, I'm being eaten by a boa constrictor."
Dawson: That couldn't happen.
Kara: What do you mean?
Dawson: They don't eat people. Here . . . let me find . . . Wait. (*Searches text and then reads.*) "Boa constrictors are not aggressive toward humans."
Kara: Oh. So what does that sentence mean to you, that they are not aggressive?

Dawson: I know they wouldn't attack because . . . this one time . . . we were at the Wildlife WorldZoo and they didn't put glass on the cage.

Kara: Tell me more.

Dawson: You know how they have snakes behind glass in those places. Well, we came to the boa constrictor and he was in there but you could put your hand right in the cage, but you weren't supposed to touch the snake. The sign said if it was well fed and comfortable, then he wouldn't come out or attack people. See, that's 'cause he's not aggressive.

Kara: Hmm. That's interesting. (*She glances down at the page and notices another sentence.*) Read this part to me.

Dawson: "Some South Americans keep boa constrictors in their houses to control rat infestations." See, I told you so.

To comprehend this text, Dawson used background knowledge, made connections, picked up important information, and made an inference about what the word *aggressive* meant. He used these various thinking processes *simultaneously,* which helped to keep his mind focused on the information presented in the text.

Students in a Guided Reading Group in First Grade Use Their Systems

A group of four children worked with Katie on an emergent-level text about several animals that were having trouble fitting into a van. Notice all the thinking these students did to make meaning of this simple patterned text.

All: "Here is Monkey. Monkey is in the van."

Antoni: Hey, I think they are going to the beach! He's got those glasses on! I wear those when I go to the pool.

Katie: Oh, yes! The goggles. Do you all see them? What are the rest of you thinking?

Cindy: Everyone wants to go to the beach.

Jose: There are too many animals. Maybe some gotta stay home.

Katie: Let's keep reading on our own and see if we can find out.
(*The students continue reading, commenting on the pictures and making predictions about the animals fitting in the van.*)

Antoni: Look! I told you they were going to the beach. (*He points to a page where there is a beach bag overflowing with snorkels, flippers, and an umbrella.*)

Jose: And Georgie Giraffe is carrying the bag. They *have* to make room for him. He has all the fun stuff!

Jackie: Hey! We got one of those! (*Pointing to the sunroof in the picture.*) My car has a hole too. Sometimes my mom opens it when it's warm outside. We're not allowed to stick our hands out.

(*They get to the last page, where they see Baby Giraffe sticking his long neck out of the sunroof.*)

Antoni: That's where he fit! I knew they would fit him in.

Katie: Now they can all go to the beach!

The children truly enjoyed this simple story. They were predicting, making connections, questioning, and inferring as they read this emergent-level text. The first graders were beginning to put together a reading process system and clearly understood that meaning is at the heart of reading. After the lesson, Katie sent the children off to read the book one more time by themselves to feel the flow of the whole story together without interruptions.

The three examples above show students using their network of strategies to make meaning out of print. Examples like these open our minds to grasping what reading process is all about.

Unlike the students in these examples, struggling readers often do not understand what they read. They do not make connections or inferences, form images in their minds, or ask questions about the text. They often don't make attempts to solve tricky words or fix up mistakes. *They do not have an efficient reading process system.* What needs to be done if a student is not showing evidence that he or she is constructing an efficient system for reading? Modeling, thinking aloud, and doing shared demonstrations are a few ways we begin to make our thinking visible for struggling readers. Throughout this book, we will give examples of lessons with ideas about how to support readers who struggle.

What Is a Reading Process System?

Figure 2.1 shows one possible way to describe the network of strategies necessary for reading. A copy of this figure can also be found on the inside back cover for easy access as you read this book. Keep in mind how difficult it is to put the complex processing of the brain into words. Take a moment to examine this circular chart. For a more detailed explanation of each of the terms around the circle, go to Appendix 1. There we have defined each word and given examples of what it looks like or sounds like when a teacher or child uses the strategy.

To visualize how reading process works (in other words, what might be happening in the brain as a child reads), imagine drawing lines among all the words around the circle in Figure 2.1, crisscrossing and connecting them all. This web that you have created illustrates how interconnected the thinking strategies are and what reading process is. As a person reads, she may *visualize* what is happening in the text at the same time as she is *predicting* what might happen next and still, at the same time, she may be *inferring* what the character is feeling. Several thinking processes are going on concurrently in the head of the reader as she makes meaning of the story; this is a reading process system at work.

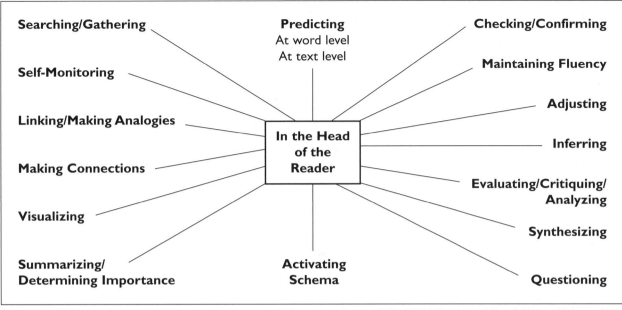

Figure 2.1
Reading Process System

Adapted from Schulman 2006, Fountas and Pinnell 2001, and Johnson 2006.

Even a beginning reader (who is not struggling) uses multiple thinking processes at once. He s*earches and gathers* information from a variety of sources to figure out the words. At the same time, he *self-monitors* to make sure the words he has chosen look right, sound right, and make sense. He may read a familiar text with *fluency*, but then *adjust* his pace and slow down in order to solve a problem.

As you study the circle chart in Figure 2.1 you may wonder, "Where's the phonics? Isn't the skill of knowing your letters and sounds a big part of this whole reading picture?" Absolutely. Phonics is woven throughout many of these strategies. For example, a child *predicts* a word by using some letter/sound information; she needs phonetic information to *check and confirm*; she is constantly *making analogies and linking* parts of words; and she *self-monitors* whether the words she is reading look right.

Some teachers teach phonics as a list of items in isolation, while others incorporate phonics into authentic reading and writing experiences. We recommend the latter for readers who struggle, because the phonics teaching is then part of the whole network of strategies. Struggling readers are often children who have stockpiled some item information (letters, sounds, sight vocabulary, and phonics rules), but don't know how to apply that information when reading continuous text. When you teach with reading process understanding, you will guide your students not only to acquire item information but also to learn how to use all the item information to gain meaning from texts. We will explore this in more depth in Chapter 4 and again in Chapters 7 and 8.

Integration of the Strategies

The following definitions of reading process come from well-known experts in the literacy field.

> *Reading is a complex process involving a network of cognitive actions that work together to construct meaning.* (Dorn and Soffos 2005, 6)

> *A literacy processing system is an integrated set of strategic actions by which readers extract and construct meaning from written language.* (Fountas and Pinnell 2006, 13)

> *The child is building a processing network that will deal with literacy tasks. He has to learn the letters and the words, and their relationship to sound, but he also has to build and expand the intricate interacting systems in the brain that must work together at great speed as he reads text.* (Clay 2005b, 102)

We want to draw your attention to a salient point that is common to all of these statements. The key to these three definitions is *integration*, or *working together*. Frequently we become so focused on learning the names and definitions of the strategies that make up the system (questioning, inferring, visualizing, etc.) that we overlook this integration. Looking only toward the strategies may cause us to be misled. We begin thinking that we can itemize those strategic actions, teaching them one at a time to students until they have acquired them all. Some schools have even divided the teaching of the comprehension strategies among grade levels. But it is the *integration,* or using them all together from the very beginning, that is crucial if students are to comprehend and read fluently.

As we begin to understand reading process, we not only need to learn about the in-the-head strategies that readers use but also must direct our attention to the *integration* factor. Without understanding integration, we risk missing the whole point.

For now, let us present a useful analogy to illustrate how a reading process system works. Many researchers have likened the network of strategies to an orchestra (Clay 2005b, Fountas and Pinnell 2006, Smith 2005, Lyons 2003). In a symphony orchestra, all the instruments blend to form incredible compositions extremely pleasing to the ear. The strategies in the head of the reader combine to make meaning of the text just as each instrument joins the musical composition perfectly in tune with the others. The Dana Foundation, as quoted in Clay, says, "Literacy involves lots of brain parts working together as a symphony and some learning is about how to feed new minor parts into the ongoing symphony" (Dana Foundation, in Clay 2005b, 102).

For the struggling reader, there is little or no orchestrated symphony of strategies going on. What is happening is more like cacophony! Have you ever been early to the symphony and heard the musicians warming up? The sounds coming from the instruments are not blended or working in smooth harmony. It's just noise. The struggling reader who has not constructed a reading process system has a head full of unrelated items bumping into each other, but not connecting or integrating. In other words, just noise.

The Process Is the Same for Everyone

In *Teaching for Deep Comprehension* (Dorn and Soffos 2005), the authors share how the process of writing is the same no matter what level writer you are. They compare the process a first grader goes through while writing a fairy tale with that of a college student writing a research paper. The same type of comparison can be done with reading process.

Imagine three students reading three different texts:

- A first grader reading a nonfiction book about penguins called *Amazing Penguins!*
- A fourth grader reading *Shiloh* by Phyllis Reynolds Naylor, a fiction chapter book
- A high school junior reading Shakespeare's *Hamlet*

All three of these students will need to do the following:

- Recognize words; figure out others
- Predict the meanings of certain vocabulary words by searching and gathering information from context, background knowledge, and other sources
- Keep a constant check to make sure what they are reading makes sense
- Use fix-up strategies when they get confused
- Activate prior knowledge and combine that information with the words of the author to derive meaning
- Make connections to other books or prior knowledge
- Attend to punctuation
- Group words into phrases
- Think about the character's feelings or thoughts (fiction) or the new information presented in the text (nonfiction)
- At times, visualize or question what they are reading
- Infer the meaning of a word or phrase, or infer what the author meant in a particular section
- Think about what they know about the structure of this text—nonfiction for the first grader, fiction for the fourth grader, and drama for the high school student
- Critique and evaluate—decide whether they like or dislike the text, agree or disagree with the information, would recommend it to others, or

would choose to read another book on the same topic or by the same author and so on

Refer back to the circle chart in Figure 2.1 and compare it with this list. Though their comprehension may have differed in range and depth because of the complexity of the text, can you see that each of the readers used an *integrated system of strategies* to understand the text?

All readers—and that includes students with learning disabilities—use the same reading process.

> *The reading and writing processes are the same for all learners. Labeled learners may have less facility with the process, may not understand what they should be doing as they read, or may have difficulty understanding the language used in books, but they do not use different processes (as they read and write) than do unlabeled learners.* (Gilles 1992, 62)

Important Points About a Reading Process System

❋ *A reading process system is composed of a multitude of strategies.* We have listed many strategies in Figure 2.1, but there are most likely even more.

❋ *Strategies are in-the-head thinking.* We can never really know exactly what happens in the head of a reader while he or she reads, but we can infer certain thinking processes are happening based on the behaviors we observe.

❋ *Every reader constructs his or her own system.* A teacher cannot put a strategy into a child's head, nor can a teacher tell a child how to integrate the strategies into a working system.

❋ *The integration of the strategic actions is crucial.* The strategies overlap, interconnect, and support each other.

❋ *The goal of a fluent reader is for the strategies to work quickly and flexibly.* Though a beginning reader's process may operate slowly at times, the goal is for it to increase in efficiency until many of the strategic actions are performed automatically.

❋ *The reader solves problems by dipping into his or her repertoire of strategies in different ways.* Each time a child gets stuck when reading, he or she may solve the problem by different means. There is no set way. How the system is used to make meaning or solve a problem differs from reader to reader and from situation to situation.

❋ *The system becomes stronger the more it is put to use.* For a reading process system to work proficiently, children need time to read often in books that are neither too easy nor too hard. By putting their system to work, that is, using strategies to make meaning of print and to solve difficulties, their network of strategies will become stronger and stronger.

The Case for Early Intervention

Mary Ann Poparad from the Illinois Reading Recovery Center stressed in a workshop how important it is to be "early rather than late." Too often, struggling readers plod through the early grades falling further and further behind. We let them spend years deepening confusions, practicing inappropriate reading behaviors, and gathering random bits of knowledge without any integration of those skills into a functional reading process system. Think about the child who continues to make an *s* backward or confuses *b* and *d* for years, the child who thinks "sound it out" is the only way to read words, or the child who reads word by word without any fluent phrasing. The more they practice their habit, the more difficult that problem is to correct.

Carol Lyons tells us that recent brain research has shown "that the brain is highly plastic and capable of reorganizing and rebuilding itself. Furthermore, the evidence strongly suggests that the earlier children are provided help, the quicker they will catch up to their peers and learn from regular classroom instruction" (2003, 172).

Doesn't it stand to reason that an *early intervention program* or a *knowledgeable teacher* would benefit such children? The earlier we can clear up confusions, the better.

An Early Intervention Program

After years of research working with proficient and struggling readers, Marie Clay developed Reading Recovery as an early intervention program. Reading Recovery teachers train extensively to work with the lowest 20 percent of children in first grade. They provide thirty-minute daily lessons to individual children. The majority (75 percent) of students reach grade level standards in just twelve to twenty weeks. Reading Recovery has had amazing results worldwide. Tens of thousands of teachers have been trained, and 1.7 million first graders have become successful readers, having accelerated their learning to reach the average reading level of their classmates. It should be noted that these numbers also include children who are labeled learning disabled.

The What Works Clearinghouse, an independent review of research, stated that "no other intervention has such an extensive research base and has demonstrated such strong results" (2008). What Works gave Reading Recovery high ratings across all four areas that they rate:

* Alphabetics
* Fluency
* Comprehension
* General Reading Achievement

Though Reading Recovery has a framework for how the lessons proceed for thirty minutes, the lesson itself is not the main contributor to the program's success. *It is much more about teachers learning a new way of thinking about reading, a way of understanding reading process.* Because of that understanding, they are able to assess students with the lens of an integrated system of strategies. That assessment helps them plan and carry out lessons that are tailored to the individual needs of each student.

A Knowledgeable Teacher

Though Reading Recovery has shown remarkable success with at-risk readers in first grade, it is not available in every school district at this point in time. Nor did Clay intend this one-on-one pull-out intervention program to be implemented with any but the most struggling 20 percent of students. We wholeheartedly support this.

Since the success of Reading Recovery is attributed to the teachers' in-depth understanding of reading process, doesn't it make sense to have as many teachers as possible broaden their vision of how reading works? Why can't we support them in becoming knowledgeable teachers of struggling readers? Pat had fifteen years' experience as a reading teacher *before* being trained in Reading Recovery, and her knowledge expanded exponentially within her first years of doing Reading Recovery. She further layered her understanding as she continued for seven years as a Reading Recovery teacher. Katie, who is not Reading Recovery trained but has read much of Marie Clay's writings and worked closely with Reading Recovery teachers, has also expanded her paradigm of how reading works and how best to support struggling readers. We want to acknowledge how much our thinking has been influenced by Marie Clay's work, and you'll see this reflected throughout this book. Lyons, Dorn and Soffos, Fountas and Pinnell, and others have shared their knowledge of reading process in their books as well. Like them, we realize that excellent early intervention programs are not available to every at-risk reader and therefore we'd like to share as much as we can about what we have learned related to effectively teaching struggling readers.

The following list outlines several things that a Reading Recovery teacher knows or does well. As you read the list, think about how this information would benefit you and the teachers in your school. Any teacher of struggling readers needs to do the following:

- ❀ Understand reading process and that each reader must construct it for himself or herself
- ❀ Plan instruction from observations and assessments
- ❀ Analyze running records with strategic actions in mind; look for what the child can do or almost does as a reader and plan to build on those factors

❀ Keep the child working on the edge of his or her learning capabilities, always requiring that the child do as much of the reading and writing work as he or she is able while the teacher handles the responsibility for the rest

❀ Maintain a safe learning environment so that struggling readers do not become discouraged

❀ Know when to model, prompt, and cut back on supports, and when to reinforce specific behaviors; in other words, move up and down the scale of help, altering the level of support in response to the child's reading behaviors

❀ Be very careful about his or her language when demonstrating, supporting, and prompting the child

❀ Teach toward independence so that the child takes more control over the reading and writing strategies

❀ Value the power of reciprocity of reading and writing; help the child see that what he or she knows in reading can help in writing and vice versa

❀ Provide opportunities for the child to practice with authentic reading and writing experiences. This time allows students to strengthen their processing ability because they are constantly using their system of strategies

We believe, as do many others, that a struggling reader has "a difficulty rather than a deficit . . . which implies that it can be altered with good teaching" (Lyons 2003, 94). And good teaching means that the instruction is specific to the exact needs of the learner. We will elaborate on the factors mentioned in the preceding list throughout this text.

What's Your Theory of How Reading Works?

Having read this chapter, has your vision of how reading works shifted or changed? How do you understand beginning reading? Do you have a theory of how children learn to read? If you haven't thought much about it, take a moment now before reading on.

A primary teacher once said to Pat, "To tell you the truth, I'm not really sure how the kids in my class start reading, but they do. Sometimes it seems like magic!" It may seem magical to some because we are unable to see all that is happening in the brain as children develop a reading process system. Keep in mind there are *visible* and *invisible* aspects to learning to read.

Basically, most literacy educators agree that there are two contrasting theories, the simple and the complex. The simple theory of reading, sometimes called the item or skills-based theory, relies on all the visible aspects. Because we can *see* the letters, words, punctuation marks, and so on, the simple theory proposes that the teaching of letters and their sounds (phonics), sight vocabulary, parts of speech, and other such visible items are paramount. The complex

Figure 2.2
Simple and Complex
Theories of Reading

A teacher with a *simple*, or *item-based*, *theory* is more likely to do the following:	A teacher with a *complex*, or *literacy processing*, *theory* is more likely to do the following:
• Value assessment tools heavily based on quantifying systems—numbers or levels that indicate whether a child is on grade level, above, or below	• Use ongoing assessment tools, such as running records, that, when analyzed properly, give information about the way the child is processing text in order to inform instruction
• Choose a focus for a lesson based on grade-level lists, curriculum guides, basal reading charts, or state standards lists	• Choose a focus for a lesson based on what the children need, keeping reading process in mind as well as school and state curriculum standards
• Use independent reading time so that children can learn how to read more books, add more sight words to their repertoire, develop vocabulary, and practice phonics skills	• Use independent reading time so that children can use their thinking system of strategies in an integrated way to make meaning and solve problems; believe that the more children use their network of strategies, the stronger their system will become
• Believe that struggling readers need more practice time on skill-and-drill phonics tasks, word lists, spelling lists, and so on	• Believe struggling readers need support and practice building a reading process system while reading and writing continuous texts

theory of reading, which we have described in this chapter, proposes that *as* the reader is learning various letters, sounds, words, and other items, he or she is also developing neural networks in the brain (the invisible part of reading), which help him or her perform strategic actions to make meaning of text.

How a teacher understands reading process determines how he or she assesses, plans, instructs, and supports students.

Whether a teacher subscribes to a simple or a complex theory of reading, we are sure that every teacher wants all children to enjoy reading; be able to make good, independent choices of books; read from a variety of genres; and become lifelong learners.

For a majority of children it doesn't matter which theory the teacher subscribes to. But our biggest concern is for the struggling readers. For them, we would argue strongly, *it does matter* which theory the teacher holds. Struggling readers need help constructing a system that enables them to be successful readers. Therefore, it is crucial that a teacher, when working with struggling readers, teach from a reading process theory that includes a network of strategies operating in an integrated way.

The aim of this chapter has been to add layers of understanding to your knowledge of how reading works. With this book, we want to add our voices to others in the literacy field who want to invite more teachers to understand reading process so their struggling readers can reap the benefits.

In the next chapter we delve into finding that place where we can best meet the needs of struggling readers as they build their reading process systems. We use Lev Vygotsky's (1978) zone of proximal development and the gradual release of responsibility model to do this.

CHAPTER 3

Vygotsky Takes a Seat in Our Classrooms

At a recent conference in Columbus, Ohio, we heard P. David Pearson urging us to accept our students for who they are. He said, "They are who they are. They know what they know. They bring what they bring." It reminded us of what we often say to teachers: "It doesn't help to blame the teachers who had the kids before you. Take the students in your class from where they are and move them forward from there." Nowhere are these statements more applicable than with struggling readers. They are the ones who need us to meet their needs at a place where they can benefit the most from our instruction. So where is that place? And how do we find it?

We have found that Vygotsky's theory of teaching and learning helps answer those questions. We rarely run into a teacher who hasn't heard something about Lev Vygotsky and his zone of proximal development. We've heard comments like, "Oh yeah, I remember something about that from undergraduate ed. psych classes." For many, Vygotskian theory of how children learn is just another one of those concepts that we once read about, perhaps studied, maybe even quoted in a college paper, but now fail to see any practical application for our classrooms.

We believe that Vygotsky's theory is important and applicable enough to warrant its own chapter. Over the past five years or so, we, and many of the teachers we work with, have delved deeper into Vygotsky's work and layered our thinking. Through conversations with colleagues and our work with struggling readers, we now have a better grasp of terms such as zone of actual development, zone of proximal development, and social speech, private speech, and inner speech. This understanding has caused a slight shift in our teaching and impacts the way we plan, instruct, and use language with struggling readers. In this chapter we will be sharing those understandings.

As you read in this chapter the examples of teachers and students working together, we hope you will reflect on the following questions:

- ❀ What is Vygotsky's theory and why should I take time to learn about it?
- ❀ When is my teaching most effective?
- ❀ How do children learn best?
- ❀ What is the zone of proximal development (ZPD)?
- ❀ What does the gradual release of responsibility model have to do with ZPD?
- ❀ How will understanding ZPD make me a better teacher of reading?
- ❀ What are the benefits for struggling readers?

What Are the Basics of Vygotskian Theory?

Lev Vygotsky was born in Russia in 1896 and died of tuberculosis in 1934 at the age of 37. In his short lifetime he published 180 works, with unpublished manuscripts totaling 300. His works were banned by Stalin and were not allowed to be read and circulated until after Stalin's death in 1953. Americans were slow to accept his theories because of the popularity of Piaget's work and behaviorist theories. More detailed information on Vygotsky's life and work can be found in *Scaffolding Children's Learning: Vygotsky and Early Childhood Education* by Berk and Winsler (1995).

In the last twenty years or so, Vygotsky's theories of how children learn have found their way into nearly every college curriculum for teacher training. Listed below are three major ideas about which he wrote extensively (Vygotsky 1978, 1986). Following the list, we elaborate on these foundational concepts, putting them into practical terms with examples that are more closely connected to you and your classroom.

* Teaching is most effective (and learning is most likely to happen) when it takes place within the child's *zone of proximal development.*
* *Language is a central tool of humans* and, when used appropriately in teaching/learning situations, can play a crucial role in children's cognitive development.
* The *sociocultural aspect of teaching and learning* is important and includes developing environments for learning that foster lots of talk, interaction, and joint projects.

The topic most written about, and the one we will address most completely from Vygotsky's work, is the concept of the zone of proximal development. Let's begin there.

Zone of Proximal Development

Have you ever wondered whether or not your students are actually learning what you are teaching? We have. We have had times when we thought we were teaching our hearts out only to realize that nothing much sunk into the children's brains. So were we really teaching then? We thought we were, but how can teaching exist without learning?

For us, Vygotsky's concept of the ZPD answers the question, Where does effective teaching really lie? Vygotsky's answer: You are doing your best teaching when you are working within the child's zone of proximal development. He defines ZPD as *where the child can do it with your help* (Vygotsky 1986). When you teach children within their zone of proximal development, they have the highest potential for successful learning. They see the task, skill, or strategic thinking modeled by you, they do it together with you, and eventually they take on the new learning independently as you back off your supports.

We have adapted a graphic explanation of ZPD from Frank Smith's book *The Book of Learning and Forgetting* (1998). Refer to Figure 3.1 as you read the following.

Figure 3.1
The Zone of Proximal
Development

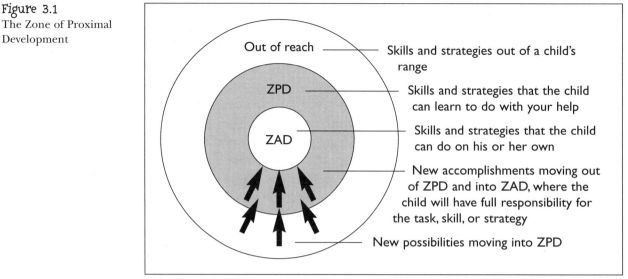

Out of reach —— Skills and strategies out of a child's range

ZPD —— Skills and strategies that the child can learn to do with your help

ZAD

Skills and strategies that the child can do on his or her own

New accomplishments moving out of ZPD and into ZAD, where the child will have full responsibility for the task, skill, or strategy

New possibilities moving into ZPD

Adapted from Smith (1998), Figure 11.1.

The innermost circle, called the zone of actual development (ZAD), represents things that the child has total control over and can easily do without your assistance. For example, Marcus, a second grader, has control over leaving spaces between words. As he writes, he leaves a space automatically before beginning his next word. He doesn't even give the idea of spacing much conscious attention. Another student, Serena, a fifth grader, attends to punctuation well as she reads. She reads with expression, letting the conventions of punctuation marks guide her decisions about how the text should sound. These are just two examples of what might be included in the child's inner circle. There are certainly more skills and strategies each of these children have total control over.

For each person, the ZAD includes all that you know, your background knowledge, and the tasks you are able to perform independently. In the case of literacy, it includes all the skills and strategic behaviors you control thus far as a reader and writer.

The outermost circle contains those things that are very much out of a child's reach at this time, what the child wouldn't be able to do even with your help. Marissa, a first grader, is just beginning to read books with patterned text. For her, learning to use context clues to figure out the meanings of unknown words would not be appropriate instruction. It's out of her reach at this time. Mohammad, an English language learner in second grade, writes with a mixture of invented spelling and a few high-frequency words but without any end punctuation. So for Mohammad, learning about indenting paragraphs is out of his reach.

Oftentimes in classrooms, students who are expected to complete tasks that are out of their reach will become very frustrated and confused. Similarly, students asked to constantly work within their ZAD using skills and strategies they have total control of become bored and take on little or no new learning.

Take a minute to digest the information about the inner and outer circles and what that might mean for you and your classroom. Have there been times when you thought you were teaching something new, but then realized that the students already knew how to do what you were asking of them? Were there other times when you felt that what you were trying to teach a student was way out of his or her zone?

The middle of the three circles is the zone of proximal development. It is here that the child can almost perform the task; that is, he or she can do it with your help. Berk and Winsler say, "According to Vygotsky, the role of education is to provide children with experiences that are in their ZPDs—activities that challenge children but that can be accomplished with sensitive adult guidance" (1995, 26). For Mohammad, the student mentioned previously, it would be better to work with him on rereading his work and listening for where end punctuation should be rather than to teach about indenting paragraphs. He would be able to address punctuation with your help, and therefore that teaching would be within his ZPD. For Marissa, the first grader, a teacher might choose to help her learn to self-monitor her predictions on those patterned books. This would probably be within her ZPD. She could learn to check if a word she predicted looked right, sounded right, and made sense.

Look back to the graphic, Figure 3.1, and you will see arrows pointing inward. These represent the skills and strategies that are moving from the *out of reach* area into the ZPD as well as those moving from the ZPD into the ZAD. As a child is constructing his or her reading process system, items, skills, and strategic actions are always moving in this manner. The more control the child gains over the task or strategy, the more that task or strategy will move toward the innermost circle where the child can do it independently.

One way to understand ZPD better is to use the following activity. You may want to try this at a grade-level team meeting. Using a blank version of the chart in Figure 3.2 (found in Appendix 2), choose one reader from your classroom. While thinking about this child, fill in at least three things under each column. What do you know about this child as a reader? What strategic behaviors can he or she perform all on his or her own (ZAD)? What are some skills or strategies he or she is ready to learn how to do with your modeling and assistance (ZPD)? And what things would you consider teaching to other children in the room, but would be out of reach for this child at this time? Discuss your chart with a partner. The chart Katie completed for one of her students appears in Figure 3.2.

A Closer Look at ZPD

Pat will never forget an example she heard when she first became familiar with ZPD. Reading specialist Barbara Anzalone told a group of reading teachers a story about three toddlers in a sandbox. First she reminded the group of the idea of making a birthday cake with packed-down sand in a bucket, a typical task performed by young children in the sand. Then she said, "Here are the

ZAD What strategic behaviors can this child perform all on his or her own—in his or her *zone of actual development?*	ZPD What are some skills or strategies this child is ready to learn how to do with your modeling and assistance—in his or her *zone of proximal development?*	Out of Reach What things would you consider teaching to other children in the room, but would be *out of reach* for this child at this time?
-uses the visual information (first and last letters) of a word to solve unknown words -predicts what might happen next in the story -stops at an unknown word when visual information is not helping	-monitors for meaning, asking "what would make sense here?" -maintains fluency, reading smoothly and with expression -checks what he has read to make sure it makes sense, goes back and rereads, putting the sentence all together	-determining importance in nonfiction text -adjusting the reading rate for different kinds of text

Figure 3.2
Individual Student
ZPD Chart

scenarios of three toddlers. After I describe all three, I want you to decide for which child is 'learning how to make a sand birthday cake' within his or her ZPD?"

Child 1. He first fills the bucket with sand, periodically patting down the sand to make it firm. When it is full and packed down hard, he then turns the pail upside down and slowly glides it off, careful not to ruin the shape he has created. Ta-Da, a birthday cake!

Child 2. She shovels a few handfuls of sand into the bucket, looks up at you, hesitates, then shovels in a few more. When the bucket is about half full, she turns it over and all the sand spills out.

Child 3. He gets in the sandbox, picks up the shovel, and starts eating the sand.

We're sure you've guessed the answer. Child 2 is ready to learn this task, but will need your help. This task is within her ZPD. She knows to shovel sand into the pail, but does not realize the need for packing it firm. She knows she will eventually have to turn the bucket over, but doesn't realize that the bucket needs to be filled to the top. With your modeling, specific language supports, and sensitive guidance, she will soon be able to do the task on her own.

For child 3, who started eating the sand, this task was probably out of his reach. Think about the times we give children work that is on a frustration level for them. A common error we make is to let children plod through books that are much too difficult for them.

Child 1 already made a perfect creation. This task was in his zone of *actual* development. Think about this. How many times have you seen teachers instruct children on work they are already capable of completing? More often than not, it's mere busy work. We do not deny that there are times when children should practice tasks that they know how to do; we just shouldn't mistake this for instruction.

One third-grade teacher we know revamped her entire spelling program when she began thinking about ZPD. She realized that she was having every child in the class do the same weekly spelling list from the text, including all the activities for those words, when almost half her students could spell all those words on Monday. She realized she was not "teaching" spelling to those students at all, but was merely having them stay busy with activities to complete.

Granted, in a classroom situation it would be difficult to have every child working within his or her ZPD every moment of every day. But we have found that when teachers understand the zone of proximal development, they strive to know their students better and try harder to vary their supports, questions, or instruction for different students. For example, Katie notes that after reading the morning message with students each day, she asks different questions of different students, supporting them in the appropriate zone. Whether asking Abir to come up to the message and circle a word with two parts or syllables or asking Melvin to find the letter *M*, like in his name, the teacher is there to support them.

Classroom Examples of Working Within a Child's ZPD

Most teachers tell us that the way they learn best is to watch another teacher as he or she teaches. Let's have a look at two excellent teachers, one working with a single child and one working with a small group.

Example 1: Kathleen and Frank

One day Pat watched literacy coach Kathleen Fay teaching first grader Frank how to self-monitor by checking the ends of words. The classroom teacher had noticed in her assessment notes and observed in her running records that Frank often neglected to check the endings of words. Though she had modeled this for the class on numerous occasions she determined that Frank needed some one-on-one instruction on this matter, so she asked Kathleen to model this skill for Frank.

Kathleen selected a book that Frank had already read a few times. He continually read the wrong verb form:

Child:	running	jumping	flying	looking
Text:	run	jump	fly	look

The text followed a pattern that went something like this:

I saw a rabbit inside his hole.
I saw a squirrel stare at me.
I saw a bird fly way up high.
I saw a possum run up a tree.

After a short chat about what they would be working on, Kathleen began by modeling for Frank.

Kathleen: Watch me read the first two pages. "I saw a rabbit in his hole." Wait. Let me check that. "I saw a rabbit in/sss/inside his hole."
(*She does the same with the next page, reading* staring *for* stare, *and then correcting it.*)
Kathleen: Frank, do you see how I'm checking to see if the word looks right *at the end?* That's what I want you to do today. Start reading here.
Frank: (*Reading from the text.*) "I saw a bird flying way up high."
Kathleen: Something wasn't quite right there. Try this page again and make sure this word looks right at the end. (*She holds her pen over* fly.)
Frank: (*Reads it correctly this time and then continues.*) "I saw a possum running up a tree." (*Rereads without a teacher prompt and self-corrects* running *to* run.)
Kathleen: Nice job checking the end of that word.

On another page, Kathleen has to prompt Frank, but does so by saying, "How do you think you did there?" She doesn't want to be the one who monitors for him; he needs to take over the checking. Then he reads the next three pages correctly. Near the end he reads *look* correctly, but glances at the teacher and says, "I almost said 'looking.'" He laughs. Can you see that Frank is taking responsibility for self-monitoring the endings of words? Kathleen took a moment to write notes about what she observed during the lesson. She will hold him accountable or reteach when necessary in future situations.

This example shows two things. First, it illustrates how the teacher was able to find the child's ZPD, knowing that the child could learn to do the checking with her help. Second, it shows the teacher's use of explicit modeling and gradual release of responsibility (presented later in this chapter)—she supported the child as he slowly took over the task of self-monitoring and made sure the endings looked right.

Example 2: Carrie and a Second-Grade Guided Reading Group

While reflecting on her anecdotal notes (more on this in Chapter 10), second-grade teacher Carrie Cantillana noticed that several students were reading in a word-by-word manner. Her running records showed that these children were able to problem solve words and self-corrected often, but their choppy reading was very much an issue. She decided a lesson on fluency was in order.

Carrie knows a lot about fluency teaching. She knows that it's not just a matter of getting students to read faster, but that it involves reading the punctuation, using correct intonation, grouping words together into phrases that would sound like natural talk, and making it sound like a character is talking when dialogue appears. Carrie realized that one quick lesson would not necessarily be enough for these students and that she couldn't do everything at once. Her first goal was to make the students more aware of how they sounded when reading. She wanted them to self-monitor themselves and decide if they sounded choppy or smooth. If they caught themselves sounding choppy, she wanted them to go back and reread that part.

As she planned her lesson, she decided on the language she would use to model and prompt the students. She chose three phrases to use:

1. Did you sound smooth or choppy?
2. Go back and put it all together.
3. Make it sound like real talking.

Instead of introducing a new book, as we often do in guided reading, Carrie chose a familiar book in order to keep the lesson within the students' ZPD. Since they would be working on monitoring their fluency, a new behavior for them, she didn't want their attention focused on solving new words. She chose a version of *The Three Billy Goats Gruff* that the students had been introduced to during a prior session. Each of the five students had read the book at least once.

Carrie had a short conversation with the students, letting them retell the story. She wanted the meaning of the book at the forefront of their minds. Then she moved to her teaching point.

Carrie: I've noticed that when some of you read, your voice sounds a bit choppy, like this. (*She reads a page from the book in a staccato manner.*) Readers sound better, and even understand stories better, when they can make their reading sound smooth. Close your eyes for a minute and listen to me read. (*She reads some sentences choppily and some smoothly, letting the students listen and then answer the question, "How did I sound that time?"*)

Carrie: To make it sound smooth, readers have to read in groups of words. Let me show you something. (*Carrie places a cut-up sentence from the book in two ways. She demonstrates. See examples.*)

Down went his horns and he rushed at the Troll.
(*She reads this in a word-by-word manner.*)

Down went his horns   and he rushed   at the Troll.
(*She reads fluently, grouping the words with her voice.*)

Carrie: Now let's all turn to page 7 and read that page together. (*Carrie's voice carries the students along as they read, "The Troll tumbled off the bridge, down, down, down, into the deep water under the bridge."*) Try it again by yourself. (*She listens as the students try to make their voices sound fluent.*)

Carrie: Today you are each going to work on sounding nice and smooth. Read in a whisper voice and listen to yourself. If you notice you are slowing down and reading in a choppy way, stop and go back and put it all together. Make it sound like real talk. I'll be coming around to see how you are doing.

Carrie moved two students to the floor and another two to a nearby table. She kept one girl next to her at the guided reading table. Because Carrie knows her students well, she realized this student would need the most help getting started. Once that student had read two or three pages, Carrie left her and moved to the other students, jotting notes in her assessment notebook as she observed each student. She continued using the same three prompts: Did you sound smooth or choppy? Go back and put it all together. Make it sound like real talking.

Both Examples

There are several commonalities between these two excellent lessons. Both teachers did the following:

Think about your day. When did you feel you were working within a particular child's or group's ZPD? When you became aware of a child struggling because the material was too far out of his or her reach, what did you do? What else could you have done differently?

❀ Used assessment to guide their instructional decisions

❀ Chose a book that fit the children and the focus

❀ Modeled with specific language exactly what they wanted the children to do

❀ Set up an opportunity for the children to practice

❀ Offered sensitive guidance during practice time

❀ Knew which student to keep by her side (in Carrie's case) for extra support

❀ Made notes afterward about what happened and how the students did. These notes will help them plan the next step of instruction.

The most important point to take away from these examples is this: When you know your students well, you can create ZPD opportunities for teaching and learning.

ZPD at Home

Parents know their children well. Some parents are natural teachers in that they know exactly how much challenge their child can handle without becoming frustrated, what to say to support their child's learning of a task, and when to back off and let the child discover something for himself or herself. It might serve us well in education to take hints from what some parents do well.

Our friend Lisa Merkel recently shared a story of how she helped her son, two-year-old Zachary, decide how to get his shoes on correctly. Although he was able to get his Crocs on by himself, he ran into trouble getting them on the right feet. She taught him to put the shoes side by side on the floor one way, take a good look, and then put them the other way and take another good look (see photos). She used language to support his noticing. When they were

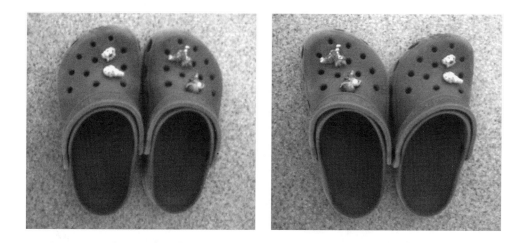

together the wrong way, she helped him notice the big space on top and how the tops of the shoes curved out. But when they were together the right way, the tops curved towards each other.

Zachary soon was getting those Crocs on the correct feet in a jiffy! Pat jokingly asked when she'd be teaching him how to tie his laces. And she said, "That'll be a while yet!" We noted how easily she knew which task was within his zone of proximal development and which was out of his reach.

Think about a time you have helped a child learn to do something new at home. Perhaps it was a household chore or a simple art craft. Or have you taught a child to ride a bike, dive off the diving board, or learn a sport? Think about the language you used while teaching the task, how you modeled it and let the child try it with your support, and how you slowly turned over responsibility to the child.

David Wood, in his book *How Children Think and Learn* (1998), presented a study he did of mothers teaching a particular puzzle construction to their three- and four-year-olds. Wood's example illustrates how Vygotsky's beliefs differed from Piaget's, the popular educational theorist of the 1920s. Piaget believed that a child's learning was limited by certain stages of development. Vygotsky disagreed, saying that though the child was not able to do the task alone, he could possibly learn to do it independently if he learned from, and was supported by, an *experienced other.*

Wood chose a task that children under the age of seven were not able to perform independently. It involved building a pyramid out of twenty-one wooden blocks that had various pegs and holes in them. Then he asked several mothers to teach this task to their three- and four-year-olds. As Pat read the study, she thought, "Whoa, if seven-year-olds couldn't do it, how were the mothers supposed to teach three- and four-year-olds?"

To her surprise, many of the children were eventually successful in performing the task alone. Wood carefully studied what the moms did in the teaching phase. He was looking to see what worked and what didn't.

Two factors definitely did not work. The moms who first tried to show the child how to do the entire task without letting the child become involved seemed to overload the child. Other moms, who depended solely on verbal directions, also frustrated their children.

On the other hand, there were certain factors that led to success:

- Raising the interest level by letting the child play with the pieces before beginning the task, and showing them how the pegs and holes fit together
- Simplifying problems by selecting some pieces and moving others aside
- Using language to point out or name a feature that the child needed to take into account
- Offering more help as soon as the child began to struggle
- Pulling back on assistance when the child was managing a part of the task alone

Wood noticed "the child [was] never left alone when he [was] in difficulty, nor [was] he 'held back' by teaching that [was] too directive and intrusive" (1998, 100). Wouldn't that be the perfect classroom? A place where a child is never held back from discovering things for himself or herself by over-teaching or by interrupting talk from the teacher? And where a child is never left alone to struggle when he or she is confused and frustrated?

We admit that in crowded classrooms it is harder to find a child's zone of proximal development than it is in the parent/child situation. And no one would expect a teacher to find it for every child in every learning situation. *But it is the struggling reader who will need this the most.* We discovered that the more we knew about a particular child's strengths and weaknesses as a reader, *and* the more we learned about reading process, the better we became at observing that child's reading to determine our next step of instruction within his or her ZPD.

Explicit Modeling, Gradual Release of Responsibility, and Their Relationship to ZPD

Teaching reading using an apprenticeship model (what David Wood calls the kind of teaching the moms did) is what working with a child within his or her ZPD is all about. *Cognitive apprenticeship* adds a slightly new dimension. When learning to read, the child is not just learning how to perform an action like doing a puzzle, hitting a ball, or putting shoes on the right feet. Cognitive development has to do with the brain. The child is learning new problem-solving tasks, new ways of thinking. He or she is learning to solve words in a variety of ways and how to use a repertoire of strategies to comprehend texts. As we explained in Chapter 2, readers need to construct this network of strategies for themselves. Teachers who learn to teach with a cognitive apprenticeship model can support readers as they build functioning reading process systems.

You may know this type of teaching as the gradual release of responsibility model (Pearson and Gallagher 1983). In *One Child at a Time* (2006), Pat shared the different language used by the authors of many professional books to describe this same concept (see Figure 3.3).

Teachers who use the gradual release model know that there are times when *modeling* the task or behavior is appropriate. For example, a teacher can demonstrate these behaviors:

- ❀ Going back and rereading what he or she has written before deciding on the next word in a writing demonstration
- ❀ Predicting a word for a blank in the morning message, choosing a few words that would sound right and make sense, and then narrowing the choice by checking which one would look right as he or she writes the first letter
- ❀ Reading dialogue, making it sound like the character and checking where the quotation marks are

Figure 3.3
Words to Describe the
Gradual Release Model

Linda Dorn and Carla Soffos ***Shaping Literate Minds* (2005)** *Modeling* *Coaching* *Scaffolding* *Fading*	**Regie Routman** ***Reading Essentials* (2003)** *Demonstration* *Shared Demonstration* *Guided Practice* *Independent Practice*
Pat Johnson ***One Child at a Time* (2006)** *Modeling* *Scaffolding* *Prompting* *Backing Off* *Reinforcing*	**Irene Fountas and Gay Su Pinnell** ***Guiding Readers and Writers* (2001)** *Show* *Support* *Prompt* *Reinforce* *Observe*

There are hundreds of demonstrations that teachers do throughout the day. During the modeling, the reading or writing work is done by the teacher; children are the observers. When a teacher models or demonstrates, he or she is providing the heaviest support for children. Take a look at the placement of the dot in Figure 3.4. The heaviest support a teacher can offer (modeling) is located closest to the out-of-reach area and just inside the ZPD area.

After one or several demonstrations, the teacher performs the task again, but this time encourages interaction from the children. Routman (2003) refers to this as the *shared demonstration* part of gradual release (see Routman in Figure 3.3). Here the students and teacher negotiate the task together. The children are active participants in learning how to do the task. Imagine the dot in Figure 3.4 moving more toward the middle of the ZPD circle.

Figure 3.4
Location of Modeling in ZPD

Figure 3.5
Location of Guided Practice in ZPD

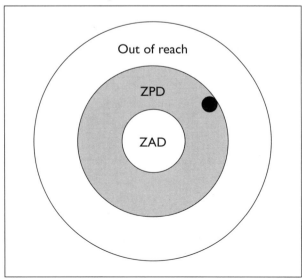

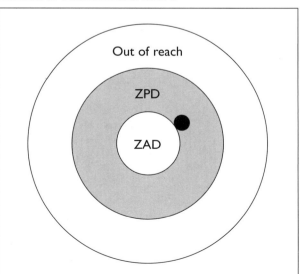

In teaching with the gradual release model, teachers must constantly keep independence as the goal. This means that after modeling and shared demonstrations, the teacher must back off the supports, lessening the amount of help he or she is giving. The teacher may do this first with some *guided practice* lessons, in which the children try what was taught. The teacher is still available for support. Notice the location of the dot in Figure 3.5, which indicates light support from the teacher during guided practice. As children take on more control, their ability to do the task is moving toward independence. The more control children have over performing the task, the more that task moves towards the inner circle, the zone of actual development.

In the books *Strategies That Work* (Harvey and Goudvis 2007) and *Reading with Meaning* (Miller 2002), the authors take us through numerous lessons using explicit modeling and gradual release of responsibility.

1. They model, using explicit language to make their thinking visible.
2. They engage the children in working on the reading behavior together.
3. They provide opportunities for the children to practice using the strategy or behavior.
4. They watch as children try it on their own and notice which children need more support.

In these texts, most of the lessons are done with a whole or small group; however, the same concept of gradual release of responsibility can also be used for one-on-one teaching with a struggling reader. The only difference is that here the teacher doesn't always move from modeling to sharing to guided participation to observing *in a straight line*. More often the teacher will have to move back and forth, up and down the levels of support based on what the child is doing. This is often called responsive teaching: responding with a certain level of help based on what the child needs at the exact moment of difficulty. We saw this happening in the classroom example as Kathleen taught Frank how to check the ends of words.

❊ ❊ ❊

We feel that when teachers take the time to deepen their understanding of Vygotsky's zone of proximal development, they will become better teachers of reading. This knowledge will support teachers as they strive to meet the varied needs of each reader and writer in their classroom.

Language Is a Central Tool

In *Choice Words: How Our Language Affects Children's Learning*, Peter Johnston says, "Talk is the central tool of [teachers'] trade. With it they mediate children's activity and experience, and help them make sense of learning, literacy life, and themselves" (2004, 4).

Vygotsky, too, emphasized the importance of using language as a tool for learning. He felt that language is instrumental in restructuring the mind and in helping learners develop self-regulation (Berk and Winsler 1995).

What does self-regulation mean for readers? It means putting the reader in the driver seat. For a child to become a proficient reader, self-regulation means that *the child* actively problem solves the print; *the child* initiates the plan for what to do when a difficulty arises; *the child* self-monitors to make sure that he or she understands what he or she is reading; and so on. If we want children to be able to act independently as they solve words and understand texts, then we need to show them how to do these things. Language aids us in this undertaking. The language we use as we demonstrate, support, prompt, and reinforce should be chosen with great care.

Teacher Language Changes in the Gradual Release Model

Let's think about the language we connect with the various parts of explicit modeling and gradual release of responsibility (modeling, shared demonstrations, guided practice, independence). During *modeling* the teacher uses language to make thinking visible. The teacher thinks out loud about whatever he or she is modeling—visualizing, questioning, inferring; searching for more information in the letters, pictures, or text; predicting a word based on what would make sense; connecting to prior knowledge; and so on. Whatever the teacher is demonstrating, he or she is basically saying the following to the children:

 Vygotsky used the terms *social speech, private speech,* and *inner speech* to describe what happens with language during a teacher/student interaction.

- Social speech: the language the teacher uses as he or she models and also the language between teacher and student as they negotiate the task together
- Private speech: the language used by the child to direct himself or herself to do the reading or writing strategic action; this is not an exact imitation of the teacher's language but the child's own abbreviated version of that language
- Inner speech: the language the child has going on in his or her head to help plan actions and self-regulate literacy behaviors; eventually inner speech turns to thought

* "Look—here's something that readers do."
* "Here is something that works for me."
* "Here's something you could try."
* "This might help you figure out a word."
* "This could help you when you're stuck."

With the *shared demonstrations* the teacher is still modeling and supporting, but the children are participating in the meaning making; they, too, are using language. Teacher and students negotiate the task together and have conversations. Vygotsky calls the language used during modeling and shared demonstration *social speech.*

When teachers work within children's ZPD, their language guides and supports the students. As the children take more control of the task, they slowly take on the language that goes along with the task. During *guided practice*, children sometimes talk to themselves, reminding themselves to do certain things as they read and write. Listen in on a first-grade classroom during literacy time and you'll hear things such as these:

- ❈ "Oops, I almost forgot my space."
- ❈ "No, that doesn't make sense."
- ❈ "I better try that again."

Vygotsky calls this *private speech*. When beginning to learn to read and write, children often talk themselves through things. This is not talk that is intended to communicate with anyone else; they are just talking to themselves to direct their own actions. Lyons (2003) writes that "private speech involves thinking and problem solving out loud, which is used for self-reflective purposes within the child's brain; one mind (brain) working alone to successfully complete the task at hand" (52).

Adults use private speech throughout life. You may find that you talk to yourself about your lost glasses—"Now where was I when I wore them last? I came into the house and I . . ." Sometimes we talk to ourselves to help us remember things, particularly when the learning is new to us. Can you think of a time when, after learning to do something new, you needed to talk yourself through the steps? Katie, a seasoned skydiver with over 300 jumps under her belt, experienced this.

> *When Katie first learned to land her parachute, the instructor and she would talk through the landing procedures before she made the jump. His instructions echoed in her head throughout the jump. She had to look at her altimeter and tell herself, "OK, I'm at 900 feet . . . I need to be over the hangar, steer the canopy that way. Alright, now I'm at 600 feet . . . I need to be over the taxiway. Whoa, 300 feet! I need to be on final approach—no more turns now! Don't look at the ground, don't look at the ground—keep my eyes straight ahead until I'm 10 feet off the ground . . . now get ready to land!"*

Vygotsky (1978) tells us that children's private speech is not a direct imitation of the adult speech. It is "not a mechanical process involving direct transfer of exact copies of adult verbal prescriptions . . . It is the child's spontaneous speech to regulate his actions" (Lyons 2003, 52). Children take on the language, change it a bit, and make it their own. It sometimes comes out as an abbreviated version of the language the adult used.

Think back to Lisa teaching Zachary how to get his shoes on the right feet. Her language of "See how the tops curve out" and "Look how the tops come together here" was taken on by Zachary in his own way. She heard him mumbling to himself during his first solo attempts. He'd say, "They're going out . . . that's not it" when the shoes were placed together backward. The private speech slowly faded away with each application of the task. Sometimes he'd just say, "Yup, got it." And when he controlled the task completely, no vocalization was needed. He just slipped those Crocs right on!

Type of Speech	Classroom Example	How It Sounds
Social Speech	Teacher uses language to model spaces during community writing. She explains the need for spaces.	"I need a space here before I write my next word." "People can't read my writing unless I use spaces."
	Teacher and child use language to interact about the task. Teacher sets up opportunities where children can direct her to use spaces.	T: What do I need to do next? C: Put a space. T: Who can tell me where to start my next word? C: Right here. You need a space.
Private Speech	Child has partial control over the action as he writes. He uses language to direct his action.	"Put my finger right here." "I need a space first." "And this . . . like this . . ."
Inner Speech	Child "talks" silently, like a voice in his head directing him.	No vocalization as child writes; he may be directing himself with inner speech.
Inner Thought	Task becomes automatic.	Child puts spaces between words without conscious attention.

Figure 3.6
A Classroom Look at
Vygotsky's Social, Private,
and Inner Speech

Eventually, Vygotsky tells us, the private speech of the child turns to *inner speech*, like a little voice inside the head reminding the reader. The last part of gradual release of responsibility, *independence*, is when the children are given opportunities to use the behavior or strategic action that they've been working on. Finally, in order for the task, behavior, or strategy to be totally controlled by the child, the inner speech turns to pure thought. Once the language in the head has become thought, the strategic action happens quickly for the child, even without conscious attention.

Figure 3.6 shows a classroom example of a teacher teaching children about leaving spaces between their words as they write.

Teachers Plan Their Language

In a recent Literacy Collaborative (LC) meeting with K–2 teachers, the LC coach asked the teachers to think about the language they would use in a specific teaching interaction with a child. She wanted them to take time to think through the process of how their language changes from modeling to prompting to observing to reinforcing.

Each teacher chose a student. Their task was to think about what teaching point would come next in that child's instruction and how they would design a lesson. Then they made a list of the language that would best support that child in taking on the new learning. Keep in mind this is not something teachers would do in their own classrooms with each child. The value comes from doing it in a group setting and discussing how their language changes from demonstration to independence.

Katie decided that Anthony needed to use known words to self-monitor and self-correct. This was important so that he could attend to the print while confirming and demonstrating one-to-one matching. She chose the guided reading book *The Leaf Boats* by Annette Smith (2006) because it had several repeating lines of text, with a small change in the pattern on every other page. There was a great deal of picture support, as well as several high-frequency words that Anthony knew.

Katie's completed sheet is shown in Figure 3.7. A blank version can be found in Appendix 3 if you would like to try this with a group of teachers.

Figure 3.7

A Teacher Changes Her Language as She Moves from Demonstration to Independence

Teaching Phase	Teacher Language
Demonstrate	• Readers have to follow the words on the page. • Use your finger—point to each word as you read. Check yourself with the words you know. • When you point to "my," you should be saying "my."
Share the Task	• Let's try this page together. Watch my finger and see how I point to each word. I made my finger match each word that I said. You try. • Make sure the word you say is the word you're pointing to.
Provide Guided Practice (High Support)	• Did your finger match what you were saying? • Find a word you know and make sure your finger matches what you are saying.
Gradually Withdraw Scaffold (Low Support)	• Did it match? • Go back and reread—make it match.
Give Specific Praise or Redirection	• You stopped when your finger didn't match the word you were saying. • Try it again—make it match.

While one lesson on this topic may not solidify this reading behavior for Anthony, planning her language this specifically helped Katie be very purposeful in her teaching. Future lessons can build on this one while keeping the prompts appropriate for the level of learning.

In Chapter 4 we will explore the language that we use as we model strategic actions and as we prompt students to activate their strategies and behaviors.

The Sociocultural Aspect of Teaching and Learning

Vygotsky believed that although children are developing on a natural course biologically and physically, they also grow because they are affected by outside factors—cultural influences. In other words, children develop cognitively by learning and interacting with others. Learning is a social endeavor. Vygotsky believed that "social interaction and children's participation in authentic cultural activities are necessary for development to occur" (Berk and Winsler 1995).

For teachers, this means setting up a classroom environment that fosters talk, having students working collaboratively, developing projects based on student interests, and encouraging students to support each other as learners. Vygotsky's idea of a sociocultural approach does not fit with a silent classroom of students all in rows, constantly working individually, with the teacher being the one who holds all the answers.

When we combine the sociocultural aspect of Vygotsky's theory with his ZPD approach, we can't help but ask, "Which type of classroom would be the best match?" We feel that a comprehensive literacy approach is definitely the best match. Such a classroom allows teachers opportunities to work with children in small groups and occasionally individually during reading and writing workshops. As you've seen from most of our classroom examples thus far, teachers who are meeting children within their ZPDs are working either in small groups or one-on-one. We will elaborate on a comprehensive literacy classroom in Chapter 5 to show how the organization and management allows teachers these opportunities.

A sociocultural environment also means that children should be actively involved in learning activities. When they work on tasks collaboratively and talk about those tasks with a more expert other, they grow cognitively. Their thinking is transformed. They learn. Lyons sums up Vygotsky's sociocultural approach to learning by saying, "Social interactions provide the platform for learning how to learn and for the development of self-reflection, responsibility, cooperation, and effective problem solving, and it is through social interactions that children develop and expand their capacity to learn" (2003, 136).

The teacher is not the only person in the room from whom children can learn something. Katie finds this to be especially true in her classroom at a school where over 75 percent of the children speak a language other than English as their first language. Katie sets up projects where the English language learners (ELLs) can work in groups with native English speakers as well as ELLs of varying degrees of ability in English. The kind of talk that goes on in the group work benefits her English language learners.

Parker and Pardini, in their book *"The Words Came Down!"* suggest setting up science and math workshops in addition to reading and writing workshops in order to support ELLs throughout the day.

> *We are strong proponents of this workshop model for several reasons. It fosters the individualized instruction that we implement in order to meet a wide range of academic and linguistic needs. It enables us to expose our ELLs to content through interactive experiences, with guided practice, during whole-group lessons. Then they have opportunities to apply their learning in small-group settings.* (2006, 36)

Is My Classroom a Vygotskian One?

In closing this chapter we decided to use a list describing what a Vygotskian classroom would look like to summarize Vygotsky's theory. By reading and reflecting on the list, you will be able to decide how much of your classroom is supported by his work.

- A classroom whose teacher understands the zone of proximal development and works hard to instruct children in their ZPD range whenever possible
- A classroom that is literacy based—where reading, writing, speaking, and listening play a major role
- A classroom where there are many opportunities for children to talk, not idle chatter, but purposeful talk that leads to negotiated meaning-making of books, poems, and student-initiated writing pieces
- A classroom where instruction follows a gradual release of responsibility model; where children are scaffolded and supported when they need it, but are left alone to discover new things when they are managing challenging tasks on their own
- A classroom where joint projects and partner work abound, allowing children to work collaboratively
- A classroom with very little rote learning activities and isolated drills
- A classroom that uses dynamic ongoing assessment focusing not only on what students can do independently but also on what they can do with the guidance of an expert other

Our aim for this chapter has been to expand your knowledge of ZPD, the gradual release of responsibility model, and other concepts from Vygotsky's work. With these understandings, your teaching will become more effective and your students will learn better. In the next chapter, we will look at supporting children in developing some of the earliest strategies for solving words.

CHAPTER 4

Beyond "Sound It Out"

Word-solving strategies are some of the earliest strategies that students take control of as they begin to build a reading process system. Students need to learn how to predict what the word in the text might be when they do not recognize it automatically. It's important that all readers, including struggling ones, actively learn word-solving strategies and behaviors.

A common question we often hear is, "What do I do or say when the child stops at a word he doesn't know?" Many teachers are beginning to realize that although "sound it out" often comes to their lips, it isn't necessarily the best response. Why not? For one, the English language is not consistently phonetic. In fact, there are many, many words (about 40 to 50 percent) that cannot be solved by sounding them out. Therefore, it is not helpful (or even fair) to a child for us to prompt with "sound it out" when the word is *said, night, know,* or any of the other gazillion words that do not follow basic phonics rules. Marie Clay says that sounding out words is "not a routine response used by an efficient reader" (2005b, 168).

Another reason for not repeatedly saying "sound it out" is that there are other sources of information that a child can use in addition to letters and sounds that can help him or her problem solve an unknown word. And if there are other ways, doesn't it seem logical that we should teach and support a child to use them as well? In this chapter, we will do the following:

❀ Take a look at those sources of information, that is, those ways to solve words in addition to phonics

❀ Give suggestions for prompts teachers can say to get students solving words

❀ Show how teachers can model using the sources of information with whole-class or small-group demonstrations throughout the day

❀ Include how this knowledge of the sources of information can be used as we assess children so that we plan well for teaching them

Our goal in this chapter is to help teachers learn ways to support children as they build early word-solving strategies and learn to read with fluency and comprehension. We also want to equip teachers with the knowledge and language to share this information with parents.

Solving Words Using All the Sources of Information

When proficient readers solve words, they do not depend solely on phonetics. Watch what happens as you read the following sentence. Think about how you would figure out the missing word (we use a blank to substitute for an unknown word with adult readers).

After losing the soccer game, Jonathan walked _____ to the car
with his head hung low and his shoulders hunched.

You were probably able to quickly put in a word that made sense, such as,
sadly, slowly, unhappily, or even *back,* because you were thinking about the meaning of the sentence. Notice that all of these choices are the same part of speech.
You knew what would sound right, based on your knowledge of spoken language. Because you are familiar with the structure of how language sounds, you
would not have put in a word like *go,* or *table,* or *pretty.* Now, suppose the word
was not a blank, but rather a smudged word that looked like this ~~_____~~ .
Since parts of letters are now visible, this would lead you to rule out *back* and
unhappily and narrow down your choices to *sadly* or *slowly.*

In this example, you automatically used a combination of *meaning, language structure,* and *visual information* (phonics) to solve the unknown word. You
drew upon these three sources of information to make a decision. Here are
explanations of each:

- ❋ *Meaning (M):* Knowledge that includes any background knowledge, information gained from the pictures in the text, or ideas gathered from the
  context of the sentence or story. Readers think about what *makes sense.*
- ❋ *Structure (S):* Knowledge that comes from being familiar with spoken language, English structure, and how it sounds. Readers choose words that
  sound right.
- ❋ *Visual (V):* Any letter/sound correspondence knowledge a person has.
  Readers check to see if the word *looks right.*

When students are just beginning to learn to read, they are often unable
to use all three sources of information simultaneously as you did in the example. Early readers, especially struggling ones, tend to lean on the sources of
information that come easiest to them. They need teachers who provide the
following guidance:

- ❋ Show them how to integrate and balance meaning, structure, and visual
  information;
- ❋ Set up opportunities for them to practice figuring out words using all the
  sources of information while reading continuous text;
- ❋ Support and reinforce their efforts. (See Figure 4.1.)

Young Children Attempt to Solve Words

Let's think about some early readers who, on occasion, may rely too heavily on
their background knowledge (meaning). They usually pay attention to the
teacher's book introduction as he or she tells a little bit about the story line

Figure 4.1
A Balance of the Sources
of Information for Word
Solving

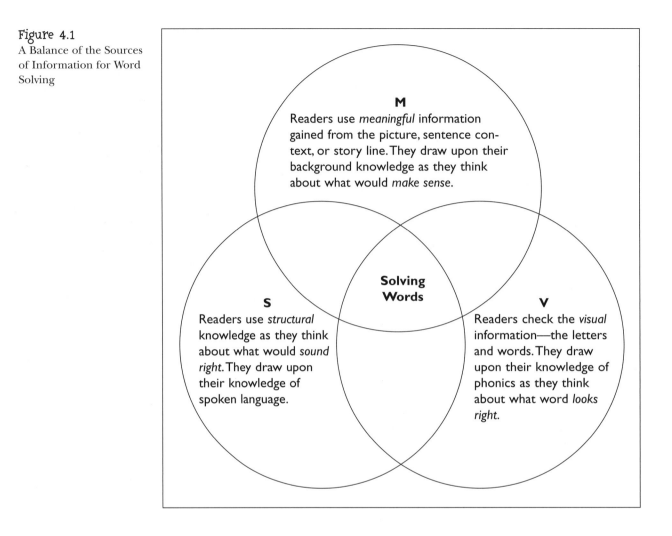

M

Readers use *meaningful* information
gained from the picture, sentence context, or story line. They draw upon their
background knowledge as they think
about what would *make sense*.

Solving
Words

S

Readers use *structural*
knowledge as they think
about what would *sound
right*. They draw upon
their knowledge of
spoken language.

V

Readers check the *visual*
information—the letters
and words. They draw
upon their knowledge of
phonics as they think
about what word *looks
right*.

before reading. They use the pictures and what they know about the topic to
predict what the text might say, and sometimes invent entire lines of text. They
may even ignore the print at times or only randomly attend to it. The fact that
they are making the story make sense carries them along. Sometimes the number of words they say does not even match with the number of words written
on that page.

The substitution words that these readers invent are often both semanti-
cally (M) and structurally (S) correct (they make sense and they sound right).
It is often difficult to separate those two sources of information. In other words,
if the child puts a meaningful word in place of the actual word in the text, it
usually is also the correct part of speech. The following substitutions were
made by students.

Child: Look at me. I am <u>sleeping</u>.
Text: Look at me. I am resting.

Child: Jasper <u>likes</u> tuna fish.
Text: Jasper eats tuna fish.

Child: Is he in the <u>door</u>?
Text: Is he in the cupboard?

Notice how the word the child says in place of the actual word not only makes sense but is also the right part of speech. In addition, you can see that the child neglects to check if the word he or she predicted began with the right letter. The child is not paying attention to the visual information.

In the following example, Rubin, while reading *Skipper's Birthday* by Roderick Hunt (1997), paid little attention to another kind of visual cue, the number of words on the page. His one-to-one matching gets off track on page 7 and he invents the text based on the meaning. He can see what Dad is doing in the picture.

Page 5:   Bobbie put up some balloons.
Page 6:   Mom made a cake.
Page 7:   Child read: Dad got a piece of bread.
           Text says: Dad took a sandwich.

Students need to learn the importance of paying attention to the visual information in print, beginning with how to notice the first letter. They also need to check their predictions against the letter information or number of words on the page. Finally, they need to take on the responsibility of checking for themselves and not waiting for someone else to monitor their errors for them.

At other times some beginning readers may rely too heavily on their phonics knowledge (V) without enough focus on meaning. When this happens the reader substitutes words that may have some of the right letters as compared to the correct word in the text, but do not make sense in the sentence. And sometimes the words he or she substitutes are not even real words, but just a garble of sounds.

These readers, when asked "What can you do if you don't know a word?" will always answer, "Sound out the letters." That mantra has become so ingrained in them that they often remain dedicated to sounding out even when it is not helping them solve the word. At times, it doesn't seem to matter to them that what they are reading is not making any sense at all. They just keep plodding on. Here are some examples:

Child: <u>That</u> you Tom.
Text: Thank you Tom.
Child: I can go <u>was</u> Father Bear.
Text: I can go with Father Bear.

One goal of teaching reading is to support all readers as they learn to use a balance of all of these sources of information (meaning, structure, and visual). In the prompting and modeling sections of this chapter, you will get some ideas as to how this is done.

Another Way to Understand the Balancing of the Sources of Information

We frequently share the explanation of the three sources of information in workshops with teachers. On occasion there are one or two participants who write something on the evaluation form or say something afterward about phonics being the most important of the three. They still feel strongly that phonics should come first. Can children really use meaning and structural information as effectively as phonics, or visual information? Here is another way of understanding the answer to that question.

In their text *Teaching for Comprehending and Fluency* Fountas and Pinnell (2006) say, "Prediction provides a forward motion, which enables the reader to spend much less attention on letters and word parts" (53). This does not mean the authors are encouraging children to disregard the letters and sounds of words. Quite the contrary. Readers should always be using as much of the phonetic information as they can pick up quickly (with *quickly* being the key word here), but they need to be doing so in combination with meaningful information. Children who take time to examine every letter of every word read too slowly and soon lose the meaning of the text. That is not how proficient readers read. Remember how you used all three sources of information yourself quite simultaneously when you solved the smudged word in the sentence on page 53.

So, what does it feel like to have meaning and structure constantly drive the reader forward? Try filling in the blanks in this story:

Once, long _____, there lived a little old _____ deep in the forest. Most days she didn't talk _____ anyone all day long and she often felt very _____.

Notice how fast and fluently you filled in words in the blanks to make this story make sense. You were able to do that because you were keeping your mind focused on the meaning of the passage. You chose appropriate words because of your background knowledge of how stories work, because you thought about what made sense, and because you've had years of experience with spoken language. You put in the correct part of speech (noun, adverb, preposition, and so on) without giving a moment's thought to what you were doing. You surely did not run through all the grammar rules you know before choosing the correct part of speech.

Also, you did not use any visual information (phonics), because we didn't include any. The ability that enabled you to fill in those blanks so fluidly is what Fountas and Pinnell mean when they say that predicting with meaning and structural information "provides a forward motion." Without meaning and structure constantly driving our understanding forward and keeping our reading phrased and smooth, we would read slowly in a word-by-word manner. But with meaning and structure pushing us swiftly across a line of text, we are in a constant state of anticipation. As fast as one word comes out of our mouth the next word has already been anticipated.

This needs to happen with children, even very young children, just as it happened with you. When children stay focused on meaning as they read, they are constantly anticipating the next word. This aids their fluency. The goal is to have them stay focused on meaning *at the same time as* they are checking the letters of the words. The internalized questions—Does it make sense (M)? Does it sound right (S)? Does it look right (V)?—play an important part as they monitor their reading. They need to be used together in an integrated way.

Knowing that it's just as important for children to use meaningful and structural information as it is for them to notice the letters and sounds, what are the implications of that for teachers? How does this knowledge do the following?

* Affect the way we *prompt* children as they are reading?
* Inform the way we *model and support* children as we are working with them?
* Affect the way we *assess* children?

Prompting Beginning Readers

Many teachers who work with beginning struggling readers find themselves at a loss for what to say when a child reading with them gets stuck on a word. It happens to all of us. Our inner voice begins to worry:

* Will I say the right thing?
* What will help him solve the word on his own?
* Is now the time that I should go with a meaning prompt or do I direct her to the letters?
* What if I confuse him further?
* Should I just give her the word and talk about it later?

We both admit to being in that exact situation at times. We have learned to be more effective with our prompting over time and with continuous practice. We thought the best way to share some of our learning with others would be to include a variety of situations we have encountered and what we actually said to each child at the point of difficulty. This is certainly not an all-inclusive list of examples of what you will come across when you read with children, but we hope it's enough to get you started.

The prompts we've included will help you build a repertoire of what to say to children as they are engaged in the process of reading. We decided to give only a few prompts for each situation. We felt shorter was better. We have heard too many complaints from beginning teachers who are given lists with as many as seventy-five prompts on a page!

The examples are set up in this manner:

* We identify something a reader does or doesn't do while reading.
* We give a scenario of that situation, including the prompting the teacher did.
* We suggest other possible prompts that you might try when confronted with a similar incident.
* And finally, we give a suggested reflection idea that relates to the situation.

Beginning reader who is not looking enough at the visual information (not using his knowledge of letter/sound correspondence to check the words)

Anthony: (*Reading.*) I can see my mom. She is washing the car. (*Text: I can see my mom. She is cleaning the car.*)

Pat: Did that look right?

Anthony: Umm. (*Long pause.*)

Pat: Read that again and check to see if this part looks right. (*Slides her finger under the second sentence.*)

Anthony: (*Reads the page again and, with just a little hesitation, is able to fix his error.*)

Pat: Are you right?

Anthony: Yeah, there's a *c* right there.

Other possible prompts:

* Run your finger under that word to see if it looks right to you.
* You know how to check that. Go ahead. (For the child who hesitates because he or she knows something is not quite right.)
* Let the first part of that word help you.
* Are you making it up or really looking? (For the child who is inventing text.)
* Sit up tall and keep your eyes over the message. (For the slouching child; teacher is unsure of where he or she is looking.)
* Don't look at me. Did *you* check to see if it looks right? (For the child who appeals to you for confirmation after he or she reads the word correctly.)
* Keep your eyes down while you're checking.

Reflection Time: Think about *who is doing the monitoring* as you work with children. In the preceding situation with Anthony, Pat was first hoping that Anthony could find his own error. But when he sat and did nothing, she knew she had to run her finger under the part that contained the error to draw his attention to it. She does not always want to be the one who monitors his errors. Eventually Anthony needs to do this for himself. Pat knows she will have to turn responsibility for monitoring over to him. For now she's supporting him in learning how to check if words look right.

 Beginning reader who uses too much visual information (V) and not enough meaning (M) and structure (S)

Emma: (*Reading very word-by-word.*) When Max came home from s - ch - o - o – l. (*Sounds letter by letter without success.*)

Katie: You know where Max was coming from. Think about the story and try it again from here.

Other possible prompts:

* Try that again from here. (Say this as you tap the beginning of the sentence. This helps the child reread to get the sentence meaning back in his or her head.)
* Sometimes the letters don't help us enough so we have to try something else. Let me show you what I'd do next.
* What are you thinking about? (Ask a question about the story, forcing meaningful thought.)
* Is that working for you? (For the child who is persistently sounding the letters without success. This alerts the child to the fact that if sounding out is not helping him or her solve the word, maybe it's time to try something else.)
* If that didn't make sense, remember it's your job to check it. (For the child who puts in garbled sounds and keeps going.)
* Try that again and keep the story in your head as you do.

Reflection Time: Think about whether you prompt in a way that will help the child *only with this book* or in a way that helps the child become a better reader. In the preceding scenario when Katie said, "You know where Max was coming from," she was specifically referring to this story. This is fine to do at times. However, the end goal is for the child to keep his or her mind on what the story is about while reading. The child needs to take responsibility for thinking about the story as a way to help him or her solve the words. You will want your prompts to become less specific over time, for example, "Think about the story." Remember, our job is not just to get the child through *this book*, but rather to help the child add strategic actions to his or her repertoire that can be used on any book.

Beginning reader who does not know all of his or her letters and sounds

Katie: (*First does a book introduction and looks at the pictures in the book together with the student. During the conversation, Katie has purposefully repeated the pattern of the text several times.*)

Edward: (*Reads text.*) I can see a zebra. I can see a . . . (*He stops before the word seal.*)

Katie: It starts like Sydney. (*Emphasizes the* s *sound as she says a fellow student's name.*) Let's try it together.

Other possible prompts:

* ❋ Let's get our mouth ready for this word together. (Or initiate the first sound for the child.)
* ❋ Is it *dolphin, seal,* or *porpoise*? (Giving a few choices of words might narrow the possibilities enough so that the child can use some phonetic information.)
* ❋ Look right here at the first letter. That will help you start that word.
* ❋ It starts like your brother's name, Sam. (Use the names of children in the class as hints or the hooks from the ABC chart.)
* ❋ Put your finger under the first letter of the word. Do you know a word that starts like that? Think about your ABC book.

Reflection Time: We do not hold students back from starting with books until they have all their letters and sounds in place. Do you? Even with only ten letters in their repertoire, we want students to have books they can read. We will continue to teach them more phonetic knowledge as we work with them on continuous texts (real books!) as well as at other times of the day, especially during writing workshop. In Chapter 7 we include information about students like this who come to us with very little knowledge of phonics, letter identification, and early book behaviors.

Beginning reader who misreads the endings of words and doesn't check

(*Katie is teaching a guided reading group with four students. They are reading a book and the text says "Jack looked for the umbrella. He looked and looked."*)

Serena: Jack lookdid for the umbrella. He lookdid and lookdid.

(*Katie notices several of the children are either reading "look" for "looked" or are saying "lookdid."*)

Katie: Friends, let's take a look at these words. (*She writes "look" on the whiteboard, and then writes "looked" underneath.*) What do you notice?

Jasmin: There's an *-ed* on the bottom one.

Katie: Yes! Sometimes words have an *-ed* on the end. *-Ed* makes some different sounds. When we say "looked," what do you hear at the end?

Michael: A *t*! But there's no *t* there!

Katie: You're right! When we say "looked," we hear a *t*. That's just how we say it. I could say, "I looked out the window and saw a bird's nest." You say that. (*The children repeat the sentence.*)

Katie: (*Writes* look, looked, looks, *and* looking *on the whiteboard, one under the other.*) Let's read all of these words together. (*They do so.*) When you read, you have to pay careful attention to what is at the end. Now go back to your book and read that page again.

Other possible prompts:

- Remember what we're working on. Be sure that ending looks and sounds right.
- You got the first part right; now check the ending.
- Did that sound like the way you say it when you are talking? (For errors like "lookdid.")
- How can you fix the last part of that word?
- Wow! You made sure that ending was just right. (For reinforcement.)
- Your brain really noticed that the ending didn't look right and you fixed it! (For reinforcement.)

Reflection Time: The preceding scenario applies to children who are ready to look at more than just the first letter. Katie knew that these students had enough word-solving behaviors under their belts to move on to checking the ends of words. Children should not be asked to look all the way across words in the earliest levels of texts (Developmental Reading Assessment 2 [DRA2] levels 1 or 2, or Fountas and Pinnell levels A and B). These early text level books are mainly for getting one-to-one matching under control, using the picture to make a meaningful prediction of a word, and using the first letter information. Further along the line, when children are doing these things on their own, you can begin working on checking other parts of the word to see if it looks right.

Beginning reader who is not monitoring for 1:1 matching

Eve: (*Reading.*) Come play with us. (*Text: Come and play baseball with us.*)

Pat: Remember, you can't just read without looking. You have to check to see if you're right. Read it with your finger this time and I bet you can fix that part.

Eve: (*As she points with her finger, her attention is drawn to the words and she fixes it just fine.*)

Other possible prompts:

- Use your finger to touch and point here.
- Remember, there has to be a word in the book for each word you say.

- ❋ Check that again by reading it with your finger this time.
- ❋ Did it match?
- ❋ Try that again, but this time touch under the words.
- ❋ Don't hide the words from your eyes. (For a child who touches on top of the words.)
- ❋ Let's try this. You touch under the words as I read this page.

Reflection Time: Some beginning readers try to memorize text. They remember what the story is about and they begin to read without focusing on the print. When we ask them to use their finger, this draws their eyes to where they should be looking. It helps them monitor for their known words. They can learn to check that the word they are saying is the same as the one they are touching. We include more information about supporting children who need to work on voice/print matching in Chapter 7. Once one-to-one matching is under control, the finger pointing while reading should be discouraged. It tends to slow down the reader. When a problem arises, it's OK for the child to use his or her finger to straighten out the confusion, but then the child should drop it as he or she picks up speed again.

Child who is ready to use some visual information beyond the first letter, but is unsure how

Carlos: (*Reading.*) I will st . . . (*Text: I will stay here. You can go and hide.*)
Pat: (*Writes* day *on the whiteboard.*) Do you know this word?
Carlos: Day
Pat: (*Writes* stay *under* day.) If that is *day*, then what would this be?
Carlos: St . . . ay. Stay!
Pat: Yes, if you know *day* you can figure out *stay* because it looks and sounds the same at the end; it just starts with different letters. Now go back and reread that page.
Carlos: (*Reads.*) I will stay here. You can go and hide.

Other possible prompts:

- ❋ Do you see a part of this word that looks like another word you know? (Point to the unknown word.)
- ❋ What do you know about that word?
- ❋ Does it remind you of a word you know?
- ❋ What could you check?
- ❋ What can you hear that might help?

Reflection Time: For struggling readers who don't automatically make connections between known and unknown words, the teacher can support them in learning to make analogies. The teacher holds some of what that child knows in his or her memory and begins to help the child link a part of the unknown word to a word that the child knows.

❀ ❀ ❀

As readers begin to take on more and more strategic actions, they continue to form their reading process systems. They begin to self-monitor themselves more often. Even the earliest readers begin to notice when things don't look right, sound right, or make sense, and they can often self-correct without teacher assistance. These are excellent times to congratulate the child. Your reinforcement will *spur on* repeated use of the strategic action that the child just performed. The following are suggestions for prompts to use after self-corrections.

> ### Reinforcement prompts after a child self-corrects an error
> ❀ Did you notice that when you _____, it helped you _____?
> ❀ Right here you were able to _____. Let's see if we can try that together over here.
> ❀ You are really being a great checker today.
> ❀ You found that tricky part on your own and fixed it.
> ❀ You must feel proud of how you fixed that all by yourself.

The best and most basic advice we can offer overall is to keep your prompts short, specific, and to the point. Less teacher talk is better. Also remember that when a teacher uses a prompt, he or she is either asking the child to self-monitor (check on something) or calling on the child to perform an act that he or she knows the child is capable of doing. For prompting to be effective, children must have control over the strategic action that is being asked of them. They can only respond to our prompts if they understand what the prompt is asking them to do. In the next section we look at how teachers model those strategic actions or use the sources of information throughout the day, thus preparing children for action when prompted.

Modeling the Sources of Information Throughout the Day

All of the strategic actions that children are expected to do when prompted can be modeled during the literacy block in various ways. Wise teachers use the language of prompts throughout the day in a supportive manner. We often begin by doing our modeling with the whole class, but we are constantly watching children to notice who needs further instruction.

Occasionally we reflect on the prompts we commonly use to make sure that our prompting language connects with the language we use during focus lessons. Then we come up with ways to model these strategic actions during shared reading, community writing time, morning message, or even while reading aloud.

In the next sections, we show a variety of ways that we incorporate strategy teaching throughout the day. We give ideas for how to teach for making sense, for using a balance of the sources of information (M, S, V), and for confirming.

Teaching About Making Sense

One thing we wondered recently was whether or not all the first graders understood what we meant when we prompted "Does that make sense?" We began using that phrase purposefully during other times of the day. After reading aloud *Amazing Grace* by Mary Hoffman (1991), Katie might ask, "Does it make sense that Grace was given the part of Peter Pan?" Or after a shared reading of the Big Book *Who's in the Shed?* by Brenda Parkes (1997a), "Does it make sense that the animals ran away from there?" The children seem to be able to answer these questions thoughtfully, with ease, and with evidence from the text to support their answers. The continual exposure to that expression "Does it make sense?" becomes quite familiar to them. Our frequent repetition also fully supports the concept that everything we read *is supposed to* make sense.

We also think aloud about making sense during writing lessons. One day when Katie was modeling in front of the children, she accidentally wrote the word *look* instead of *took*. As she was rereading her sentence to decide on her next word, she read aloud, "'We look the subway to . . .' Wait a minute! 'We *look* the subway.' That doesn't make sense. Let me fix that. 'We *took* the subway to DC near the museum.'"

If you're not one to make errors often, you can easily make the same kind of error intentionally. During shared reading or when reading aloud, just substitute a wrong word, but quickly show how you monitor yourself for making sense. After fixing the error, tell the children how important it is for readers to always be listening to themselves as they read, even when they are reading quietly inside their heads. Tell them, "If you read something that doesn't make sense, it's your job to go back and fix it."

Some teachers may feel awkward or fake making a purposeful mistake in front of students. Don't overdo it with this idea. The children will catch on soon enough. Except for these occasions of visibly showing what it means when something doesn't make sense, we rarely make purposeful errors in front of students. However, we always grab onto that teachable moment when we make the kinds of mistakes that readers and writers inevitably make. These are great authentic teaching opportunities, and a chance to show your students how self-monitoring really works.

Teaching for Balance of the Sources of Information

In our prompting examples you saw that we often prompted the child to use the source of information that he or she was neglecting when trying to solve the word. In our teaching we need to model for the students how we use all the sources of information—meaning, structure, and visual—in an integrated way.

Children may find it easy to use the picture, but using the picture *and* the first letter(s) requires more modeling. Here is how Christy Hermann demonstrated this to her K–1 students. She was reading a Big Book that gave clues about an animal on one page, and the answer on the next page. On one page the children could see the picture but the word was covered with a sticky note. For example, the children predicted that the picture was a crab or a lobster. Christy asked them, "What would you expect to see at the beginning if the word is *lobster*?" "What would you expect to see at the beginning if the word is *crab*?" Then she revealed the first letter, which helped the children use first-letter and picture information together.

Along the same lines, teachers can use symbols to represent various strategic behaviors. We introduce the symbols to the children on strategy cards (see photo) and show how we use them. The symbols represent, in order: (1) checking the picture, (2) thinking about the story, (3) going back to reread, (4) checking the first letter(s), (5) checking known parts of the word, and (6) rereading to check and confirm. (Appendix 4 provides a copy of the strategy card that you can reproduce.) We leave the symbols on a small chart nearby so that the children can refer to them when we ask the question, "What can we try?" Once the children become familiar with the strategies the symbols represent, we remove the chart. We don't want the use of the chart to slow the students down. The strategic actions need to become second nature to the children.

Another way to model using a balance of the sources of information can be done during shared reading. While rereading a familiar Big Book, we might change a word in the text with white correction tape. For example, cover the word *neighed* in the sentence, "'Who's in the shed?' neighed the old gray mare." Then write the word *yelled* on the white tape. Now cover over that word with another strip of white tape. The students then have to predict words that would make sense (M) and sound right (S) for that blank. They can't depend on remembering the word of the text from past readings, because you've changed it. After collecting several suggestions from the students, we show them the first letter so that they can narrow down the choice with phonetic information (V). We would always end by saying something like, "You're right. The word *yelled* makes sense and sounds right, and it looks right too."

One last possible way to teach for balance is to use your morning message. The day before a field trip to the zoo, a line in Katie's morning message said, "Do you think the animals at the zoo will be active tomorrow?" When the children got to the word *active*, they all stopped. Katie asked, "What can we do to help ourselves with that tricky word?" One child suggested starting the word like /a/ in *apple*, another suggested rereading from the beginning of the sentence, and a third child said he saw the word *act*.

Katie felt confident that her modeled lessons were beginning to transfer over and the children were self-initiating problem solving. During independent reading time she was noticing that many of the children were starting to use all three sources of information.

Teaching Confirming

If we are going to expect children to respond to our prompts with certain behaviors, then we need to teach them the behaviors. They will not instinctively know how to reread to confirm or use their finger to run under a word to see if the letters look right. We need to model these actions. Struggling readers, in particular, need explicit modeling, and oftentimes more than once.

Modeling the rereading of a sentence or part of a sentence encourages children to do the same. This can be done when reading from a chart the class created or from a Big Book, or as we are writing in front of the children. Include your reason for rereading, as in the following examples:

❀ During a writing workshop mini-lesson, we often say, "I better reread what I'm writing here to make sure this sentence is making sense and sounds right."

❀ While reading together in the Big Book *The Enormous Watermelon* by Brenda Parkes (1997b), Pat said, "I want us to read that line again. It has bold letters. That means the author wants us to read those words louder." (Everyone rereads together emphasizing the bold words.) "Now that sounded right!"

❀ After the children collaborated on a shared writing of a note to the other first-grade classes about their worm habitat, Katie said, "Now let's reread the whole thing one last time. We want to make sure it all sounds right, looks right, and makes sense."

We try never to assume too much when working with beginning readers. For children to be able to independently check and confirm words as they read and write, we have to be sure they know *where to look* and *how to perform that task*. There are some children who don't know what you mean when you ask them to find the *beginning* or *end* of the word. Remember to model, as in the following examples:

❋ We often use the phrases "the first part of the word," "the last part of the word," or "find the first letter or last letter" when writing with the children or during a word study demonstration.

❋ Sometimes during shared writing we'll say, "I'm going to run my finger under that word and say it slowly to make sure it looks right." For example, when the class was composing a letter to the parents about their upcoming poetry reading, Katie stopped after writing *invited*. "You are all invited. Hmm. Let me check to see if that looks right." She ran her finger slowly under the word. "I'm listening to see if the letters match what I'm saying. In . . . vi . . . ted."

❋ When writing a letter to parents together, we might suggest two ways to say a phrase or sentence and then ask the children, "Which way sounds right to you?" For example: "On Friday we are going to the Pumpkin Patch" or "On Friday we going to the Pumpkin Patch."

It's important to weave our strategy teaching into a variety of components throughout the day. In Chapter 5 we elaborate on the components of a comprehensive literacy framework. If we expect children to predict, search for, and gather information from the various sources of information; reread; and check and confirm predictions, then we need to model how to do those things. These opportunities will serve to familiarize the students with the language of prompts.

Keeping MSV in Mind as We Assess

Our focus in this chapter was to teach and prompt children to use meaning, structure, and visual information (MSV). So one aspect of how we assess early beginning readers is to remain alert for how they are using such information. A running record, or any miscue analysis system, is a wonderful display of what the child does when he or she comes to unknown words. Whether the child is successful in solving the words or not, we can tell a lot by examining the attempts, errors, and self-corrections that are recorded on these assessment forms. Even without running record knowledge, it's easy for any teacher to take note of the word the child mistakenly read in place of the word in the text.

Here are some examples of substitutions:

Child:	goes	seeing	kids
Text:	comes	looking	children

These examples tell us that the child is using a fair amount of meaningful information when reading but needs to be encouraged to look more at the letters and use that knowledge too.

Child:	<u>great</u>	<u>nest</u>	<u>going</u>
Text:	grass	need	good

These examples suggest to us that the child is not using enough meaningful information. The errors have some of the right letters, but most likely do not make sense in the sentence. This child needs more help holding on to the sentence meaning or story line as he or she stops along the way to figure out a word.

Examining self-corrections (SC) will also show us how the child is beginning to cross-check one source of information against another.

Natalie:	<u>Matthew</u>	<u>looked</u>	<u>around. / SC</u>		
Text:	Matthew	looked	excited.		
Timmy:	<u>Up / SC</u>	<u>the</u>	<u>box</u>	<u>says</u>	<u>Mom.</u>
Text:	Open	the	box	said	Mom.
Lupita:	<u>Off</u>	<u>went</u>	<u>the</u>	<u>three</u>	<u>little. / SC</u>
Text:	Off	went	the	three	bears.

Resources About Taking Running Records

Running Records for Classroom Teachers by Marie Clay (2000).
One Child at a Time: Making the Most of Your Time with Struggling Readers, K–6 by Pat Johnson (2006).
On Solid Ground: Strategies for Teaching Reading K–3 by Sharon Taberski (2000).
Running Records: A Self-Tutoring Guide by Peter Johnston (2000).

When Natalie said *around* in place of *excited*, she used meaning and structure, but then she fixed it with visual information. Take a minute and think about what happened in the two other instances.

These are just a few examples of observing student errors to see how a child is using the sources of information. Further training is necessary for teachers to become adept at taking and analyzing running records; there is certainly more to it than what we've suggested here. The sidebar contains a few books with more information on learning how to take and analyze running records.

Valuable information can be acquired through analysis, especially when we see consistent patterns emerge. This information directly leads to our instructional decision making. We discuss this in more depth in Chapter 10.

Wrapping Up MSV

Many teachers use the word *decoding* to mean the figuring out of words that kids do. We tend to stay away from this word because by its very definition, *decode* means that there is some specific code to be translated. And, as mentioned earlier, English is not an easily decodable language. To us, *decoding* means that only phonics is being used, and we hope we've shown in this chapter that all students need to use a balance of meaning, structural, and phonetic information simultaneously as they figure out words.

Even students who are reading at higher than primary-grade levels need to use a balance of all the sources of information (MSV) when solving words. Upper-grade students may need more teaching on *how words work* and on *taking words apart*, but they *still* need to balance that detailed visual word attack with meaningful and structural information. In fact, all readers solve words by these means.

CHAPTER 5

A Comprehensive
Literacy Framework

Margaret Mooney (1990) speaks of the importance of including reading and writing *to children, with children,* and *by children* in every teaching day. We agree that this is the most supportive framework for literacy instruction. This is nothing new, however. In fact, most teachers are probably familiar with the components of this framework. Fountas and Pinnell (1996) write about *balanced literacy*; Schulman and Payne (2000) refer to their classroom environment as *comprehensive literacy*; Keene (2008) describes a *literacy studio*, which, at its very foundation, has reading and writing *to, with,* and *by*; and Boushey and Moser (2006), "The Sisters," incorporate these elements in their "daily five."

Throughout our book, we refer to this classroom environment as a *comprehensive literacy framework*. We prefer the word *comprehensive*, meaning "complete and broad," over the word *balanced*, which can lead some teachers to believe that each component is given equal time. Although we recommend that all components be included, the frequency and duration of each component will differ based on the needs of your students.

If teachers are going to support their hardest-to-teach readers as they learn to build a reading process system, then the classroom environment must allow time for teachers to do just that. Within a comprehensive literacy framework, teachers are able to reach all children, including struggling readers, by addressing various needs in multiple instructional ways.

In this chapter, we describe each of the components of a comprehensive literacy framework. However, we do not go in depth on how to implement the organization and management of each component. There are many professional texts already published that support teachers in setting up the classroom in this manner (see sidebar). Our focus is to show two aspects:

1. How *reading process* is woven throughout each component
2. How *struggling readers* are supported within a comprehensive literacy classroom

Later in the chapter, we discuss the reciprocity of reading and writing. While the focus of this book is on reading process and struggling readers, we felt it necessary to include writing as a key component in reading instruction. Finally, we take a look at a primary classroom where a comprehensive literacy framework is in place. Our goal is for you to see how teaching within this approach helps all students build an effective reading process system throughout the day.

Professional Resources About a Comprehensive Literacy Framework

Guided Reading: Making It Work by Mary Browning Schulman and Carleen daCruz Payne (2000).

Guided Reading: Good First Teaching for All Children by Irene Fountas and Gay Su Pinnell (1996).

"The Words Came Down!": English Language Learners Read, Write, and Talk Across the Curriculum, K–2 by Emelie Parker and Tess Pardini (2006).

More Than Guided Reading: Finding the Right Instructional Mix by Cathy Mere (2005).

Reading To, With, and By Children by Margaret Mooney (1990).

On Solid Ground: Strategies for Teaching Reading, K–3 by Sharon Taberski (2000).

The Daily Five: Fostering Literacy Independence in the Elementary Grades by Gail Boushey and Joan Moser (2006).

The Components of a Comprehensive Literacy Framework

Figure 5.1 shows the components of a comprehensive literacy framework. Each component serves a purpose in reaching all students in their literacy acquisition. Such an environment, which encourages student independence, will give the teacher opportunities to meet with small groups and individually with children.

Figure 5.1
Components of a
Comprehensive Literacy
Framework

Reading To, With, and By Children	Writing To, With, and By Children
Read-Aloud Shared Reading and Interactive Read-Aloud Guided Reading Independent Reading	Morning Message Community Writing Independent Writing

Read Aloud: Reading *To* Children

Quite some time ago, Shelley Harwayne, author of *Lifetime Guarantees* (2000) and other great texts, asked us in a workshop to think about our *nonnegotiables*. She wanted the participants to reflect on those parts of their day that they were unwilling to give up no matter what. Reading aloud topped our list then, and it still does.

Many teachers hold firm to the belief that reading aloud should only be for the pure enjoyment of books. Others use the read-aloud time to teach and model. We support a combination of the two. For us, there are two kinds of reading aloud: the *traditional read-aloud* and the *interactive read-aloud*. In a traditional read-aloud we come together as a community and the teacher models for the children what the language of books *sounds like*, what loving a book *looks like*, and what being lost in a story *feels like*. This time may not be attached to any curriculum objectives or academic standards. Rather, it is simply a time to share and enjoy a fabulous book with your students.

In an interactive read-aloud, the teacher reads the text with a clear instructional purpose in mind, engaging the children in conversation before, during, and after the read-aloud. Teachers use this type of read-aloud to model comprehension strategies, such as making connections, activating prior knowledge, questioning, and so on. Because we value interactive read-aloud time with children so highly, we delve further into this component in Chapter 6. You will see how all students, including struggling readers, can talk about and process texts within a supportive community, as we nudge them to comprehend a higher level of text than they are able to read on their own.

Although we provide time for focused talk during an interactive read-aloud, we don't discourage the children's spontaneous responses or reactions to the text during a traditional read-aloud. For example, Katie recently read the book *Skippyjon Jones in the Doghouse* by Judy Schachner (2008) to her class as a fun, traditional read-aloud to end the day. She was not planning on using it for a particular teaching focus, but watch what happened.

This book is a story of a mischievous Siamese cat who gets in trouble and is sent to his room. Once there, he goes into his closet and, through his imagination, takes journeys as a bold and fearless Chihuahua. As Katie was reading this fun book to her class, Jose said, "Hey, Skippyjon Jones is just like Max in *Where the Wild Things Are*!" (Sendak 1988). Katie hadn't even thought of that connection, but he was absolutely right, Max and Skippyjon Jones both take wild, imaginative adventures after being sent to their rooms. Although she was not teaching a lesson on making connections, Katie certainly stopped and acknowledged the connection and reinforced the idea that readers make connections to help them understand and enjoy what they read. This natural talk will occur frequently during all read-alouds, and we encourage it, as these comments authentically show what readers do when enjoying and interacting with text.

All kids need to be read to, but it is especially beneficial for your struggling readers. Some have not had rich literacy experiences before entering school. Some English language learners may have been read to in their home language, but have had little exposure to English. And, sad as it may be, some children have never been read to at all prior to entering school. With read-alouds, all of these students get multiple opportunities to hear book language while being mesmerized by an expert reader reading an enjoyable text. Teachers share their passion for reading to encourage all students to make reading a part of their lives. A traditional read-aloud is one way to do this. And it's a whole lot of fun!

Shared Reading: Reading With Children

Don Holdaway (1979) introduced shared reading, an interactive reading experience, as a way to imitate the typical bedtime story. The purpose of shared reading is to make texts accessible to all children, allowing them to experience what it feels like to be a proficient reader. It is a time for us to teach about the reading process and serves as a gateway to guided reading and independent reading. Enjoyment of the story is important, and children are encouraged to participate in the shared reading experience.

If we want to support children as they build an effective reading process system, then we must show them what it looks like when a proficient reader is using his or her system. Shared reading provides us with a place to do just that. It is an opportunity for teachers to "provide a solid foundation for reading and writing. At the same time, it fosters a sense of community, as children collaborate to talk, think, listen, and join in on the reading" (Parkes 2000, 12). This is especially beneficial to our most struggling readers as they are guided by a teacher in putting together an integrated reading process system and are part of a community of readers.

The shared reading text must be large enough for all children to see—a poster, chart, Big Book, or text projected on an interactive whiteboard or displayed with an overhead projector. The teacher does the reading and encourages the children to join in on a refrain or some other known part of the text. While the first reading may be done for enjoyment, repeated readings provide multiple opportunities for the teacher to model a reading strategy, skill, or behavior as the children are supported in a low-risk setting. Teachers think aloud to help children see what goes on in the head of a proficient reader.

A focus for a shared reading lesson could include, but is not limited to the following:

- ❀ Comprehension strategies such as visualizing, questioning, activating schema, monitoring and correcting, and predicting at the word level or the text level
- ❀ Concepts about print such as voice-to-print match, left-to-right reading with return sweep, reading the left page before the right, and punctuation and what it means for the reader
- ❀ Meaning, structure, and visual sources of information to solve words and comprehend
- ❀ Searching and gathering information to support word solving or comprehension
- ❀ Word work and word study analogies
- ❀ Fluency
- ❀ Nonfiction text features such as italics, graphs, diagrams, and bold print
- ❀ Nonfiction text formats such as cause and effect and questions and answers
- ❀ Genre study

Professional Resources About Shared Reading

Shared Reading for Today's Classroom: Lessons and Strategies for Explicit Instruction in Comprehension, Fluency, Word Study, and Genre by Carleen daCruz Payne (2005).
Read It Again! Revisiting Shared Reading by Brenda Parkes (2000).
Perspectives on Shared Reading: Planning and Practice by Bobbi Fisher and Emily Fisher Medvic (2000).
Text Savvy: Using a Shared Reading Framework to Build Comprehension, Grades 3–6 by Sarah Daunis and Maria Cassiani Iams (2007).
On the Same Page: Shared Reading Beyond the Primary Grades by Janet Allen (2002).

This is not an all-inclusive list. In fact, any of the strategies on the circle chart in Figure 2.1 can be modeled for children through a shared reading lesson. There are several excellent books that illustrate the many instructional possibilities for shared reading and its importance as a component in a comprehensive literacy approach (see sidebar).

Actively engaging children in reading a familiar text can support them as they begin to transfer the strategies into their own reading and writing. Sometimes Katie uses the shared reading experience to springboard into a word study activity. Notice that in the following lesson she is not focusing on a specific item or sound, such as /ch/ or /cr/. The idea is to get across a *concept*—that a

reader can break words apart into smaller parts and examine them. Rather than do such an activity with unknown words or nonsense words in isolation, Katie takes the words from a familiar shared reading text. Let's see what this looks like.

Children in Katie's class have heard the Big Book *In the Tall, Tall Grass* by Denise Fleming (1995) several times. This book contains some difficult vocabulary, but because of the many rereadings, the children are now familiar with phrases such as "Crunch, munch, caterpillar's lunch." By pulling out some of these tricky words and examining them together as a group, Katie is able to demonstrate for the children how to take words apart. Moving the parts of the words around with magnetic letters allows her to model how words are built with various chunks (see photo).

As they work on these, the children are able to connect a part of a word to a known word. Vanessa notices that /un/ is in *fun*. Anthony notices that *tall* is a little like *ball*. Brenda points out that /ch/ appears at the beginning of Charley's name, and also at the end of *crunch* and *munch*.

As Katie sends the children off to read and write independently after the lesson, she reminds them to look for parts they know as they are solving words. This activity, of course, is one of many on this concept.

Shared reading is often used to model a comprehension strategy. In the following example, Katie uses a Big Book to model questioning. She shows the class the cover of *Fabulous Frogs* by Linda Glaser (2000) and begins the lesson.

Katie: I have a book to share with you about something a lot of you are interested in—frogs! When I first found this book, I wondered what this book might teach me. I had a lot of questions about frogs. I wondered what kind of frogs would be in this book and if I would learn about how frogs were born. Take a minute to turn and talk to your partner about what you are wondering. What questions do you have?

After the children turn and talk, Katie calls on several children to share their questions. She records the questions on a piece of chart paper.

Lucy: Where do frogs live?
Sam: What do frogs eat?
Celeste: Why are the frogs on the cover blue?
Katie: Wow! What great questions you all have! I can really tell you are think- ing about what you would like to learn about frogs. You are getting your minds ready to read by thinking about what we might find out while read- ing this book. That's a really good thing that readers do before they start to read. I wonder if those questions will help us keep our minds focused on the information in this book. Let's search for some answers, and if you have any more questions as we read, we'll write those down too.

They begin to read the book, stopping to record more questions and talking about the answers they find along the way. Later, Katie finds a good stopping point in this nonfiction Big Book.

Katie: Let's stop reading for today. But first, let's go back and look at the ques- tions you asked. Let's see which ones have been answered. We'll write the letter *A*, for *answered*, after those questions. If there are any questions that haven't been answered yet, we will leave those on the chart for tomorrow. If they still aren't answered when we finish the book, we'll put an *MR* next to them, meaning that we need to do *more research* to find the answer. You can look in other frog books, in the library, or on the computer to see if you can find out the answers.

The class talks about the questions and everything they have learned so far from this book. The children are excited about continuing the reading the next day, in hopes that their other questions will get answered. If they are not, they will love going to other sources to find the answers. Although Katie would not record questions on a chart every time she reads a nonfiction Big Book nor require readers to write this information down while reading independently, occasionally keeping track of their thinking allows them to revisit the reading work and helps children learn how questioning can help them understand what they are reading.

The shared reading experience provides a time for struggling readers to try reading strategies or build concepts within a safe environment and with the support of the teacher and other readers. Even for adults, doing something with a group gives us support and confidence and often the courage to do something we wouldn't try on our own. Katie found this to be true when training for her first 100-mile bike ride. It was much easier, and certainly more enjoyable, to train with friends who were experienced cyclists than to train alone. Shared reading has a similar confidence-building effect on struggling readers.

Guided Reading: Reading *With* Children

Reading with children in small groups or one-on-one is known as guided reading. The teacher guides the readers in texts that are at their instructional level, appropriately challenging them to put their reading process system to work. Every child is in the role of reader with his or her own copy of the book and reads at his or her own pace. The students work at solving the words and comprehending the text with support from the teacher. In order to make sure that guided reading meets the needs of your struggling readers, you will need to pay attention to several important factors:

- ❀ How to give supportive book introductions
- ❀ How to choose a focus for your guided reading lesson
- ❀ How to schedule groups so the struggling students get the attention they need
- ❀ How to keep the rest of the class engaged in literacy activities while you are meeting with small groups

The Importance of a Quality Book Introduction

When we gather children together for a guided reading group, we want to be sure to set the stage for a successful first reading. We need to make sure that the book we have chosen for this group is one the kids will want to read. Can they relate it to a personal experience? Are they interested in the topic? Will you be able to help them connect this book to background knowledge? Is it a good match for this group of kids?

After you have chosen a good text, you will need to focus on giving a quality book introduction. Regardless of the level of the text the children are reading, it is our job to prepare them and help them get their minds ready to read and think about the text. We use our introductions as a way to support readers in processing a text that is at their instructional level—slightly more difficult than their independent reading level. Book introductions should accomplish several goals:

❀ Set the children up for success on the first reading

❀ Include authentic social interactions and conversations

❀ Powerfully support ELLs and struggling readers and ensure that the children have the language and ideas needed to understand and enjoy the book

❀ Include deliberate teaching moves

The book introduction is different from a page-by-page "book walk" in which you or the students are simply talking about what the children see on each page. Instead, you keep meaning at the forefront of the conversation and engage the children in *thinking* before reading. There are some common steps for a book introduction. Choose which of the following are appropriate for the readers you are working with:

❀ Always give the title of the book and talk with the students about what it might mean.

❀ Give a short summary: the big idea. Keep this meaning statement short and concise. For example, "This book is about three billy goats who want to cross a bridge but are frightened by the troll who lives underneath. Let's read to see how they trick the troll to get across the bridge." (See Chapter 7 for more on meaning statements in early emergent books.)

❀ Hook the children with a comment or question to encourage their talk. Make sure to connect to their prior knowledge, interests, or wonderings. For example, "This book is about a boy who has a pet who is always getting into trouble. Have you ever had a pet who caused problems in your house?"

❀ While conversing, allow the children to predict and negotiate the meaning of the text while looking at a few pictures or looking through the book on their own. For example, "Do you think the boy will be able to keep his pet after it has caused so much trouble?"

❀ Use some of the vocabulary from the text in your conversation, especially if there are words that some of your students will not have experience with. For example, words like *hearth* or *scarecrow*.

❀ Practice an awkward language structure if needed. For example, the meaning of "off you go" may be unfamiliar to children, even if they can read the words.

❀ Ask the children to predict and locate a word if necessary. You may have the children turn to a specific page and see if they can find that word. For example, on a page with a picture of a helicopter you might say, "What do you think *helicopter* might start with? You say it. What might it end with? Do you think it will be a long word or a short word? Now see if you can find the word *helicopter* on this page."

❀ Mention and remind children of the teaching focus. This has been determined based on what this group of children needs in order to continue developing their reading process system. For example, "As you are read-ing, remember when you are figuring out a tricky word to make sure that what you say looks right and makes sense in the story."

❁ Save some things for the children to problem solve on their own. We want the children to use this time to practice using their systems. We need to make sure there are opportunities to do so.

The Importance of Having a Focus

Guided reading lessons have a specific focus for instruction. The decision about what to choose for an instructional focus is determined from your ongo-ing assessments and is based on what the children need to learn next as read-ers. The focus is intended to add to the readers' repertoire of strategic actions and behaviors. Guided reading is for readers to develop "systems of strategic actions for processing increasingly challenging texts" (Fountas and Pinnell 2006, 373). Once teachers understand more about how reading process works, they become more adept at choosing the instructional focus of a guided read-ing lesson. As in shared reading, any of the instructional foci that make up a reading process system can become the focus for a lesson (see the list on page 75), as long as you base the focus on the needs of the students in that group. Remember, we are teaching the *readers*, not the book.

Throughout the guided reading session, the teacher also plays the role of observer, watching and recording how the children are putting their reading process systems to work. We need to observe struggling readers carefully and notice which strategies they are secure with, which strategies they are begin-ning to use, and what they need to learn next. The information the teacher records helps to plan future instruction.

Considerations for Scheduling Groups

Guided reading gives teachers the flexibility to work with children in small groups or one-on-one on very specific instructional needs. This flexibility is essential when considering the needs of our hardest-to-teach children. Struggling readers need to be provided with many opportunities to handle text at their own level and, therefore, need to meet with the teacher often. In the reality of a classroom with twenty-five or more kids, many teachers start their guided reading groups each day by meeting with their larger groups of more proficient readers. But we find that this leaves little time for the smaller groups of children who are having the most difficulty. Take a look at the sample chart (Figure 5.2) of how Katie schedules a typical week of guided reading sessions.

Notice that Katie's priority is given to her most struggling students, as she meets with them daily. She meets with groups B and C four times a week, while

Figure 5.2
Guided Reading
Schedule

Monday	Tuesday	Wednesday	Thursday	Friday
A	A	A	A	A
B	C	B	B	open
C	open	C	C	B
D	E	D	E	D

A = 3 students on DRA level 3 (least proficient)
B = 4 students on DRA level 5
C = 6 students on DRA level 9
D = 6 students on DRA level 12
E = 5 students on DRA level 16+ (most proficient)

her more proficient readers (groups D and E) receive small-group instruction two to three times per week. Although she has grouped by levels on this particular chart (Figure 5.2), other weeks she groups by specific needs. The groups remain flexible, changing weekly or as the needs of the students change. Occasionally she might have a student who does not fit exactly in one of the groups. That student may participate in two different groups—one slightly below where his or her needs are, and one slightly above. Note that there are also two open spots for Katie to use as individual needs arise.

In all honesty, it is rare that the schedule works out this perfectly because of the inevitable interruptions that are out of our control, such as fire drills, assemblies, and so on. Our intent here is to bring your attention to how often struggling readers need to be met with, and the importance of being purposeful in your planning for your guided reading groups. Being fair does not always mean equal time with the teacher. It means providing children with the kind of instructional support required for them to continue to develop as readers.

What Are the Other Kids Doing?

As a classroom teacher who mentors new teachers in the school, Katie is often asked, "But what are the other kids doing while the teacher is instructing a guided reading group?" Katie has done different things every year, depending on the group of students and what they can manage independently. Some years she uses structured literacy centers, but other years, with a different make-up of the student population, she chooses not to use centers. However, one thing she believes strongly is that students need to be engaged in authentic *reading* while she meets with groups. They may be reading independently, with buddies, following along in a book at a listening center, or reading charts, Big Books, and other shared reading texts around the room. How you decide to do this in your classroom will depend on the grade level, time of year, and the needs of your students. To learn more, take a look in one of the many resources that describe

Professional Resources About Guided Reading

Guided Reading: Making It Work by Mary Browning Schulman and Carleen daCruz Payne (2000).

Guided Reading: Good First Teaching for All Children by Irene Fountas and Gay Su Pinnell (1996).

Growing Readers: Units of Study in the Primary Classroom by Kathy Collins (2004).

The Daily Five: Fostering Literacy Independence in the Elementary Grades by Gail Boushey and Joan Moser (2006).

Literacy Work Stations: Making Centers Work by Debbie Diller (2003).

guided reading and the use of centers or other literacy activities that kids can do while you are meeting with small groups (see sidebar).

Regardless of the way you choose to structure your guided reading time, there are two important factors to keep in mind:

* Make sure you address the needs of all of your students, especially your struggling readers, during the guided reading sessions.
* Remain flexible as a teacher, so that you are willing to change things such as the schedule, instruction, or the groupings if something is not working quite right.

Independent Reading: Reading *By* Children

A comprehensive literacy framework includes time for independent practice. Many teachers make the best use of this time by providing students with a selection of books that are matched specifically to each child.

In primary grades, teachers often use book boxes or book bags—collections of books that children have read previously in guided reading groups or have chosen from the classroom collection. The books are a combination of

teacher-selected and student-selected texts. They are neither too easy nor too hard and provide just the right level of challenges for children to practice integrating strategies as they build a reading process system. If children are not spending a significant portion of their day engaged in texts that allow them to practice the strategies we are modeling, then we cannot possibly expect them to take on these strategies and use them independently. "To become skilled at almost any activity requires extensive and continual practice" (Allington and McGill-Franzen 2008, 22).

All students can benefit from rereading familiar texts. Rereading helps build fluency and allows children to think deeper about the texts. We are always amazed at how much more children notice and think about on the second or third reading of a book. Frequent, familiar reading gets the system working faster and stronger. It also builds confidence and a feeling that, "Yes, I *am* a reader!"

During independent reading time, the teacher confers with children. He or she observes how the children approach reading and how they are using their strategies. Careful observation lets the teacher see how the child is processing. This guides instruction as he or she plans for guided reading groups as well as whole-group instruction.

Although we make sure that the books in the children's hands are just right for them during independent reading, it is important to have a different time in our day for children to read self-selected books that are not necessarily leveled. Katie has two separate times in her day when children can read anything they choose (see the sample schedule that begins on page 91). They love to peruse the latest *Ranger Rick* magazine, the huge *Ripley's Believe It or Not* book (Packard 2002), and all the fiction, nonfiction, and poetry books in the classroom library. Many children choose books that are challenging for them, but it is during this time that children freely enjoy the pictures and/or the words in books of their choosing.

If our ultimate goal is to have children become proficient readers, then we must make sure that there is a great deal of time and choice within our independent reading time. Readers need to enjoy a variety of texts, choose favorites, and live the life of a reader. At the same time, they need to practice the strategies that readers use so that they too can experience success as readers and continue to strengthen and expand their network of strategies. As Tony Stead says in his book *Good Choice!* (2008), "By establishing a time for independent reading from the onset of the school year, children not only build up stamina for reading but also see it as an important and pleasurable component of their daily lives" (5). The professional books in the sidebar

Professional Resources About Independent Reading

What Really Matters for Struggling Readers: Designing Research-Based Programs by Richard Allington (2005).
Growing Readers: Units of Study in the Primary Classroom by Kathy Collins (2004).
The Power of Reading: Insights from the Research by Stephen Krashen (2004).
Reading Essentials: The Specifics You Need to Teach Reading Well by Regie Routman (2003).
Good Choice! Supporting Independent Reading and Response, K–6 by Tony Stead (2008).
Beyond Leveled Books: Supporting Early and Transitional Readers in Grades K–5 by Karen Szymusiak, Franki Sibberson, and Lisa Koch (2008).

emphasize the importance of giving all students, including your struggling readers, time for independent reading.

Morning Message: Writing *To* and *With* Children

The daily morning message is a time for writing *to* children as well as reading and writing *with* children. It is important to note that there are many ways to do morning message, including Responsive Classroom's *Morning Meeting Book* approach (Kriete and Bechtel 2002) and the ways described in *Getting the Most Out of Morning Message and Other Shared Writing Lessons* (Payne and Schulman 1998). Some teachers choose to write the message ahead of time, others write the message with the students, and still others do a combination. Katie routinely writes her message to the children (*writing to*) ahead of time, with opportunities for them to interact with the message while reading it and while writing parts of the message as well (*writing and reading with*). In this way, their morning message is highly interactive.

The message is written as a friendly letter from Katie to the class, and can be written on chart paper, the overhead projector, or an interactive whiteboard. Children need to be able to write on the message and all of them need to be able to see it. Katie's messages are typically three to five sentences, with a few blanks for the children to fill in words or letters, as well as an occasional survey question or place for all children to write on the message. The content of the message can be wide and varied; it does not have to be about the daily schedule. (See Appendix 5 for examples of morning messages.)

Katie purposefully plans what the focus of the message will be and makes sure that the text is engaging and of high interest to the members of the class. Her class reads the message together first, saying a soft "hmm" for each blank word. Then Katie calls on different children to fill in the blanks, circle something they notice, or explain what they are thinking. She is particularly mindful of the varied needs of her students. She can differentiate her instruction and better meet the needs of her most struggling readers by calling on them to interact in a way that is appropriate to their individual needs.

Katie tries not to do too much with one message. This is a quick and focused time of the day. It's all too easy to get carried away and find yourself spending thirty minutes on the message! Even though she may have one skill or strategy in mind,

Possible Teaching Points for Morning Message

- Writing communicates a message
- Self-monitoring
- Checking and confirming
- Maintaining fluency
- Linking and making analogies
- Predicting
- Word endings and beginnings (suffixes and prefixes)
- Days of the week
- Capital and lowercase letters
- Punctuation
- Concepts of word and letter
- Hearing and recording sounds in words
- Parts of words
- Contractions
- Homonyms and homophones
- Left-to-right and top-to-bottom (directionality)
- High-frequency words
- Strong verbs or new vocabulary words
- Spaces
- Format and parts of a friendly letter

the talk from the children oftentimes calls her attention to something totally different. She changes direction if she feels it will benefit the students. It is important to remain flexible.

A morning message will vary depending on the grade level, the needs of the students, and the purpose. Katie makes sure that the messages she writes are meeting the needs of her particular group of students, and for that reason they change over time. Ideally, morning messages get more challenging as your students are able to handle increasingly difficult texts.

A morning message can be used to teach a multitude of skills and strategies (see sidebar on page 84). It's another time for teachers to model an integrated system of strategic actions and to support readers and writers in developing their own systems. The list in the sidebar is just a starting point; you may want to brainstorm possible teaching points for morning message with your grade-level team. Be careful not to use the ideas as a list of topics to "cover," but rather use them as a reference as you match purposes with what your students need.

One great thing about the morning message is that it becomes another familiar text in the classroom for the children to reread.

Community Writing: Writing With Students

Community writing is a time to write together as a class, or in small groups, with all students' contributions given consideration. The writing pieces are generated from authentic talk, shared experiences, or inquiry-based projects. Children may share the pen with the teacher while composing the text (also called *interactive writing*), or the teacher may write while the children orally compose the text (also called *shared writing*). Andrea McCarrier emphasizes the community aspect by saying, "As collaborators in the process, students become a 'writing community' with the support of skilled teaching, making decisions together as they move from ideas to oral language to messages they want to write" (2008, 67).

Community writing pieces often are read and reread *while* composing and *after* completion. The finished pieces are used as familiar texts for children to practice putting together an effective reading process system.

When writing the pieces, children are given many opportunities to practice strategic reading and writing actions and skills:

- ❋ Saying words slowly
- ❋ Listening for sounds
- ❋ Clapping out parts of words
- ❋ Putting spaces between words
- ❋ Writing strong leads or endings
- ❋ Including a beginning, middle, and end
- ❋ Using dialogue

❋ Rereading
❋ Checking and confirming
❋ Linking (making analogies with words while spelling)
❋ Self-monitoring
❋ Using text structures of various genres

Within the context of community writing, the students not only learn about letters, sounds, and how words work but also about decisions writers make, such as what to include, how to best structure a sentence to make a point, or how to organize thoughts on a topic.

Community writing can take on many different forms and genres. We create stories, invitations, thank-you notes, lists, retellings of familiar stories, observations of science experiences, and reflections on math problem-solving strategies—just to name a few. These texts are occasionally made into books that the children take home and reread to their families. The children become very familiar with community writing pieces because they are meaningful, generated from common experiences, and read and reread many times. In Katie's room, these texts become favorites in the class library and are enjoyed throughout the year.

Writing together is an excellent time to teach children within their zone of proximal development (see Chapter 3), especially when sharing the pen. You can ask different children to be responsible for different parts of the message. While Jesse may be ready to write the letter *J* since his name begins with it, Sophie may be ready to write the whole word *went* since it is a high-frequency word she has been learning.

Community writing can be done in all subject areas, as long as it comes from an authentic shared experience and is surrounded by a great deal of conversation. Recently, Katie's class conducted a series of observations in their butterfly garden. They worked in small groups, with each group observing a specific plant weekly over the course of a month. Each week they took pictures of the plant, measured the plant, talked about what they noticed, and then wrote a summary of their observations together. The following section describes one of these small-group lessons.

Butterfly Garden Observations April 24, 2009

Katie gathered together a small group of four children and the photo they'd taken of the plant they were observing. She started the lesson with a conversation.

Katie: What do you notice this week? (*Looking at the photo.*)
Olivia: There are lots of buds!
Yasmin: Those make flowers, right? Like in that book we read.

Anthony　Alexander

Olivia　Lucy

April 24, 2009
We saw buds. There are old
bRANches. We Think there
will be flowers!

Katie: Yes, we read that yesterday. What kind of flowers do you think will come from the buds?

Anthony: They are green, so green flowers?

Katie: Maybe. We'll have to keep watching. What else do you notice?

Alexander: Lots of dead stuff on it. Is it dead?

Olivia: Those are from before. From winter, you know? When the plant was resting in the winter. The plant is not dead, just the stuff is dead.

Katie: What do you think will happen with the dead stuff?

Yasmin: It's old branches. They'll fall off when the new ones grow.

Katie: Hmm. Good thinking. We'll have to keep looking for that. Maybe we'll know more next week when we observe our plant. I heard you make two important observations this week. You noticed the buds and the old branches. You also made an important prediction—that the buds will turn into flowers. Let's start writing your thoughts down so we can keep track of your thinking. How could we start?

Alexander: We saw buds?

Yasmin: Yeah, let's start with that.

Katie: OK, "We saw buds"—how many words is that?

Anthony: Three! (*Claps his hands for each word while saying the sentence.*) We saw buds.

Katie: We saw buds. What is the first word in our sentence?

Anthony: *We!* I know that one!

Katie: Great, Anthony. Why don't you start. (*Hands him the marker.*) Show me where you will start the first sentence. (*Anthony points to the correct place on the paper,* *the left-hand side.*) Awesome! Write *we*. I'll bet you can write it fast. (*Anthony writes* we *quickly on the paper, and even knows to begin with a capital letter.*) Good job! So what will come next? Let's say our sentence again. We saw buds.

Yasmin: *Saw.* Sssss.

Katie: What do you hear at the beginning of *saw*?

Yasmin: *S.* Like Sonia!

Katie: Great! Where are you going to put the *s*?

Yasmin: I have to leave a space so the words aren't all smushed up. (*Yasmin uses two fingers to leave a space and starts to write the letter* s. *Then she hands the marker back to Katie.*)

Katie: Wow, I noticed you made a lowercase *s*! Good thinking, since the word *saw* is in the middle of the sentence. (*Katie quickly writes the* aw *to complete the word to keep momentum going, since she knew the* aw *was out of Yasmin's reach.*) Let's read what we have so far. "We saw . . ." What comes next?

Alexander: *Buds*! (*He turns and looks at our science word wall.*) It starts the same way that *butterfly* starts. *B*!

Katie: Yes it does. Come on up and show me where you will write the *b*.

Alexander: I have to make a space so people can read it. (*He uses his fingers to make a space and Katie hands him the pen to write the letter* b.)

Katie: Good job! Now what do you hear next? Let's say that word slowly. B . . . u . . . d . . . s.

Alexander: *D?*

Katie: Yes, you do hear a *d*, but there is another letter first. (*She says the word slowly again, emphasizing the /u/, and then takes the marker and writes the letter* u.) Now we hear the *d*. (*Alexander writes the* d.)

Katie: Let's read what we wrote. "We saw bud . . ."

Kids: *S*!

Olivia: We need an *s* because there were lots of them!

Katie: Yes we do. Anthony, can you finish the word *buds* for us? (*Anthony comes up and writes the* s. *He also adds a period.*)

Katie: Let's read the whole sentence now and check to make sure it makes sense and sounds right.

Katie and the small group continue to finish the next two sentences in a similar way. She guides the conversation, reminds the children what they talked about, and encourages the children to read and reread what they have written. When they finish the writing for the day, they all read the entire piece one last time to make sure that it says what they wanted it to say. While she focused on letters and sounds during this writing, Katie always keeps meaning at the forefront and shows the children how writers read what they have written to make sure they are clearly communicating the message. All the children in this group participated during this fifteen-minute lesson.

This shared experience, coupled with a great deal of conversation throughout the unit, made the pieces of writing a meaningful class project that many children returned to often. The students learned much about the science content and informational writing as well.

Writing these observations as community writing pieces supported Katie's struggling readers during the writing process and encouraged them to write the parts they were confident with. Since they had participated in creating the text, it also gave them another text that they could read. Community writing serves as another place for readers to practice using their system of strategies. To see more ideas for community writing projects, see the photos in Appendix 6.

Independent Writing: Writing By Children

Professional Resources About Writing Workshop

About the Authors: Writing Workshop with Our Youngest Writers by Katie Wood Ray, with Lisa Cleaveland (2004).

Study Driven: A Framework for Planning Units of Study in the Writing Workshop by Katie Wood Ray (2006).

The Art of Teaching Writing by Lucy Calkins (1994).

Units of Study for Primary Writing: A Yearlong Curriculum (Grades K–2) by Lucy Calkins and colleagues (2007).

Of Primary Importance: What's Essential in Teaching Young Writers by Ann Marie Corgill (2008).

Writing Workshop: The Essential Guide by Ralph Fletcher and JoAnn Portalupi (2001).

The Writing Workshop: Working Through the Hard Parts (And They're All Hard Parts) by Katie Wood Ray, with Lester Laminack (2001).

Boy Writers: Reclaiming Their Voices by Ralph Fletcher (2006).

A Fresh Look at Writing by Donald Graves (1994).

Assessing Writers (2005) and *How's It Going? A Practical Guide to Conferring with Student Writers* (2000) by Carl Anderson.

A Place for Wonder: Reading and Writing Nonfiction in the Primary Grades by Georgia Heard and Jennifer McDonough (2009).

Especially for Kindergarten Teachers

Talking, Drawing, Writing: Lessons for Our Youngest Writers by Martha Horn and Mary Ellen Giacobbe (2007).

Already Ready: Nurturing Writers in Preschool and Kindergarten by Katie Wood Ray and Matt Glover (2008).

Engaging Young Writers, Preschool–Grade 1 by Matt Glover (2009).

In order for children to become writers, they must be given lots of time to practice. In many schools, children are given an independent writing time daily, also known as writing workshop. They are in charge of topic selection, negotiating the content, writing the words on the page, and illustrating the text.

During writing workshop time, the teacher confers with young writers and meets with small groups with similar needs in guided writing groups. Touching base one-on-one with students as he or she circulates in the room, the teacher engages in a variety of supports, from helping one child stretch a word, to encouraging another child to give his character a name, to nudging yet another child to add description to her piece.

Besides the many writing mentors who originally influenced our thinking, such as Donald Graves, Shelley Harwayne, Lucy Calkins, Georgia Heard, and Ralph Fletcher and JoAnn Portalupi, we also use many current resources for developing our individual writing time. We have listed many classic and current resources in the sidebar.

Writing independently and then reading what was written gives children the chance to self-monitor to see if what they have written makes sense, sounds right, and looks right. Active engagement during writing workshop helps a child build a network of strategies and begin to see the connection between writing and reading. All of the skills and strategies that have been introduced and practiced together during community writing are put to use while writing independently.

Reading and Writing Reciprocity

Reading and writing are different processes that share a reciprocal relationship. Knowing this, and making sure that our teaching is informed by this, can help our most struggling readers learn to develop strategic behaviors in writing that will help them in reading as well. Marie Clay says, "Writing can contribute to the building of almost every kind of inner control of literacy learning that is needed by the successful reader" (1998, 130). Clay also reminds us that these reading/writing connections don't happen by accident. A teacher must be knowledgeable about this reciprocal relationship and scaffold instruction in a way that supports struggling readers to use what they know in reading to help them in writing, and vice versa. With our goal being to help children develop an effective reading process system, we would be remiss if we did not utilize writing as another way to reach this goal.

We want our *readers* to make sure what they read makes sense, sounds right, and looks right. We also want our *writers* to make sure what they write makes sense, sounds right, and looks right. Take another look at the circle chart in Figure 2.1. How many of these strategies do we use in writing? Writers *and* readers need to use these skills and strategies:

* Self-monitor
* Check and confirm
* Activate prior knowledge
* Know that text is read and written from left to right, top to bottom, and that there are spaces between words
* Link and make analogies while writing; look for known word parts when reading
* Search and gather information
* Predict what letter or word will come next
* Use punctuation correctly
* Generate (in writing) and recognize (in reading) high-frequency words quickly
* Be familiar with beginning, middle, and end
* Understand genre
* Understand text features
* Understand text formats

According to Marie Clay, "Writing can foster reading competence and vice versa if the learner becomes aware of the reciprocal nature of these acts. Reading and writing can be learned concurrently and interrelatedly" (1998, 138). Concepts of print such as directionality, spaces, and letter formation can become clearer to a child when he or she is writing. These concepts of print are then transferred to reading and result in a better understanding of how texts work. For example, a teacher working with a child on putting spaces between her words can then take that new learning over to reading and use it to help the child see the importance of one-to-one matching. Likewise, when a child is able to self-monitor for meaning in his reading, the teacher can help transfer this knowledge into writing, making sure the child is rereading for meaning and self-monitoring his own writing. Emily Rodgers emphasizes this point in saying, "Learning to read can be supported and accelerated through writing experiences because they share common items of knowledge and involve similar problem-solving activities" (Rodgers in Scharer and Pinnell 2008, 206).

Putting It All Together in a Typical Day

With such a comprehensive approach to teaching literacy, how does this all fit into a typical day? While Katie does have a specific reading and writing workshop time, she continues to teach literacy throughout the day. She wants her students to see writing and reading not only as something they do in school every day, but as tools to make sense of the world. Integrating literacy in all subjects helps children see the importance of learning to read and write and provides meaningful opportunities to practice and explore reading and writing.

The following is a schedule of how a typical day might look. Katie uses this general framework to set up her classroom regardless of the grade level she is teaching. Under each item, there is a brief explanation and then the specific components of a comprehensive literacy approach that are included in that time frame are bulleted. While we know every school has a different daily schedule, we hope you can see the possibility of teaching literacy throughout the day by this example.

Sample Daily Schedule

8:40–9:15 Explore Time

As children enter the room each morning, they are given time to reconnect with one another, start their day with an activity of their choosing, and make the sometimes difficult transition between home and school. They are engaged in a variety of self-selected activities: reading any book from the classroom library; retelling stories with puppets; writing; participating in a mock store/post office or other imaginative play; working on inquiry projects; using math manipulatives; doing individual research; working on computers; painting, drawing, and other creative play; or working on literacy and math activities. During this time, Katie interacts with the small groups, observing oral language development and encouraging exploration of multiple forms of literacy. For example, after a field trip to Washington, DC, several children made the buildings they saw out of blocks and then made a map to retell their trip. Katie might also do a quick assessment, such as a running record or anecdotal notes while reading a book with a child, during this time. There are a variety of literacy-rich activities going on throughout Explore Time.

* Independent reading
* Independent writing

9:15–9:30 Morning Meeting
The class gathers in a circle to greet one another and discuss the schedule for the day. Then Katie shares the morning message with the class.

* Morning message
* Shared reading

9:30–10:30 Reading Workshop
Katie starts the workshop with a short focus lesson, which may include an interactive read-aloud or shared reading. She then sends the children off to read independently while she confers with children and meets with guided reading groups. Children may also meet in book clubs, do buddy reading, read from the class library, or work in literacy centers during this time. The workshop ends with a whole-group sharing time.

* Interactive read-aloud
* Shared reading
* Independent reading
* Guided reading

10:30–11:30 Writing Workshop
Katie starts the workshop with a short focus lesson, which may include an interactive read-aloud, shared reading, community writing, teacher modeling, or a conversation. She then sends the children off to write independently while she confers with children or meets with guided writing groups. The workshop ends with a whole-group sharing time.

* Interactive read-aloud
* Shared reading
* Community writing
* Independent writing

11:30–1:30 Specials, Lunch, and Recess

1:30–2:30 Math Workshop
Katie starts the workshop with a short focus lesson and then sends the children off to work in small math groups or with partners while she confers with children and meets with guided math groups. Literacy is integrated in math through interactive read-alouds and by recording the class's thinking with community writing pieces. The workshop ends with a whole-group sharing time.

❀ Interactive read-aloud
❀ Community writing

2:30–3:30 Science and/or Social Studies Workshop

Katie starts the workshop with a short focus lesson and then sends the children off to work on a variety of science or social studies research and inquiry projects while she confers with children and facilitates explorations and projects. The workshop ends with a whole-group sharing time.

❀ Read-aloud
❀ Interactive read-aloud
❀ Shared reading
❀ Community writing
❀ Independent reading
❀ Independent writing

Notice that there is not a set time for each component of a comprehensive literacy framework (shared reading, guided reading, independent reading, and so on). It is up to the teacher to plan how to incorporate all the elements throughout the day. One way teachers in our school have done this is through the use of a weekly planning sheet (see Appendix 7). On this form, we can plan our week, making sure to include all components. The amount of time given to each component may vary. For example, in kindergarten and the beginning of first grade, more time typically may be spent on community writing and shared reading. As children move into second grade, you may reduce the time spent on these components and increase the time in independent reading and writing and interactive read-aloud.

All children need all of the components as part of their literacy instruction. How you structure this will look different depending on your grade level, the time of the year, and, most importantly, the needs of your students.

What Kind of Environment Supports a Comprehensive Literacy Approach?

Throughout this chapter you have read about the components of a comprehensive literacy approach and have seen that these components work best in a classroom that values meaningful conversation, student choice, and a strong sense of community. Children must be allowed many opportunities for independence to practice building their own network of strategies while the teacher is working with small groups and individual children in their zone of proximal development. A classroom must be carefully designed to support this kind of teaching and learning. There are many resources that address how to set up your classroom's physical space as well as resources on how to build a strong community of independent learners. Please see the sidebar on page 94 for some wonderful books on these topics.

Professional Resources About Building Your Classroom Community and Physical Space

Teaching Children to Care: Classroom Management for Ethical and Academic Growth, K–8 by Ruth Charney (2002).

Classroom Spaces That Work by Marlynn K. Clayton and Mary Beth Forton (2001).

Spaces and Places: Designing Classrooms for Literacy by Debbie Diller (2008).

Reading with Meaning: Teaching Comprehension in the Primary Grades by Debbie Miller (2002).

On Their Side: Helping Children Take Charge of Their Learning by Bob Strachota (1996).

Learning to Trust: Transforming Difficult Elementary Classrooms Through Developmental Discipline by Marilyn Watson and Laura Ecken (2003).

Designs for Living and Learning: Transforming Early Childhood Environments by Deb Curtis and Margie Carter (2003).

Responsive Classroom Web Site and Books: www.responsiveclassroom.org

Some of the essential items we consider in the physical environment to support students in all K–4 classrooms are the following:

* Tables or desks grouped together
* Large open space for the whole class to sit on the floor in a circle and for children to work on the floor with clipboards and/or pillows
* Small teacher table and/or workspace in a corner or as a shared space in the room—as opposed to a large teacher desk dominating the room
* Books in baskets grouped in a variety of ways and bookshelves throughout the room
* Print-rich environment with anchor charts, community writing pieces, artwork, and meaningful displays hanging on the walls; little to no commercially prepared charts and posters
* Photographs of children, their families, and their school community on the walls
* Organized way of keeping community supplies (crayons, pencils, markers, scissors, etc.) available at all times—labeled and stored where they are easily accessible to students
* Writing folders, book boxes, math journals, science journals, and other supplies neatly labeled and organized for easy access by the children
* Evidence of student interests and thinking on charts and photographs in the room so that one gets a sense of who belongs to this community

Katie has organized her room in this way throughout her teaching career, when teaching grades ranging from first through eighth grade. You can adapt these basic guidelines to whatever grade level you are teaching and the students you have in a particular year. The important thing is to have your physical space support the teaching and learning you and your students are doing. The Reggio Emilia approach to teaching asserts that the classroom environment is the "third teacher," along with the children and parents/teachers (Gandini 1998). How we plan and organize our space can certainly help or hinder our efforts to establish a community of learners working within a comprehensive literacy approach. Take a look at how Katie organizes her classroom space on page 95.

As Katie reflects on her current first-grade class, she realizes that only a comprehensive literacy approach allows her to meet the needs of students like these:

> Quent, an above-average reader and writer who excels at individual research on any animal
>
> Joseline, who is already reading and comprehending Magic Tree House books
>
> Jasmine, a quiet child who is learning English as a second language, is on grade level, but can always use more vocabulary building
>
> Randy, a talkative, bright child who has a learning disability and struggles with being able to recall what he has read
>
> Melvin, a student from El Salvador who recently arrived mid-year, has never been in school before, and speaks no English
>
> Angie, a native English speaker who came to first grade with meager knowledge of letters, sounds, and concepts of print
>
> Antonio, a child with significant directionality and sequential order issues

With twenty-four such varied and unique children, a comprehensive literacy classroom is the environment that works!

CHAPTER 6

Interactive Read-Aloud:
Talking Our Way
Through Texts

For many readers who struggle, reading is not yet seen as something enjoyable, fun, and meaningful. It is our job to change this. In Chapter 5 we discussed the importance of reading aloud for enjoyment and to hear the language of books while honoring the natural talk that grows from a good book. This chapter will elaborate on reading aloud by showing how to use it for a more focused instructional purpose. Using a picture book to teach is commonly called an *interactive read-aloud*. This purposeful, planned instruction provides the teacher time to model the reading process through think-alouds and interactive discussions as he or she helps readers, struggling or otherwise, engage with books in a safe, risk-free environment.

Interactive read-aloud is a critical piece of our literacy instruction for all readers. Our English language learners (ELLs), who are certainly not all struggling readers, need to hear many books read in English. They become more familiar with book language and they hear the cadence and flow of how English sounds. These ELLs, along with our most struggling readers, need multiple opportunities to see how the reading process works. Interactive read-aloud provides these opportunities.

Children's listening or receptive levels are much stronger than the level of books they can read independently. They can understand, learn from, and converse about texts that are well beyond their own individual reading capabilities.

Take a look at the following scenario. Consider the diversity of learners in your classroom and think about how this interactive read-aloud lesson allows all children to participate. Also notice how the teaching is woven into the reading experience.

Author! Author! A Classroom Scenario

The reading lamp is lit, and the children are huddled together on the rug, squirming and chatting and being, well, like first graders! Read-aloud time is about to begin.

Katie: Friends, this weekend, I went to a book festival in Washington, DC. I was so lucky! I got to see some of our favorite authors. David Shannon, author of *No, David!* and our other favorite David books; Doreen Cronin, author of *Click, Clack, Moo;* and Jon Scieszka, author of *The True Story of the Three Little Pigs!* and *Robot Zot!* (*Holds up these texts.*)

Carlos: You did?

Jennifer: You *really* saw them?

Zameer: In real life?

The children are amazed that Katie actually saw the people they view as famous stars. From the very first day of school, she has shared books from a variety of authors and always reminded the children that they are authors too, just like the authors of their favorite books. Children need to know that authors are real people who live normal lives and write about topics they love. Katie continues:

Katie: Jon Scieszka was so awesome. He read one of his new books from the Trucktown series. And do you know why he wrote these books? He said it was because he and his three brothers loved to play trucks and smash things up when they were kids. It reminded me of how many of you love to play with our Matchbox trucks and the blocks, and I just knew I had to get this book for our class. So today, we're going to read *Smash! Crash!* by Jon Scieszka. And guess who illustrated it? David Shannon!

Randy: Cool!

Andy: I could tell! The pictures look like *No, David!*

They are hooked. Every one of their squirmy first-grade bodies is mesmerized by the cover of *Smash! Crash!* (Scieszka 2008). Katie begins to read the book with expression, trying her best to imitate how Jon Scieszka read it at the book festival. She turns the pages, slowly lingering on the pictures, and invites the kids to join in on the repeating phrase "Smash! Crash!" on alternating pages.

"Read it again! Read it again!" rings out as she closes the book. She laughs, knowing that a book is a hit when she hears the "read it again" refrain. They certainly will revisit this book, but for now Katie wants to know what the kids are thinking and how they will respond to what they just heard. "Turn to your partner and take a few minutes to share what you're thinking," she says.

The kids scoot around to sit eye-to-eye and knee-to-knee and the talk begins. Practicing this particular routine has gone on since the first day of school, so they pair up quickly. The talking time is not to answer Katie's questions, nor is it for her to do a check on who was listening. Rather, the talk serves a variety of purposes. It's a time for the students to negotiate the meaning of the text together; to share their thoughts, opinions, and connections; or to make predictions of what's to come. They support each other as they dig deep to construct that meaning.

On this particular day their conversations go in many directions. Katie overhears some partners talking about the illustrations. Others mention that they like how Jon Scieszka repeated the line, "Smash! Crash!" Many are making connections, since the book reminds them of games they play with trucks at home. A few of the girls discuss how strong the girl trucks were in the text.

It's the second week of first grade, and Katie is pleased that the conversations stay on track, even if it's only for a few minutes. It takes many attempts and repeated modeling of how readers talk about books and behave in a discussion group to get quality discussions going. From our experience in using interactive read-aloud, we know that once the children can stay on topic and respectfully talk and listen to each other, we can go even deeper in our conversations with other books.

So Many to Choose From

There are so many good children's books out these days. Just walk into your local or school library or neighborhood bookstore and you will be over-whelmed by the number of uniquely illustrated and beautifully written picture books, both fiction and nonfiction. Consider collecting titles of books you might want to use with students from a variety of resources:

- ❀ Texts by favorite authors
- ❀ Recommendations from other teachers
- ❀ Online sites such as www.childrenslibrary.org, www.carolhurst.com, and www.readingyear.blogspot.com
- ❀ Nonfiction texts: The Orbis Pictus award winners are always excellent choices and are listed on the National Council of Teachers of English Web site (www.ncte.org).
- ❀ Books related to curriculum topics for your grade level (National Council of Teachers of Mathematics [www.nctm.org], National Science Teachers Association [www.nsta.org], National Council for the Social Studies [www.socialstudies.org])
- ❀ Reviews in magazines, professional journals, or newspapers
- ❀ Lists of books that have won awards such as the Newbery or Caldecott, or books listed on the International Reading Association Web site (www.reading.org)

With all these titles and recommendations, how does one go about choos-ing a good interactive read-aloud text? For us, *why* we select a particular book is intricately woven with *the purpose* for which we plan to use that text. Here are some purposes we consider:

- ❀ Use for a *think-aloud* when guiding students to become familiar with strategies such as inferring, questioning, visualizing, or other strategies in Figure 2.1 (see sidebar on page 102 for more on *think-alouds*)
- ❀ Connect one text to another
- ❀ Learn about character development, setting, or plot
- ❀ Build a classroom community/culture
- ❀ Connect with a content-area curriculum topic
- ❀ Help students discover ideas for new writing topics
- ❀ Examine an author's craft
- ❀ Study a particular genre, author, or topic of interest
- ❀ Have fun with the playful language of the text
- ❀ Notice descriptive language and expand upon new vocabulary

We usually stay away from the pop culture books featuring the cartoon characters or other TV-related books. Instead, we look for books that show sit-uations from multiple perspectives, books that have both girls and boys as the

Tips for an Effective Think-Aloud

- Choose a text that is interesting, engaging, and a good match for the strategy you are spotlighting (see Chapter 8 for more information on spotlighting a strategy).
- Roughly plan your think-aloud beforehand. Use sticky notes to mark a few good stopping places.
- Be flexible and willing to stop and think aloud at any point if you feel it would be beneficial to the group.
- Use a signal to show kids when you are reading and when you are thinking aloud—Katie puts the text facedown in her lap when she is thinking aloud; other teachers may look off into the distance.
- Be clear with your language. Use phrases such as *I wonder . . ., I think . . ., I predict . . ., I'm not sure about . . ., and This part made me think about . . .*
- Be authentic—don't invent or make up forced connections.
- Show and talk about how you use the strategy to help you understand what you are reading.
- Don't overdo your think-aloud by stopping too often. Make sure you keep the flow of the text and meaning intact.

main characters, and books that don't portray stereotypes. We tend to pick books with beautiful literary language and engaging illustrations. We bring our knowledge of our students' lives and interests into play as we select texts.

Teachers need to watch the diet of books they are reading to children, being careful to keep it balanced. Be wary of falling into the trap that one kindergarten teacher fell into when she told Pat, "I only pick my read-alouds based on what we're studying." She was searching the library for all the "apple and pumpkin" books she could find. For a period of three straight weeks her students were fed only apple and pumpkin books! While it is certainly wonderful to use read-aloud books in all areas of the curriculum, we want to make sure our children are exposed to a wide variety of texts. We personally start our math and science workshops with a daily interactive read-aloud that relates to the topic we are studying, but this is in addition to books that we use in reading and writing workshops that are for a purpose not related to content-area curriculum.

Junko Yokota says that the books we bring into our classrooms should be both "windows and mirrors":

> *Mirrors let readers see reflections of their own lives: windows let them see others' lives. Seeing oneself represented in literature engenders a sense of pride, it encourages a reader to take more interest in a book and feel a sense of involvement in literary discussions that follow a reading selection. Books that act as windows allow readers to see experiences that are different from their own lives and stretch the range of experiences that we have had.* (2002)

Books can be mirrors into our selves, our culture, our life experiences, and our community. Children need books that reflect who they are as people and that reflect what is happening in our world, our school, and our daily lives. Children need to see themselves in the literature they read and that is read to them. It values who they are and lets them know they are not alone in this world.

Books can also be windows through which children see new opportunities, different worlds, and varied experiences. Books can take us places we may never get to go, meet people we may never have the chance to meet, and take imaginary journeys all over the world. Children need books that allow them to view aspects of our world through different perspectives so they can learn to accept and appreciate diversity. Children's literature has exploded in the past ten years, and now it is quite easy to find quality children's books that accurately represent different cultures, lifestyles, and historical events.

We have included some of our favorite books for you in Appendix 8. Please see this list as a starting point as you create your own favorite list of books to use with students. It is the passion that you bring to a text that will transfer over to passionate young readers.

Let Them Talk

Interactive read-aloud time is the perfect setting for having students actively involved in talking and thinking about texts. An effective interactive read-aloud has children talking *before, during,* and *after* reading. The conversation that occurs throughout these read-alouds is rich with the potential of impacting student learning and making the interactive read-aloud an important teaching time. We practice turning to our neighbor, sitting knee-to-knee and eye-to-eye, and *building a conversation* with our partner (Cole 2003, Nichols 2006). This opportunity allows children to share their thinking with one other person and challenges them to go beyond just telling their partner what they think. There's a sort of "give-and-take of thought that grows" (Nichols 2006, 49).

For struggling students or students who are learning English, this chance to talk is especially beneficial and provides a strong language model. All voices can be heard in a safe and supportive setting. In Katie's room, students can be heard speaking in English as well as in a variety of native languages.

We listen carefully to the conversations and then ask several students to share with the whole group. They love this sharing time. Reading is social, and children want to talk about what they have just heard. As teachers, we need to value the importance of thinking and talking about our thinking as a means of constructing ideas, negotiating meaning, and developing structures for independent thought. Because we always keep the reading process strategies in mind (Figure 2.1), we are constantly aware of the kinds of thinking that readers do as they read. It is this network of strategies that we know our students are building as they develop as readers.

Comprehension is just as important with beginning readers as it is in later grades. Many teachers in grades 3–6 have told us that their students read the words, but are not thinking as they read. Inviting talk during interactive read-aloud time provides children with opportunities to do the kind of thinking and talking that keeps readers engaged in the text. We can all create *active comprehenders* right from the start.

Nudging the Talk

Before we begin an interactive read-aloud, it's important to build background knowledge to enable students to focus on what we are going to read. Kathy Collins (2004) refers to this as getting our mind ready to read. We model this during interactive read-aloud and help children see how this helps us understand and enjoy what we read. Here are some of the questions we may ask:

* What do you think this might be about?
* Look at the cover. What do you notice?
* Where do you think this story takes place?
* What might we learn in this book? (nonfiction)
* Who do you think the characters are?
* Can you think of any words we might hear in this book?

Turning and talking to a partner allows all the students to participate in preparing to read and gives them a chance to connect to the book personally as they activate and share their prior knowledge.

For example, before reading *Pumpkin Circle* by George Levenson (2002) one October day, Katie and her students looked at the cover of the book together. Then partners turned and talked about what they thought the book might be about. Children were chatting, using their background knowledge of pumpkins. Several kids shared recent experiences of visiting a pumpkin patch with their families. They used words such as *seeds, vines,* and *stem.* This talk supported our English language learners by giving them the chance to hear some of the book's vocabulary from their peers before the read-aloud started. Everyone's prior knowledge was activated by the time the reading began. This helped them build a deeper understanding of the pumpkin life cycle and heightened their interest and exposure to key vocabulary.

During an interactive read-aloud, as well as *after* the book is finished, we may stop and ask the children to turn and talk. We ask questions or make comments to spur on their conversations about texts. Early discussions may get started with questions or comments like the following:

* What are you thinking?
* Talk about what you like about this book so far.
* What do you think will happen?
* Has anything like this ever happened to you or someone you know?
* Does this story remind you of anything?
* Does this character remind you of anyone?
* What are you picturing in your head?
* What are you picturing might happen at the end?
* What are you wondering about?
* What do you notice in the illustrations?

❀ What does that graph tell you?
❀ What do you already know about _____?
❀ What did you learn so far?

Questions and comments like these support students to think, connect, predict, visualize, and wonder as they participate in the interactive read-aloud and as they reflect after the reading.

As students are able to respond to those previous questions and begin to think beyond the literal meaning of the text, we know they are ready to dig deeper into stories with questions like these:

❀ How did the character change from the beginning to the end of the book?
❀ Is the author trying to tell us something with this story? Or with this information (nonfiction)?
❀ Why might _____ (character's name) have acted that way?
❀ What would you have changed?
❀ Is the author trying to convince you or change your mind about something?
❀ How was the problem solved? How else could it have been solved?
❀ What message or big idea is coming across from this book? How do you know that? Why do you think that? How can you justify that with evidence from the text?
❀ Do you have any thoughts on the words or phrases the author chose to use?
❀ How is this book like our class, our school, our town, or our world?
❀ Would you recommend this book to someone? Why? Why not?
❀ What questions are you left with? What are you still wondering?

Questions like these support students in their attempts to act as proficient readers as they engage with and think about text. Proficient readers *do* infer about the characters, setting or plot; think beyond the text and let the authors' words affect them; and critique, evaluate, and analyze texts and make decisions about whether to agree or disagree.

Teachers need to challenge students to be active readers from the very beginning—readers who read broadly and think deeply, and who realize that reading is an action sport (Keene and Zimmermann 2007). Meaningful talk, an integral part of an interactive read-aloud, allows our youngest readers to experience what all readers do as they read independently. It nurtures their comprehension by giving them the time, space, and sometimes direction to do the kind of thinking that will support them in becoming proficient readers.

How Do I Sound?

Whether you are doing a traditional read-aloud or an interactive read-aloud, anyone can learn to be an engaging reader. Katie considers herself a person who reads aloud quite well now; however, that wasn't always the case. As a student teacher many years ago, she remembers her cooperating teacher, a master story-teller, telling her to "slow down and feel the story." While she was certainly a competent reader back then, she wasn't being responsive to the children and to the story while reading aloud. She was reading in very much the same way that she read silently. Her cooperating teacher's advice, coupled with years of watching kids' reactions to books, has helped Katie develop expertise. She now knows when to slow the pace and whisper, when to change her voice to fit the characters, and when to read a page's ending with a pounce!

We've sat entranced at conferences listening to teachers such as Mem Fox, Shelley Harwayne, or Lester Laminack read aloud; we've also heard some powerful tales woven by teachers right in our own building. Over the years, as we emulate these role models, we've paid attention to what they do as they read. We've noticed that teachers who read aloud well do the following:

- Adjust the rate, pace, and volume of their voice to the story, slowing down at suspenseful or thoughtful parts and speeding up when the story moves faster
- Change their voices to match the characters
- Use gestures to help with comprehension and enjoyment, especially for English language learners
- Show the illustrations in picture books and sometimes linger on a page so that children can experience the illustrations with the words
- Read slowly enough to allow children to create images in their own heads and process the story as well as make predictions and think about the story
- Put their own passion for reading into the story

Take the time to watch and listen to your colleagues or to authors reading aloud. You can do this in your own building, at conferences, at book signings at local bookstores, or on author websites. As with most skills, with practice you will improve or refine your ability to do a quality and engaging read-aloud.

We are reminded of a story that Bernice Cullinan told in her book *Invitation to Read: More Children's Literature in the Reading Program* (1992). She tells how the only thing she felt confident in as a young teacher was reading aloud. She realized the significance of this much later in life when she ran into a student she had had in first grade. He was grown with children of his own. He told her, "When I read aloud to my kids before bed, it's your voice I hear in my head." What a high compliment for Cullinan; we would be honored to receive a similar one.

Every time we do a read-aloud, it is not for the purpose of teaching reading process. As mentioned in Chapter 5, there are many times we read aloud books for sheer enjoyment. Talk amongst the children will naturally happen. Teachers need to see reading aloud to children "not as a reward, but as a birthright of the literate society in which they were born" (Harste 1992, 10). By adding purposefully planned interactive read-alouds to your instruction, you gain the opportunity to model what readers do and how readers think. Multiple experiences such as these establish a solid foundation for children as they become independent readers and thinkers.

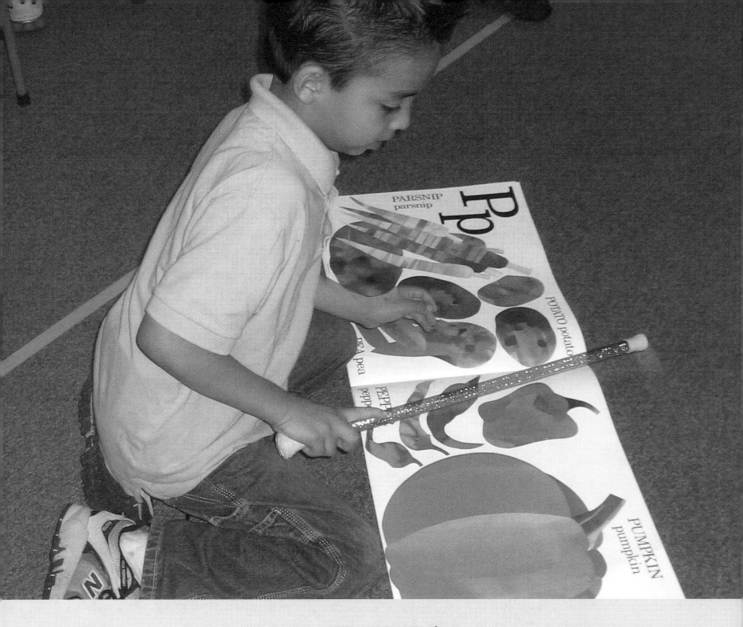

CHAPTER 7

I Thought I Knew
How to Teach Reading,
but Whoa!

A t the school where Katie presently teaches and where Pat used to teach, the students come from more than forty countries and speak more than twenty different languages. For 75 percent of them, English is not their first language. Many families fall below the poverty line and live in crowded apartments. Some parents are literate in their own language; some are not. Many of the children arrive at the school door with limited school-based literacy skills and experiences.

One school year, Katie was asked to mentor a wonderful first-year teacher, Rachel Coelho, who came to the school with multiple strengths. She was knowledgeable about our county's curriculum and understood the social needs of young children. She was confident and eager to start her new career. She was thoughtful, reflective, and committed to teaching. But since Rachel had done her student teaching at a school where most students were reading quite proficiently, she was unprepared for what awaited her at this school.

"I have kids in my class who don't know how to hold a book and some who only know five to ten letters out of all the uppercase and lowercase letters! One or two can't write their names! I started reading with a couple of kids on the very lowest books [DRA2 level 1s], but I felt like I was just reading to them and they were memorizing. I'm not sure they are even looking at the words. I thought I knew how to teach beginning readers, but I feel lost! I need help!" Katie could hear the frustration in Rachel's voice as she came to meet with her after school.

Though Rachel verbalized her frantic plea, we suspect that there are many teachers, new or not-so-new, all over the country feeling a similar panic in silence. Many new teachers come out of their education programs excited to start their own classroom, full of innovative ideas, and ready to make a difference in children's lives; however, some are at a loss as to what to do with those children who are the biggest challenge. Other experienced teachers may have come from an upper-grade classroom and may be teaching beginning struggling readers for the first time. The lucky ones teach in a district that provides expert coaches or ongoing mentorship programs. Others are left on their own to figure out how to reach these students. As a result, many of these at-risk children fall behind even more.

In this chapter we focus on the struggling readers at the emergent levels (DRA2 levels A–3), *regardless of their grade level,* who need lots of support as they learn to take on the earliest strategic actions. We will cover several topics in this chapter:

* ❋ How teachers can recognize these beginning struggling readers
* ❋ What the early reading behaviors and strategies are
* ❋ How to best teach these students who are lacking early literacy behaviors, strategies, or skills
* ❋ How a book introduction might look at the earliest levels

We close the chapter by giving suggestions to any teacher challenged with teaching the most struggling beginning readers.

Finding a Starting Point

Katie's school uses a variety of assessment tools during the first few weeks of school. Based on the needs of the K–4 children, some or all of the following (based on Clay's [2007] Observation Survey tasks) are used:

- Letter Identification: Children are shown a page of all the capital and lowercase letters, listed in random order. They identify as many letters as they can by the letter name, sound, or a word, such as *cat* for the letter *c.*

- Writing Vocabulary: Children are asked to write all the words they know and can generate independently in a ten-minute period. The teacher can make suggestions by category with prompts such as, "Color words? Family names? Number words?" The teacher can also ask about specific high-frequency words. "Can you write *mom,* or *go,* or *me*?"

- Hearing and Recording Sounds in Words: The teacher dictates a sentence that contains a multitude of sounds. Teachers use Clay's sentences from *An Observation Survey of Early Literacy Achievement* (2007). The sentence is read word by word, and the children write down as much as they can. Teachers are looking to see what letter/sound correspondence the children are aware of.

- High-Frequency Word Assessment: Children are shown a list of high-frequency words and asked to read the ones they recognize immediately by sight.

- DRA2: Children read from benchmark books in the Developmental Reading Assessment, 2nd edition kit (Beaver 2006). At the earliest levels, they are also asked to find specific words and letters on a page and are assessed on their knowledge of the concepts of print.

Rachel quickly learned how to give several of these assessments. Some can be given in small group, but others require one-on-one administration. She had not yet received training on giving the DRA2 tests required by our school district, so our school provided a literacy resource person to do that testing for her. It was about that time, after all the assessments were gathered and the literacy resource person helped Rachel understand her DRA2 results, that Rachel's panic set in.

Katie suggested that she start with what she knew—reading aloud to children, shared reading with Big Books and poems, community writing, and giving time for children to read independently each day in books of their choosing. The time for small guided reading groups would come later. As children looked at or read books independently, Rachel could notice more information about each child. Because she had not done her own DRA2 testing, she needed this time to gather a sense of each student's strengths and weaknesses before grouping the students by needs. It was a relief for her to know that she didn't have to set up her small guided reading groups within the first month or two of school.

If you are a K–4 teacher and have children struggling with beginning reading strategies, take a deep breath. Blaming previous teachers or the child's home situation serves no purpose, so let those thoughts go. Know that these students *do* have strengths; it just may take a bit longer for you to discover them. You can be the person who makes a difference in their lives by starting them off with a positive attitude about themselves as readers. Carol Lyons (2003) knows full well what often happens to these at-risk children if they don't get off to a good start: "They become embroiled in negative spirals of failure, deepening emotional challenges, and continued failure that often results in behavior problems" (144). No teacher wants that. Lyons asks all of us who work with these students to acquire three positive, self-fulfilling stances:

* Expect that the lowest-achieving children *can* learn to read and write.
* Support children as they *learn how to learn.*
* Believe that *you are the one* who will teach this child to read and write.

What Are the Early Key Strategies and Behaviors?

Marie Clay (2005b) says, "There are no set teaching sequences: there is no prescription to learn this before that" (2). We must remain responsive to the needs of each child, making sure we are linking what they already know to new learning. We always want to take the children from where they are and move them forward as readers and writers. So, where do we start?

For many of us, our first thought is to begin with the letters and sounds. In fact, most basal and commercial primary reading programs begin here. Although knowledge of phonics is certainly an important piece of beginning reading, we know that there are other concepts that are equally essential:

* Directionality and one-to-one voice/print match
* Thinking strategies while reading, such as *searching and gathering* information in order to *predict* words and text
* Letter identification and phonics
* Phonemic awareness
* The difference between *words* and *letters*
* Self-monitoring; checking and confirming while reading
* Early fluency

In the following sections, we give specific examples of how to teach these concepts within a comprehensive literacy framework.

Directionality and Voice/Print Match

Knowing which way text is read is a critical early literacy skill. In English, we read from left to right and top to bottom. It's not important that the students be able to verbalize this, they just need to be able to do it automatically. They also need to know that we have to read the words on a page in the order in which they are written. In other words, we have to have a one-to-one correspondence, or voice to print match, of the text to the words we say. If there are four words in a sentence, then we have to say four words when we read. There are several ways that teachers model directionality and one-to-one matching within the context of meaningful reading work.

Using an enlarged text (Big Book, morning message, chart, text on the overhead, or interactive whiteboard) with students, we explicitly model where to start reading. We use a pointer or a finger saying to the children, "Here is where we need to start reading. Make your words match your finger." Pointing to the text as you read together will provide a model for correct directionality, and touching under each word will help children make a one-to-one match in their reading. Clay advises that while modeling, you should be "precise and consistent in your own movements, and give deliberate, exaggerated demonstrations for a short period" (2005b, 7).

Some Big Books have too much text or the words are too close together to use for this purpose. We choose texts with clearly defined spaces between words. And similarly, when we write our morning message we exaggerate the spacing. Notice the difference in the two morning messages in the photos below.

If you have many students who need directionality and one-to-one matching support, simple poems with little text also work quite well. There are many nursery rhymes that we don't use because they are too wordy. Also, some of the language and sentence structure in nursery rhymes is not appropriate for our English language learners.

Take a look at the two poems in the photos on the next page. Which one would be more beneficial

Humpty Dumpty

Humpty Dumpty sat on a wall;
Humpty Dumpty had a great fall.
All the King's horses
And all the King's men
Couldn't put Humpty together
again!

to students needing voice/print match support? Can you see that it is much easier for the child to get control of voice/print match when touching under "Apple green / Apple red" than it is to touch under "All the king's horses / And all the king's men"?

You can use a pointer to read the poem and then call on a child to come up and point while the class reads. You may have to hold the pointer with some children.

Reading a number line or a 100s grid is a skill most of us teach in math. Kids can benefit from taking a pointer and moving it across and down the number grid while counting and learning the numbers. Start with a number line from one to ten. Then move to a 100s grid where they have to do a return sweep. This helps children see how their eyes move across and then down the page, modeling the same directionality and one-to-one matching that we do when reading.

For most children, the preceding shared reading experiences will be enough for them to take on directionality and one-to-one match independently. However, there will be a few children who will still show some confusion, so for them we suggest you try the following:

❋ Take a sentence that the child has composed orally and write it on a sentence strip. This may be a sentence to go with a picture he or she has drawn. Cut the words apart and arrange them on a table or desk with exaggerated spaces between the words. Demonstrate reading the sentence, pulling each word down as you say it. Next have the child read it, touching and pulling down each word. You can keep these cut-apart sentences in envelopes with the sentence written on the front of the envelope. This makes a great take-home activity for the child to practice with his or her family.

* Do small-group instruction using beginning patterned texts (Fountas and Pinnell levels A/B, Reading Recovery/DRA2 levels 1/2). These texts are written for the purpose of developing one-to-one correspondence. They have one line of print, a consistent pattern, and high picture support. A small-group reading lesson for children in these texts can sometimes look more like a shared reading lesson. They read along and point as you read the text aloud. You may say, "Check to see if your finger is on *my* as we're saying 'my.'" If you're working with a single student, you may ask her to "hop on my finger," by following your lead in pointing to each word as his or her finger rides along on top of yours.

* Use texts with students' names to begin teaching the child to self-monitor his or her one-to-one matching. For example, early in one school year Katie made a baseball book with Sammy. He loved illustrating it and then read it repeatedly. Each page had one line of text, as follows:

> Sammy can swing.
> Sammy can hit.
> Sammy can run.
> Go, Sammy, go.
> Sammy can slide.
> Home run, Sammy!

Sammy recognized his name well, so he could point to the words, making sure he was saying "Sammy" when he pointed to his name. On the pages where the pattern changed, he looked carefully to find his name as he read those pages with Katie. The Book Builder software by Pioneer Valley

Books (http://www.pvep.com/software/) is a wonderful resource that allows you to make custom books with the names of your kids. You can also make these books ahead of time on your computer and use photographs of the kids or let them illustrate the book. (See Appendix 9 for examples of teacher-made books.)

❋ Reinforce directionality and one-to-one matching during writing workshop. When a child is rehearsing orally what he or she is planning to write, we can help him or her point to the paper to indicate where he or she will start and which way the story will go. It's important to catch a child who has directionality issues *before* he or she starts writing right-to-left on the page. We may have to use a visual cue, such as a green dot, placed on the paper to indicate where the child should begin writing. We discontinue these heavy supports as soon as a child demonstrates control over directionality.

Thinking Strategies

The way we choose to spend our time with students sends messages to them about what reading is all about. If most of our time is spent with letter identification activities and words on cards, children quickly begin to believe that learning to read is about saying the words right. That's why we choose to begin with reading real books and writing authentic messages together. In this way, the message we send to children is that reading and writing are meaning-making activities.

Thinking about reading is emphasized every time we read with students. From the very first time they see the cover of a book, we want them to anticipate what the story might be about. Readers draw upon their background knowledge and what they see in pictures to predict story line. This begins to establish a sense that readers are always thinking.

Most children realize that the words and pictures in a book work together. However, for those who are slow to make that connection, we have to help them *search and gather* information from the pictures and use their background knowledge in order to learn to *predict* the words of the text. At times, we have to accept an invention of text as evidence that the child is beginning to use meaning to predict.

Let's examine the following example. Jackeline is shy and quiet and does not take a risk to predict a word she doesn't recognize. She is just beginning to learn that the picture is one place she could search and gather information to make a prediction about what the words might say. In the book *The Shopping Mall* (Randell, Giles, and Smith 1996) the family goes to a variety of stores. It is evident in each of the pictures what kind of store they are in. When reading this book with Jackeline, Katie modeled on several pages how she would look over at the picture to get an idea of what kind of store they were in and, therefore, what the word in the text might be. When they came to a page where the children were in a book store, the text read:

We went to the book store.

Katie asked Jackeline, "What kind of store are they in now?" She answered, "A reading store." For Katie's purpose, this was an acceptable answer, though not an exact match to the text. Her teaching point at this time was to get Jackeline *to predict* based on the pictures, something she had been reticent to try. Though some people may argue that this is teaching the children to randomly guess at words, we disagree. It is important early on that the child learns to *search and gather* to make meaning. These emergent texts are very dependent on picture support to make meaning. In the near future, when Jackeline is learning to use the pictures *and* first letter information together, Katie might answer her prediction by saying, "You're right. It might be a reading store or a bookstore. Let's look at the first letter and see which one looks right."

When working with students in beginning-level texts, you may think there are not many things to discuss. However, we encourage teachers to have conversations with children around these simple patterned texts. Teaching children that readers think about what they read needs to start from the very beginning. For example, if the text says, "Mom is swimming. Mom is running" and so on, we can involve the students in a conversation about the things their moms like to do. Without taking the time to do this, we miss opportunities to get students to make connections, infer, and ask questions about what they are reading.

Letter Identification and Phonics

Phonics has to do with learning letters and the sounds that correspond with them. Many letters make a variety of sounds, and different letters or letter combinations can represent many sounds. Knowing this, teachers usually start with the most common sound or two for each letter, and teach flexibility with letter sounds as the child continues to grow as a reader and gains more confidence with text.

Phonics is used while figuring out words during reading and while spelling words when writing. Rather than spend an immense amount of time with letters and sounds in isolation, we teach as much phonics as we can while reading and writing continuous text—during community writing, shared reading, independent writing, and guided reading. Frank Smith says that the easy way to learn words or letter/sound correspondence is "not to work with individual words at all but with meaningful passages of text" (1994, 2). (Review the community writing vignette in Chapter 5 and notice how the teacher wove letter work into the writing experience.)

There are many concepts that can be taught through names:

- Connections between letters and sounds
- Letters can be written in two ways (upper and lower case, like *David*)
- The same sound can be represented by different letters (*Jasmin*, *Gerald*)
- Word versus letter ("Olivia's name is a *word*. How many *letters* are in this word? Let's count them.")
- Long and short words ("Jackeline's name is a long word. Bo's name is a short word.")
- Words have parts ("Let's clap Alexander's name. Let's clap Ann. How many parts?")

Adapted from Fullerton (1997).

To help teach letters and sounds, we start with something the children are very familiar with: their names (see sidebar). According to Susan Fullerton (1997), "For almost every young learner, knowledge of one's name unlocks a multitude of understandings. A name forms a link in helping a child learn about print." Making a class name chart, highlighting the first letters in children's names, and referring to the chart throughout the day as a way to develop letter knowledge helps children make links between what they know and what they are learning. If they know Lucy's name starts with *L* and says /l/ at the beginning, they can use that information when writing *like* or other *l* words during writing workshop time.

When we are reading in beginning-level texts, engaging in a community writing piece, or working with a child while writing, we can use prompts like these:

- ❀ It starts like *Michael*.
- ❀ Let's get our mouths ready to start like *Sarah's* name.
- ❀ What do you hear at the beginning of *dinosaur*? Does it start like *David*? Look at our name chart and see what letter that is.

❋ Whose name starts like *sun*? (Making connections between the name chart and the ABC chart.)

An anchor ABC chart is a useful tool for teaching letter identification and phonics. Most primary classrooms have a chart displayed that shows the letters of the alphabet along with pictures. Our county's ABC chart is standard in every school, which allows for children to see the same thing year after year or as they move from school to school. This chart should be displayed in a place where the children have easy access and where you can refer to it quickly during community writing and/or shared reading. In fact, you may want to have several of these charts displayed—one next to your whole-group area or easel, one in the writing center, and small individual copies in each student's writing folder.

The ABC chart is a resource to help all students, especially your most struggling readers. It supports them in making concrete links for the letters and sounds. Even though there is only one hook for each letter on the chart, it is a starting place. Having a hook for each letter helps children while they are reading beginning emergent texts. They can check the first letter of the word and think of a word they know that starts like that.

Nowadays there is a wealth of beautiful and engaging ABC books. We recommend flooding the room with them, particularly if you are a kindergarten teacher or have a class with many students who still need to develop a sense of letter/sound correspondence.

Every once in a while, a few children will continue to confuse letters or will not be able to remember which letter is which despite all your efforts during reading and writing times. For them, more intensive work may be needed. We have found that a small amount of time learning specific letter features will give these children a way for their brains to make sense of what they are looking at. By letter features, we mean that some letters are made with sticks (*t, v, w, x, y, l, i*), some are curvy (*c, s, e, o*), some have sticks and balls (*b, d, p, q, a*), some have sticks and humps (*h, n, m*), and so on.

Keep in mind that when young children are learning to look at print, this is the first experience where order and directionality matter. Prior to their encounters with print, they are used to recognizing things in their world in various positions. Think about it. There is really no sequential order or direction that matters when viewing a toy car. The child will recognize it whether it is facing forward, backward, or upside down, and it is still a toy car, no matter what position it is in. However, with printed text, such as words and letters, order and direction do matter. A *c* is only a *c* when it is facing this way. An *s* is not an *s* if it is written backward.

Children who have severe issues with letter identification can be taught how to look at print by sorting and manipulating magnetic letters based on features:

❋ Curvy letters
❋ Letters made with sticks

* Letters with circle parts
* Letters with sticks and balls
* Letters with sticks and humps
* Letters with tails
* Tall letters
* Short letters

When doing these sorting activities, we are not asking the child to identify any letter. It is merely a time to examine the features of letters with them. We place several letters (starting simple, some with sticks and some with curvy parts) on a cookie sheet or magnetic board (see photo).

We handle the letters, exploring them with our fingers, and have the child do the same. We describe what we're looking at to the student. "Look at this one, it's so curvy. Or this one; it has two sticks." We encourage the child to talk about the letters using this vocabulary too. After examining the letters together, we ask the child to separate them as fast as he or she can: "Put all the ones with curvy parts over here and the ones with sticks over here." The aim is to have the child become faster and faster with this activity. Though we may only do this work for five minutes each day, we add a few more magnetic letters each time. However, we continue to keep the task easy for the child by saying: "Today let's see how fast you can separate the curvy ones, the stick ones, and the ones that have sticks and balls."

This preliminary work helps train the child's brain to notice specific features about letters *before* the child is asked to memorize which letter is which. Eventually, as children learn to write and recognize each letter, you can describe it with the language you used to help them examine the features of

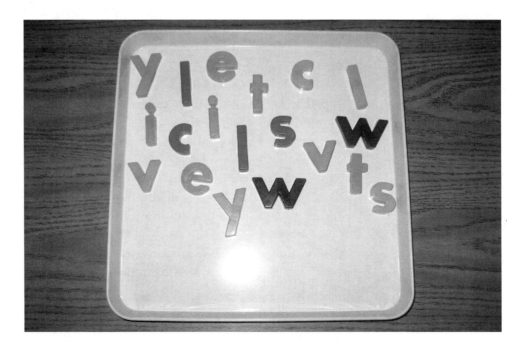

letters. "Watch me make an *h*. It has a stick and a hump." This connection between the language and the kinesthetic movement helps children hold on to the new letter forms as they are learning them. *Remember, intensive work such as this is not for the whole class.* It is only for a struggling reader who is having extreme difficulty with letter identification and/or formation.

Another activity to help children with letter identification is to start with their known letters. Line up the magnetic letters (usually about five to ten known ones). Model for the child how to say each letter quickly as you pull it down the magnetic board. Now ask the child to do the same. Mix them up and try again. You want the child to get fast and fluent with this activity. Add to the collection of letters as children add to their repertoire of known letters. A variation on this task is to have the child pull down the letter as he or she says a hook for that letter—such as *c/cat, m/mouse, s/Sydney*.

Some of the preceding activities—sorting letters by their features or pulling down known letters quickly—are easy for a volunteer to do with the children needing this extra intervention. It is much more beneficial when these children are engaged in these activities with an expert adult rather than being left on their own at a center. Our most struggling readers need the guidance of adults to make sure they are not learning and practicing bad habits.

By having an instructional aide or volunteer parent work with students on the preceding activities, you are able to spend more time with the struggling readers on reading real books or supporting them while writing.

While reading books at Reading Recovery/DRA2 levels 1–3, you may need to supply the first sound for the child when he or she comes to a tricky word. Or you can support a child while writing by narrowing the choices, as in this example:

Katie: (*Notices a child has written "I l" for "I like" and is now stuck.*) What are you writing today, Amanda?

Amanda: I'm saying, "I like flowers," but I don't know anything for flowers.

Katie: Let's say it together slowly. (*They do that several times together, but still the child cannot name any letter sound.*) Look up at the ABC chart. Do you think *flowers* starts like *fox* or like *girl*? Flowers/fox or flowers/girl? (*She emphasizes the beginning sounds for the child.*)

Support like this for a child who has limited letter/sound knowledge still leaves some phonics work for him or her to do. We want to use these supports as long as they are needed, making sure to pull back support once the child is able to do the work independently.

Having your students engaged in real reading is how they are going to become readers. Although our most struggling readers need some explicit instruction in learning letters and sounds, we recommend that the rote activities be done in very short time periods. Doing letter/sound work *only* in isolation, with no links to reading and books, will not accelerate the literacy development of struggling readers.

Figure 7.1
Phonemic Awareness
Versus Phonics

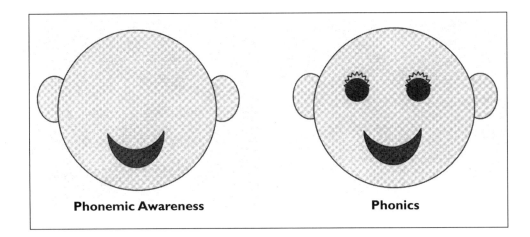

Phonemic Awareness

There is much confusion about the difference between phonics and phonemic awareness. *Phonics* is the relationship between written and spoken sounds and letters. *Phonemic awareness* is the understanding that spoken words are made up of distinct sounds and that these sounds can be manipulated. When Fairfax County (Virginia) Public Schools train their kindergarten teachers, they use a visual to show the difference (see Figure 7.1).

Phonemic awareness refers to hearing and noticing things about the sounds (ears), and being able to manipulate the sounds (mouth), but it does not include being able to identify the letter (eyes). For example, phonemic awareness is when the child knows that *tiger* goes with *table* because they begin with the same sound. The child would not have to know that they both start with what we call the letter *t*, or that *t* says /t/. Once you ask a child to connect a letter with a sound, you are focusing on phonics.

There is an abundance of information currently circulating on phonemic awareness. Kindergarten and some first-grade teachers (depending on the needs of the students they have) use many games, chants, and activities that are fun and quick and can be integrated throughout the day in meaningful literacy experiences. Here are a few ideas:

❀ While reading the Big Book *Dan, the Flying Man* by Joy Cowley (2001), which the children have heard many times, a teacher may pause at the rhyming word and allow children to fill in the word orally.

❀ While reading aloud the picture book *Me First* by Helen Lester (1995), a teacher may draw the students' attention to the alliteration: "Pinkerton was pink, plump, and pushy. [He enjoyed] bouncing off bellies, stepping on snouts, and tying tails."

- ❁ Some teachers sing and chant phonemic awareness songs as children are cleaning up, such as "Willaby, Wallaby, Wara—An elephant sat on Sarah" or "Down by the Bay" (Raffi 1999), which has lines like, "Did you ever see a bear combing his hair? Did you ever see a whale with a polka dot tail?"
- ❁ Some teachers play games while standing in the lunchroom line by asking children which one doesn't belong: "table, top, ball, or tiger."

One drawback of phonemic awareness activities is that in some classrooms children are spending too much time doing these activities when they may not need them or in place of spending time doing real reading. Elaine Garan (2007) writes, "The federal government's research warns against too much emphasis on phonemic awareness. In fact, as little as five hours of training a year is more effective than programs that use more than eighteen hours of training in a year" (85). Five hours a year for the students—divide that by 180 days! Our county suggests, "These enjoyable experiences are well suited for use during classroom transitions and unexpected available moments" (Fairfax County Public Schools 1998). In other words, do them while standing in line, transitioning to activities, or such times when an extra few minutes become available at the end of the day, right before gym class, and so on.

By the beginning of first grade, phonemic awareness instruction should only be targeting those children who still need it (again, keep ZPD in mind). Usually such children are beginning to write and cannot distinguish separate sounds in words.

One September in her first-grade class, Katie had three students who seemed lost during community writing experiences. They were unable to grasp how the other children were hearing the *first sound* when the class was saying words slowly together. Katie worked with them in a small group with the following activity. She placed three picture cards on the table (sun, table, pig). She gave each child a handful of Bingo chips. Then she asked them to listen to the word she said. They were to put their chip on the picture card that matched the beginning sound. This took a lot of modeling on Katie's part. When she said, "pencil," she had to model by saying "pencil/sun, pencil/table, pencil/pig," overly emphasizing the first letter sound. She continued saying words that began with *s*, *t*, or *p* as the children listened for the matching beginning sound. It only took two or three sessions with these children on this activity before they began to catch on. It was not necessary that Katie play this game with every single letter. The children were able to grasp *the concept* of how to listen for the first sound in words.

The reason this was effective was because Katie was able to focus on what these children needed. In order to participate in community writing and independent writing, they needed to know how to listen for the beginning sound of a word. We want to make sure that we are teaching phonemic awareness in a way that will transfer to real reading and writing.

The Difference Between Words and Letters

Have you ever had a child come up to the morning message and circle a word when you've asked him or her to find a letter? Being able to differentiate between a letter and a word is an early concept of print. Students eventually need to be able to respond to prompts like these:

❋ Look at the first letter in this word.
❋ Get your mouth ready for that first letter.
❋ Check the last letter.
❋ Can you find a word you know?

Most children will pick up the difference between words and letters right away, but for some we will need to intervene. There are several ways to bring students' attention to this quickly and effectively.

During morning message, call on children to find and circle the letter that their name begins with. If a child begins to circle a whole word that begins with that letter, say, "John is a *word*. It's your name. It starts with the letter *J*. Can you write *J* at the beginning of your name?" Wait as the child does this on the whiteboard. "Good, now can you find the letter *J* in the message?" You can also ask children to circle known words: "Can you find and circle the *word the*? Can you find the *word to* in our morning message?" Keep in mind that the letters *I* and *a* are also words and that this might be tricky for some children.

When creating a community writing piece together, make your language clear and concise to emphasize the difference between a word and a letter. For example, if the students have decided on the sentence "Snow is on the playground," you might say, "I'm going to write the *word snow*. What letter should I start with?" Some children will call out "*S*." "You're right, *snow* starts with the same *letter* as *Sarah*. Say it slowly. *Snow*. Watch me write it. Now let's read the word *snow*."

For a child who confuses the concept of word and letter, you may need to spend an extra few minutes while reading with him or her in an emergent level text. Ask the child to frame known words with two pointer fingers: "Show me the word *mom*. Now find the word *is*." It's okay if the child needs to find the word by using the pattern of the text. Some children will need to say the whole sentence and touch and point to the words "Dad is driving" in order to find the word *is*. After the child finds a word, ask him or her to find the first letter.

Manipulating magnetic letters to form known words is another useful activity that children can work on with your guidance in a small group or one-on-one. They can also work independently after you've instructed them on taking letters and putting them together to make words. Katie keeps magnetic letters and cards with students' names and each child's picture in a literacy center. Children can read the students' names and then take the letters and put them together to make names. Children love using the name and picture cards, and it is another opportunity for them to see that when you put letters together, you form a word.

Making sure the concepts of *word* and *letter* are secure will keep children from having unnecessary confusions as they move into more difficult texts.

Self-Monitoring

Ultimately, as children build a system of strategies, they develop a sense of self-regulation; that is, they keep a constant check on themselves to see if what they are reading makes sense, looks right, and sounds right. This self-monitoring in proficient readers is evident in several ways:

- They stop because something they read is not quite right.
- They fix an error.
- They reread to get more information to help solve an unknown word.
- They reread to rearrange the phrasing, pacing, or intonation of a particular sentence.
- They take a moment to check the picture or the letters in the word, and so on.

Clay reminds us, "Effective monitoring is a highly skilled process constructed over many years of reading. It begins early but must be continually adapted to encompass new challenges in text" (2005b, 108).

Every once in a while you come across a student who is very reluctant to take on her part of the reading work; she does not do the monitoring, checking, and confirming that a reader needs to do. She looks up at you for confirmation with every attempt she makes. You can almost see her head swinging from the text to you, her eyes darting to catch a glimpse of your face to affirm that she's on the right track. This dependency is one of the worst things that can happen for a young reader. The best thing is to catch it early and encourage self-monitoring from the very start. The following ideas will help you support children in taking on self-monitoring behaviors so that they will check and confirm for themselves.

When working with the whole class one day, Katie shared this story: "I was in a 100-mile cycling race when my bike tire went flat. Do you think I kept going?"

Of course, the kids called out, "No, you can't do that!" They then told Katie all the things that would happen if she kept riding on a flat tire.

"Well," Katie said, "you are right, boys and girls, I did have to stop and change my tire. If not, my problem would only have gotten worse and I never would have finished the race. You know, that's a lot like reading. If something doesn't feel quite right when you are reading along, you need to stop, go back and fix it. Otherwise, if you ignore it and keep on reading, you will lose the meaning of the story and eventually not understand anything you have read."

When reading a Big Book, you can model how readers are always checking to make sure that what they read makes sense, looks right, and sounds right. We use questions or statements like the following:

- ❊ Did that make sense?
- ❊ Did that sound right?
- ❊ Did that look right?
- ❊ Hmm . . . (after reading a word incorrectly) something didn't make sense there. I'm going to go back and reread to check myself.
- ❊ If something doesn't seem quite right, I want to make sure I go back and read it again.
- ❊ It's the reader's job to do this kind of checking.

For our most struggling readers, we will need to do extra modeling, prompting, and supporting for the development of self-monitoring. Sometimes we need to model running our finger under a word to see if it looks right. We want to encourage students to do the same when they are unsure if they predicted the right word. Nudge them by saying, "You said _____. That made sense. Now see if it looks right. Run your finger under that word."

Some of the earliest self-monitoring by children begins to happen when we make books for them, changing the word *I* to their name, as in this example.

I like apples.
I like bananas.
I like hamburgers.
Randa likes cookies.
I like pizza.
Randa likes food!

For Randa, who is just beginning to recognize the word *I* and her own name, you can almost see the aha moment. She reads along as if she has the book memorized, with the pattern being the same. And then on the fourth page she does a double take as she notices her name in the place of *I*. We always compliment the child by saying, "Wow! I saw you take a good look at that. You are starting to do some awesome checking!"

Remember to reinforce any checking and confirming behaviors as children begin to take them on. It's important that they begin to self-initiate these behaviors early.

Early Fluency

Fluency is reading with appropriate phrasing, intonation, speed, pace, and attention to the punctuation. Fluent readers think and process what they read quickly so as not to lose the meaning of the text. We want readers to learn early on that reading should sound smooth, have expression, and reflect the meaning of the text. It's important for beginning readers to practice and become confident with sounding fluent. We don't want to wait until our students are reading higher-level texts to show them how important it is to be fluent. There are many ways to teach fluency in a whole-class setting, as well as when working with students in small groups.

Be careful with the text you choose when focusing on fluency. Texts with characters talking make it easy for children; texts with sing-song patterns are also helpful for beginning readers. Sometimes you will notice books in which the publisher has already arranged the words on the page with proper phrasing. These, too, are appropriate texts.

When reading with children, we use the following prompts to support fluency:

* How do you think you sounded?
* Put these words together. Make it sound like talking.
* Was that smooth or choppy? (Use this when the reading sounds smooth and when it doesn't—we want the child to listen to himself or herself and be aware of how his or her reading sounds.)
* Look at this mark. (Point to punctuation.) What does it tell you to do with your voice?
* Make it smooth, like when you read _____. (Refer to a favorite book that has been read often.)
* Can you read it quickly?
* Can you make it sound like the character?

Katie recently teamed up with an ELL teacher, Kent Buckley-Ess, for a series of lessons to help improve fluency. They divided the class into two groups, each with a mixture of reading abilities. They chose Big Books that lent themselves well to choral reading. Each book had repeating lines of dialogue and was highly engaging to the children.

Kent and Katie each worked with one group, reading the book to the children first and then practicing it chorally. The students then suggested some lines that they thought needed more practice. Kent and Katie encouraged smooth reading and talking like the character when dialogue was involved. The children practiced rereading the books in their groups and then came back together as a whole group.

Each group took a turn performing their book for the other students. After the readings, the audience helped the performers reflect on what went well and which parts of the books sounded the best. The children loved this "performance" and really took to heart the comments from their peers.

Kent and Katie did this several times over a period of weeks. Each time the reading got even better. It seemed that having an audience, as well as the reflective discussions, were making an impact on the children's fluency. Although Katie was fortunate to have another teacher to work with, you could also do this on your own, working with one group at a time, or with an individual student.

The daily morning message, familiar Big Books, favorite poems, and community writing pieces are all opportunities to practice reading fluently. When we read these together, we talk about making sure it sounds smooth, like real talk, not "robot reading." We practice putting together groups of words into phrases and reading at a good pace. Effective readers, even at their earliest levels, read in phrases rather than word by word (Allington 2005).

Reading the punctuation correctly can help readers give the words of the text the proper emphasis and intonation. There are many opportunities in just about any Big Book to have students notice punctuation:

- Quotation marks that tell us that someone is talking
- Question marks that tell us to make our voice sound like we are asking a question
- Commas that tell us to take a quick pause or a breath
- Exclamation points that tell us to put excitement into our voices

Most children enjoy this work and catch on quickly to the hints that punctuation provides for meaning making.

For our most struggling readers, some intensive small-group or one-on-one instruction may be necessary to help develop fluency. When a child is reading a book with you, model how a phrase should sound. For example, even short phrases like "Come on" or "Wake up, Mom" or "Go away, little white rabbit" need to be modeled for some children. Stress from the very beginning that reading needs to sound smooth and not choppy. We don't want children ever to develop the habit of word-by-word reading. While children will read a new book slower since the text is unfamiliar, we want to make sure they are becoming more fluent after each rereading. (For an example of a fluency lesson, please refer to pages 37–38 in Chapter 3.)

A visual representation of the way we group words with our voice may also help struggling readers. Use a pocket chart to show readers how the words look when grouped into phrases. Select a repetitive line from a favorite story or poem and write it on a sentence strip. Take the cut-apart words and group them together in the way that they should be read (see photo on page 127). Read the sentence fluently and then have the children try reading it, emphasizing the phrasing.

When you are reading with one child, you can use your left thumb or a piece of a sentence strip to "push the words." On a familiar text, cover the words from left to right as the child reads them, moving the child at a quick pace. This will help the child move along and not pause at each word. Again, this high level of support should be abandoned as soon as the child is taking on the new learning.

Book Introductions at the Earliest Levels

In Chapter 5, we shared how to give an effective book introduction for guided reading lessons. These introductions are essential for your students reading at an early emergent level as well. However, they can present some difficulty because of how these texts are written. The texts at the earliest levels (Fountas and Pinnell levels A and B or DRA2 levels 1 and 2) were written for the purpose of teaching directionality and one-to-one match. It might be difficult for teachers to see a story within these patterned texts. And yet, if students are going to use meaning from the start, it is our job to build meaning and make these very basic texts into a story. This may involve inventing a story that goes with the text in order to interest the children and get them thinking as they are reading. Without this, we risk sending the message that reading is simply saying the words on the page or memorizing a patterned line rather than a meaning-making activity. As Clay puts it, "The child should feel that he is a reader, not just a 'rememberer'!" (2005b, 101). A sample of an early text with a repetitive line might look like this:

> This mom is a police officer.
> This dad is a teacher.
> This mom is a nurse.
> This dad is a plumber.
> This mom is a banker.
> This dad is a chef.
> This mom is a singer.
> My dad is a clown!

At first glance, you may not think there is much of a story here. The words match the pictures—something we want our readers to realize and use to help them solve words. There doesn't seem to be much going on. However, we can provide a book introduction to support the readers. For example, for the preceding example, you could say, "Once there was a little boy, just like you, who was trying to decide what job he should have when he grew up. He thought about all the moms and dads he knew and he picked the job that was the most fun. What job do you think would be the most fun?" Most children can relate to this, giving the students a strong sense of a story line.

Maryann McBride, Reading Recovery Teacher Leader from South Carolina, brought this story invention idea to our attention at a recent Reading Recovery conference presentation. She told us that before reading the book *I Like to Eat*, in which the pictures show a bear eating a different food on each page, she told the children about bears who hibernate. Then she asked, "Can you imagine how hungry that bear will be when he wakes up after sleeping all winter? Let's read and find out all the food he eats!" McBride is a master at hooking children into stories. She said, "Meaning is the most important piece. It's the ultimate check that all is well" (2009). For all readers, but especially those who struggle, this needs to be the message we send with our book introductions from the very beginning.

Asking children to read these repetitive books just for the purpose of acquiring more high-frequency words works against their innate sense of searching for meaning and our ultimate goal of having them see that reading is meaning making. Marie Clay says, "The child's need to make sense of the world gives an overarching intactness to all this learning" (1991, 40).

Suggestions for Teachers

Any teacher who finds herself in a situation similar to Rachel's, the teacher we met at the beginning of this chapter, needs the support and guidance of more experienced teachers. Oftentimes, however, teachers find themselves on their own while trying to figure out how to best meet the needs of their students. Perhaps a teacher is intimidated by being the new kid on the block, is too overwhelmed by all the demands of teaching, or is too shy or embarrassed to ask for help. Whatever the reason, if you are a teacher faced with the challenge of teaching the most struggling students, we hope the following suggestions will support you.

- ❋ Observe another teacher. Watching a lesson or seeing how a teacher interacts with a small group or an individual struggling reader is one of the most beneficial things you can do. You can do this during your planning period, or ask for substitute coverage for part of the day. Make sure you plan time afterward to talk with that teacher and reflect on what you noticed.

✸ Ask for help with your most struggling students. If you have a student who really has you stumped, see if you can arrange a reading specialist or more experienced teacher to work with this student once or twice and give you suggestions of where to go next. Oftentimes, another set of eyes can be just what is needed to see what strategies are in place and what needs to be taught next. Some schools focus their team meetings around students. They discuss running records, writing samples, and other assessments so that teachers can put their heads together for the most struggling students (more about this in Chapter 10).

✸ Make sure the books in students' book boxes are ones they can read. All children, but especially our most struggling, need to spend time on real reading. You may have to make books for these children until they are ready for level 1 texts and beyond. See Appendix 9 for examples of teacher-made books to give you some ideas. (See also pages 111–114 in *One Child at a Time* [Johnson 2006].)

✸ Celebrate every learning achievement your struggling readers make. Give them opportunities to shine so that they begin to develop a sense of self-efficacy. They need to believe they can learn to read and write and develop a "can-do" attitude. Building strong self-esteem and a positive attitude can help accelerate the learning.

✸ Take the time to get to know all of your students, and use this knowledge to connect with the kids—especially your most struggling. If you know that a child loves insects, find lots of books on this topic, or make books if you can't find any that the child can read on a favorite topic. When struggling readers begin to see a purpose for learning to read, they become motivated and don't view reading as just a task they are unable to do.

✸ Find ways to make learning to read easy. Frank Smith says, "The main thing we learn when we struggle to learn is that learning is a struggle" (1998, 13).

✸ If you have children who are learning to speak English, don't immediately assume they are struggling readers. Find out if they are literate in their home language. Ask questions about the country they came from, using student translators or other adults in your building who speak their language. Use book introductions as one place to support their budding English vocabularies and their experience with book language.

✸ Continue to grow and learn as a teacher. There are many professional books written that can help you reach the children who are hardest to teach. Ask your reading specialist or a knowledgeable teacher to recommend a few and consider joining a discussion group focusing on one of these texts. (See sidebar on page 130 for a few books on this topic.)

✸ Attend conferences of organizations such as the National Council of Teachers of English, Reading Recovery Council of North America, and the International Reading Association, as well as many other small, local conferences. These give you the opportunity to network with colleagues

Recommended Texts (In addition to those in the sidebars of Chapter 5)

One Child at a Time: Making the Most of Your Time with Struggling Readers, K–6 by Pat Johnson (2006).

Teaching Struggling Readers: How to Use Brain-Based Research to Maximize Learning by Carol Lyons (2003).

When Readers Struggle: Teaching That Works by Gay Su Pinnell and Irene C. Fountas (2009).

A Sense of Belonging: Sustaining and Retaining New Teachers by Jennifer Allen (2009). (For literacy coaches or anyone who mentors new teachers.)

and listen to experts share valuable knowledge about teaching reading. Take advantage of these opportunities and pursue professional growth and development.

Focusing on your challenging students will make you a stronger literacy teacher. Take time to reflect on what is working for these students and what needs to be adapted to better meet their needs. Be sure to talk with colleagues and share frustrations as well as celebrate successes. Our hardest-to-teach children can also be our hardest-to-love, because often these children have developed severe behavior issues as a result of academic and social frustrations. These children need our time, energy, and *love*. And it's worth every bit of that to see the light in their eyes once they see themselves as readers.

CHAPTER 8
Comprehension: The Bottom Line

Ask any teacher "What's it all for?" and we're sure he or she will tell you that the end goal of all reading instruction is for the students to be able to comprehend what they read. Highly proficient readers, having developed a functioning reading process system, will automatically and flexibly apply that system to any text in order to understand it. Our job is to see that every student eventually develops a reading process system (see circle chart, Figure 2.1) that will help him or her comprehend texts and fix up any problems that arise while reading. As we explain in this chapter, many average readers will need some support to do this throughout the elementary grades, and struggling readers will need a considerable amount of support.

In recent years, several authors—Keene and Zimmermann (2007), Tovani (2000, 2004), Miller (2002), Harvey and Goudvis (2007)—have brought the comprehension strategies to our attention. The information has helped teachers name what our brain does as it makes sense of text. Readers make connections, question, visualize, draw inferences, critique the text, and so on as they read. But there are also numerous cautions in the literature on this topic. Some literacy experts worry that naming and isolating strategies for students will interfere with fluent processing. Others warn that trying to simplify how reading process works can lead to misinterpretation by teachers. Still others caution that all this strategy instruction is taking the pleasure out of reading. Such worrisome information can confuse any teacher. As Harvey and Goudvis (2007) write, "Comprehension strategies are not an end in themselves, but rather a means to understanding. Our classroom instruction must reflect this" (33).

We have seen and heard some misinterpretations related to comprehension strategy instruction—schools that divide the strategies among the grade levels; others that designate which books should be used solely for which strategy; or schools where teachers seem to be going through the motions of strategy instruction without having a watchful eye on what the students might actually need. Here is one cautionary tale.

When Pat's grandniece, Colleen, was in fifth grade, she was an avid reader. Her teacher, in her second year of teaching, assigned the students a half hour of reading each night. In addition to the reading, students were told to write a paragraph about a connection, another paragraph about a mental image, and a third paragraph with questions they wondered about while reading. The teacher had obviously heard something about the strategies that readers use. There is no doubt she made the assignment with all the best intentions, trying to encourage reading at home and having a response page that let her know that the reading was actually done. But, needless to say, this assignment was ruining the pleasure that this voracious reader used to get from hours of nightly reading. If she already comprehended well, what purpose did the assignment serve?

Shari Frost (2009) alerts us to problems circling around strategy instruction. She attributes these to lack of long-term staff development, knowing that to fully understand strategy instruction would take hours of training: "Deep understanding of comprehension instruction will require at least a year of focused professional development." Frost describes some teachers as having only "awareness level knowledge of strategy instruction" (2009). Despite the many misinterpretations, Frost asks us *not* to throw out strategy instruction or discount it entirely. She still believes that quality instruction is possible. And so do we.

While facilitating conversations with elementary school teachers around the topic of strategy instruction, we have found that these kinds of questions frequently arise:

- ❀ Which students need strategy instruction? All? Some? And do students need to be metacognitively aware of which strategies they are using?
- ❀ What does integration of the strategic actions mean?
- ❀ If strategies are the in-the-head thinking that readers do, then can we really *teach* a strategy?
- ❀ What does comprehension strategy instruction look like when it is done well?
- ❀ How can teachers help students make the leap from guided practice to using their system of strategies independently?

In this chapter we examine the thinking and the teaching behind comprehension strategy instruction. We show ways to safeguard against misinterpretation by answering the preceding questions. We also illustrate effective teaching that supports many readers, not just struggling readers, as they build their own network of strategic actions to help them comprehend texts.

Who Needs Strategy Instruction?

For some of us, it took until high school or college to build an efficient reading process system and figure out ways to help ourselves comprehend more difficult texts. Pat actually witnessed this firsthand in college. If you saw her grades through elementary and secondary school, you would have thought she was a top reader. In actuality she was barely average. She and her classmates were not expected to think beyond the literal level of text. In fact, many of them were quite surprised when one quirky high school English teacher suggested that *Huckleberry Finn* and *Moby Dick* were about more than runaway boys and hard-to-catch whales.

When Pat entered college, she naively took philosophy as an elective her first semester and ended up in a class with seniors reading Descartes, Nietzsche, Kant, and others. Completely lost doesn't even describe how she felt when reading these authors. For the first month she just read words with no comprehension whatsoever. Then when confronted with her first D ever on a midterm, she knew she had to do something. She immediately spent hours in the library rereading all the assignments, stopping to paraphrase what she read, making connections when she could, posing questions and searching for answers, inferring, and so on. No one told her this was what she needed to do. In fact, she can only put names with the strategies she applied now that she's looking back on the experience. Pat figured it out because she had a functioning reading process system and knew that when the going got tough, she had to put it to use.

The truth is that most of us became competent readers without ever having anyone name the comprehension strategies for us. However, Pat wonders if she had had teachers who made her more aware of self-monitoring her comprehension, would she have caught herself sooner? If teachers throughout her schooling had shown her ways to fix up her confusion, would she have implemented those strategic actions from the start?

Most professional books about comprehension strategies suggest that we shouldn't just sit back and wait until high school or later for students to figure things out. They propose starting early, making the strategies visible for students at younger grades. Why not let younger students in on the secrets of what successful readers do when confronted with passages they don't understand?

We agree that comprehension strategy instruction has a place in elementary classrooms, but we raise these questions: Is prolonged strategy instruction necessary for every student? and Does the child need to name which strategies helped him or her comprehend? We have heard many stories about top readers in classrooms asking their teachers questions like these:

- I already know how to make pictures in my mind as I read, so why do I need to practice that?
- I already comprehend the story. Why are you stopping me to ask what strategies I used?

In the second edition of *Mosaic of Thought*, Keene and Zimmermann (2007) answer this dilemma by suggesting that teachers use more difficult texts with these extremely proficient readers: "Generally, with children who are avid readers, providing them with more challenging texts is key so that they can experience how consciously using the strategies can help them grasp the material" (43). We have a slightly different perspective on this. To us, these top readers already have a fluent, automatic, subconscious system at work. Even if presented with difficult text, their system would still function, perhaps needing only minimal teacher involvement. Just because a text is more challenging doesn't mean that the child's system will disappear or stop functioning—especially if it's been working like a well-oiled machine all along. Such students will *not* need to know the names of the strategies or consciously perform a strategic operation in order to approach that more difficult text and understand it.

We take to heart Peter Johnston's message that "as teachers we have to decide *what* to be explicit about for *which* students and *when* to be explicit about

Katie carries a vision with her of what these conversations can grow into. In past years, she has taught grades first through fifth and because of this, she has already experienced the depth to which these conversations can go. After looping with a class from first to second grade, by the end of last school year her second graders were inferring naturally, questioning the text, searching for evidence to support their opinions, and identifying the big idea or theme of books. There's no way this group of first graders is ready for all of that yet, but she will be able to guide, model, and facilitate these beginning students as they learn to push back at texts and get to the heart of the piece (Nichols 2006).

As Katie squeezes their stuffed bird gently to play a song, which serves as their signal to come back together, the first graders stop their conversations and turn back to look at her. She asks if someone would like to share.

Lucy: I didn't think I'd like the book when I saw the cover, but it was really good!

Jackeline: My brother likes truck books, but I don't. This one was fun. The girl trucks were really strong!

Zameer: I like how he said "Smash! Crash!" so many times. It made it fun to hear and fun to read.

Katie: You know, that's something you could try in your writing. Authors sometimes repeat certain words to make their story sound better. You could try to write like Jon Scieszka today.

In this short lesson, Katie shared her passion for learning about favorite authors and books, talked about where authors get their ideas, read a wonderfully engaging book, invited conversation about the book, and planted a seed that may nudge some of these first graders to try a repetitive line in their own writing. She will revisit the book, and children will clamor to keep it in their personal book boxes so they can read and retell it. Some will act it out in their dramatic play center. And Katie will most definitely hear the lines "Smash! Crash!" when the children play with the Matchbox trucks and cars. This interactive read-aloud provided multiple avenues for student learning.

Of course, simply picking a book off your shelf and reading it to your students is not what makes the interactive read-aloud such an essential piece of literacy instruction. Rather, its power comes from the combination of several factors:

- ❁ Carefully selected texts for clearly defined instructional purposes based on students' needs
- ❁ Time provided for meaningful conversation around these texts by teacher and students
- ❁ Expressive oral reading

The rest of this chapter will expand on these three ideas.

it" (2004, 8). For a top reader whose reading process system is operating fluently at a subconscious level, it could very well interfere with his or her processing if asked to slow down, learn about a particular strategy, name it, and learn how it works. Readers don't need to be metacognitively aware of how they were able to comprehend as long as they *did* comprehend. Marie Clay (2005b) warns us not to overdose on requiring children to tell us how they went about self-correcting an error or how they solved a particular problem. She writes, "Asking the child to talk about how he is thinking or acting slows up the in-the-head solving. It interferes with the fast responding that is essential for fluent reading" (114).

If explicit comprehension strategy instruction isn't for top proficient readers, who, then, is it for? We feel that the most effective use of strategy teaching is for the struggling reader who has no idea what the successful readers around him or her are thinking about as they read. This struggling reader is busy calling the words, but not doing the thinking necessary for comprehension. He or she is memorizing a line of text just in case the teacher asks a question. He or she is the one *not* engaged with the text—*not* talking back to it, questioning it, laughing at it, being moved by it, putting himself or herself in the character's shoes, experiencing emotions in reaction to the story line, using background knowledge to make sense of new information, or making pictures in his or her mind to be right there with the characters.

If struggling readers are taught the kinds of thinking that readers do, they could very well add those strategic actions and behaviors to their own repertoire. It isn't always a fast process, but it can be done. In *One Child at a Time*, Pat tells the story of working with Sam for most of his fifth-grade year to get an effective reading process system underway.

Thus far in this section we have focused on two groups of readers, the strugglers and the highly proficient. We recommended the need for explicit strategy instruction for the struggling readers and advised toning down the amount for top readers. Yet, between the two groups—struggling readers and extremely proficient readers—is an incredibly large body of students who could also benefit from exposure to comprehension strategy instruction in doses relevant to their needs. With effective instruction, this group of students could learn to use the following skills:

- ❀ Better infer information from text
- ❀ Distinguish important parts from nonessential information
- ❀ Pick up on subtle humor, sarcasm, or underlying themes
- ❀ Make links from one text to another in order to improve comprehension
- ❀ Expand their knowledge of various topics by activating and adding to their schema
- ❀ Examine an author's perspective or a character's point of view

Sibberson and Szymusiak were driven to write *Beyond Leveled Books* (2001, and 2008, with Lisa Koch) and *Still Learning to Read* (2003) to help teachers realize that there are many skills and strategies that we can continue teaching students in grades 2–5. Their ideas and lessons are aimed at this large middle group we have just described. "Transitional readers are not struggling readers. They simply need a new set of strategies for reading more complex texts . . . [They are] competent readers who need the support of thoughtful and purposeful instruction" (2001, 3). What we admire about these authors is that they are always careful to follow the students. They don't decide on teaching inferring, or point of view, or special features of nonfiction texts because it happens to be the next item on the curriculum guide lists. They watch their students. They look to see what seems to be confusing the students in their reading and develop the lessons from there.

As you consider strategy instruction for your students, think about why it's necessary and for whom. There is a certain danger in focusing too narrowly on each strategy for six to eight weeks with the entire class. How can every child in the class be in need of only that one strategy for six to eight weeks? Itemizing strategy instruction can be just as ineffective as teaching phonics in isolation. We have to be careful not to run the risk of deconstructing reading process to the point of no return. For students to comprehend, they need to use all their strategies in an integrated way.

The Integration Factor

It is not that difficult to get a child to practice a strategic action (such as questioning, visualizing, making connections, or searching for further information) when a teacher calls upon him or her to do so. But that is not enough. The aim of an accomplished reader is to have the strategic actions work together in an integrated way (Clay 2001, Lyons 2003, Fountas and Pinnell 2006). Harvey and Goudvis (2007) say, "The last thing we want to do is limit kids' thinking, directing them away from one strategy because we happen to be teaching another" (34). As you focus on one strategy, be sure to encourage children to use the other strategies that they already control.

There is no set way to go about comprehending. A reader does not first activate background knowledge, then make a connection, then visualize, and so on. Remember the metaphor we used in Chapter 2 on page 18 when we asked you to create a web in your mind connecting all strategy words around the circle chart in Figure 2.1. There is nothing linear or sequential about how the reading process works for each individual when it is fully integrated.

In order to have an efficient and integrated reading process system, the child must *self-initiate* the strategies, using them when he or she deems necessary to understand a text or solve a problem while reading. Peter Johnston (2007) says, "The child is the active protagonist who generates strategies and solves problems" (67). We need to constantly teach toward independence in order for students to become these active protagonists.

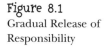

Figure 8.1
Gradual Release of
Responsibility

Modeling `--------------------------▶` You do it *for* them.
You think aloud.
You tell how it helps you.

Shared Demonstration `----------▶` You still initiate.
You do it *with* them.

Guided Practice `-------------------▶` You give practice time *to* them.
You listen, watch, and guide.

Independence `--------------------▶` You *do not* initiate.
You wait, watch, and then take action.

In the same article, Johnston writes, "The teacher's job is not delivering knowledge, but arranging for the problem to be manageable, sustaining the child's problem solving attempts emphasizing flexibility" (2007, 67). When you *arrange for a problem to be manageable,* you set up opportunities for the students to practice using the strategic action when they are reading continuous text. Guided reading is the perfect place to provide these opportunities. After a book introduction, be sure that there is still enough reading work for the children to do. The students need practice putting their systems of strategies to work. The teacher is present to support the students' *problem-solving attempts.* To *emphasize flexibility,* the teacher gives the children wait time to comprehend text on their own, using their strategies when they need them. The teacher can also prompt a child to consider a variety of ways to solve problems, encouraging flexibility.

Take a minute to examine the chart in Figure 8.1. For all of the first three parts of the gradual release model (explained in Chapter 3) the teacher initiates the strategy application. But during independent reading time, the teacher does not. The teacher waits, watches, converses, and then takes action.

This independent time is allowing the teacher opportunities to see what the children can apply on their own. As the teacher meets with individual students, he or she notices, through discussion about the books, which students comprehend and which cannot. The way the teacher responds to each student will depend on the assessment of how that student comprehends. For students who show evidence of solid comprehension the teacher can take these actions:

❁ Ask for more information to encourage the child to elaborate on his or her understandings: "Tell me more about the relationship between Will and his grandfather."
❁ Reinforce a strategy the child used: "When you told me about the type of person [character's name] was, you did a nice job of piecing together information from a lot of different places in the book."

❋ Compliment the child in a way that lets him or her know that meaning making and original thought are valuable: "Your insight about _____ is topnotch. I'm not sure I would have thought about it that way. You must feel proud of the thinking you're doing while reading."

❋ Ask for a prediction: "What do you think will happen next? How will [character's name] get out of this situation or solve this problem?"

❋ Ask the child where he or she will go from here: "What's your plan for tomorrow?"

For students who are showing evidence of confusion or lack of comprehension, the teacher can respond in these ways:

❋ Help the child pinpoint where he or she stopped comprehending: "Show me where you started to get confused. Let's look at that part together."

❋ Encourage the child to focus on a strategy that the whole class had used in an anchor lesson: "Do you remember the other day when we all came up with questions [or some strategy that you think would help at this time] before we started reading that article on tornadoes together?"

❋ Refer the child to a chart in the room: "Look at this chart. What were we doing yesterday when we made this chart? How did that help us understand _____? Could you use that idea right here where you are stuck?"

❋ Support the child in making a link from that anchor lesson to what he or she is now reading: "Do you think if you have some questions in mind, like we did the other day, it will help you understand this part better? Let's try it."

❋ Model for the child right then and there what you want him or her to try; in other words, back up and reteach: "Watch me _____." "Let me show you how I would _____."

❋ Make note about what the child is unable to do and which strategy or strategies might help this child in the future. Be sure to include the child in additional small group work on the topic.

Can We Really Teach a Strategy?

Clay (1991) tells us that we cannot put the strategies into the head of the child. Each reader constructs his or her own reading process system. So in response to the question, "Can we really teach strategies?" the answer would depend on how you view the word *teach*. If teaching means just *telling* and then hoping the students will catch on, then, no, you can't teach a strategy. However, if teaching, for you, means that the teacher does the following, then, yes, you can teach a strategy:

❋ Models a particular strategy and makes his or her thinking visible to students

❋ Continues with shared demonstrations, encouraging student involvement

❋ Follows that with some guided practice for students who need more focused attention and support

❋ And finally, allows time for the students to talk about how the strategy helped them comprehend

In other words, your teaching would stay true to the gradual release model described in Chapter 3.

Some teachers ask, "But is it okay to pull out a strategy, one at a time, and focus on just that one for a short time?" They worry that if a reader's network of strategies is supposed to work in an integrated way, then isolating one strategy might not be such a good idea. Keene and Zimmermann (2007) suggest "turning the volume up" on one strategic action for a while; Dorn and Soffos (2005) call it "spotlighting" a particular strategy.

We agree that turning the volume up or spotlighting any of the strategies can be done very effectively. But we are also cautious as we develop lessons because of the warnings from Fountas and Pinnell (2006), who say that sometimes the teaching can become "heavy-handed." So where do we draw the line between *spotlighting* a strategy and doing too much *heavy-handed teaching?*

We see the difference relating to two factors: (1) how the strategy is presented and (2) whether or not the students are given the time, opportunity, and support to internalize the strategy.

1. The teacher needs to begin with a desire to make meaning of a particular text, always keeping the focus on meaning, and then present the strategy as something that contributes to his or her understanding of the piece. Fountas and Pinnell (2006) say, "Readers' attention must be on the meaning of the text rather than on how to make their brains perform a particular operation" (45).
2. The students need to experience the strategic action working for them. If they are not able to feel its usefulness, they will be unlikely to use it at another time.

Take a look at the differences in the spotlighting and heavy-handed examples shown in Figure 8.2. Later in this chapter we present lessons on questioning and visualizing. These show how spotlighting a strategy can be done effectively and not become heavy-handed.

Another way of looking at effective comprehension strategy instruction is to compare it to the kind of teaching we do when encouraging beginning readers to take on early word-solving strategies (see Chapter 4). Here teachers use explicit modeling and the gradual release concept. We teach and encourage students to use a balance of the sources of information; we want them to use meaning, structure, and visual information quickly and without much conscious attention. But their processing is usually slow and deliberate *before* it

Figure 8.2
Spotlighting Versus
Heavy-Handed Teaching
of Strategies

Spotlighting	Heavy-Handed
Teacher introduction: I'm going to read this poem on the overhead projector and you can follow along. I'd really like to understand this poem as well as I can. One thing I try when I'm reading is to make a picture in my mind of what the words make me think of. I'll think out loud about the images I'm getting in my mind and see if that helps me understand this poem.	Teacher introduction: We've been studying different strategies that readers use. This week I'm going to teach you about visualizing. Visualizing is when you make pictures in your mind as you read. Listen to me read this poem, and I'll tell you about the pictures I'm getting in my mind.
Teacher gives time for students to talk about how the strategy helps them understand a particular part of a story, poem, or article during shared demonstrations and guided practice. The teacher also uses assessment and observation while the students read independently to find evidence that the students have taken on the strategy or behavior.	The teacher treats the strategy as the end goal in and of itself. He or she offers practice time on texts to "do" the strategy rather than emphasizing meaning making of texts. The assessment is done on tasks the child performs *at the request of the teacher* rather than on the strategy use during the child's independent reading.

becomes fast and fluent. It's the same with teaching comprehension strategies. Some children need us to walk them through how a reader actually makes connections, questions, or visualizes as he or she reads. Eventually we want students to use those strategic actions quickly, but again, for some students, the processing may need to be done slowly and deliberately *before* it speeds up.

What Good Strategy Instruction Looks Like

Given the popularity of certain texts, DVDs, and workshops on the topic of teaching comprehension strategies, we'd guess that every teacher has at least one "making connections" lesson up his or her sleeve. We are therefore assuming that the readers of this text have had some experience with developing lessons focusing on a particular strategy. The sidebar on the next page lists many books that contain well-written lesson ideas.

It is easy for teachers to copy comprehension strategy lessons; imitation is certainly a possible place to begin. In time, as teachers gain further understanding about the integrated reading process system, they will become more adept at assessing students' reading to decide which kind of strategy support is needed by which students at any given time.

**Professional Resources
About Comprehension Strategies**

Reading With Meaning: Teaching Comprehension in the Primary Grades by Debbie Miller (2002).

Strategies That Work: Teaching Comprehension for Understanding and Engagement, 2nd ed. by Stephanie Harvey and Anne Goudvis (2007).

Mosaic of Thought: The Power of Comprehension Strategy Instruction, 2nd ed. by Ellin Oliver Keene and Susan Zimmermann (2007).

Still Learning to Read: Teaching Students in Grades 3–6 by Karen Szymusiak and Franki Sibberson (2003).

Shared Reading for Today's Classroom: Lessons and Strategies for Explicit Instruction in Comprehension, Fluency, Word Study, and Genre by Carleen Payne (2005).

The Primary Comprehension Toolkit (K–2) and *The Comprehension Toolkit (3–6)* by Stephanie Harvey and Anne Goudvis (2008).

Growing Readers: Units of Study in the Primary Classroom by Kathy Collins (2004).

One fact that many researchers agree upon is that learning to read needs to be an active process and that effective instruction includes lots of time and opportunity for student conversations with the teacher and with each other (Harvey and Goudvis 2007, Keene and Zimmermann 2007, Nichols 2006, Miller 2002, Collins 2004). As Fountas and Pinnell (2006) put it, "Deep thinking cannot be generated through exercises, but it can be supported through authentic conversation surrounding texts" (108).

Shared demonstrations with enlarged texts are a perfect place where these conversations can develop. Regie Routman (2003) finds that many teachers are moving students too quickly to independence after the modeling stage. Perhaps some proficient readers can make that leap after only one or two teacher demonstrations, but many children would benefit immensely from interactive demonstrations:

Shared demonstration is routinely ignored as a rich teaching context. Shared reading is ideal for showing how text works . . . In shared reading (usually the whole class, but also in small groups or with a single student), I model and guide students in all aspects of reading to comprehend—fluency, figuring out words, thinking, questioning, predicting, rereading. I rely on shared reading at every grade level as the medium for the bulk of my reading demonstrations. (Routman 2003, 132)

Let's not miss out on the powerful learning opportunities that shared demonstrations offer.

In the next sections, you'll follow teachers doing modeled lessons as well as shared demonstrations on questioning and visualizing. We easily could have chosen any of the strategies, such as making connections or activating schema. Here, though, the particular strategy isn't important. We want the focus to be on the design of the lesson and the language used rather than on the particular strategy chosen. As you read the lesson scenarios, look for commonalities among the lessons. These common elements will help you when planning strategy instruction of your own.

Keep in mind that no matter which strategy is the focus of your lesson, you need to feel confident that it is something that you honestly use as a reader and something that the majority of your students need. Why teach for it if it's not something proficient readers use?

Questioning

Take a minute to think of a time when you use questioning. When Pat recently read *Loving Frank* by Nancy Horan (2008) (about a long-term affair that Frank Lloyd Wright had), she constantly had questions in the back of her mind: Will his wife grant the divorce? Will he marry his mistress? How much of this fictionalized account is really true?

What is your experience with questioning? When reading mysteries, do you wonder, "Where was that character when the murder was committed?" or "Could the police be wrong about the time of death?" When else do you use questioning?

Just the other day, Katie's eye caught a headline in the *Washington Post* about the future of funding for the magnet program at her school. She couldn't help but ask questions. "What programs might get cut?" "Will we still be able to maintain our Black Box Theater?" "Has this already been decided or is it still in the talking stage?" She had to read the article to find those answers.

The voice in our minds that asks the questions as we read helps us stay engaged with the information in the text. That voice leads the reader to search for answers. Without that questioning voice, some readers' minds may stray from the text.

To help a class of third graders realize how much the strategy of questioning could help them comprehend, Pat started by doing a modeled lesson. She used the Sandra Cisneros story "My Lucy Friend Who Smells Like Corn" from the book *Woman Hollering Creek and Other Stories* (1991). Pat began by saying this to the students:

Pat: I remember the other day when we were all discussing the short story "Eleven." Our conversation helped all of us understand that story so much better. I'm going to read another story by Sandra Cisneros today, but I won't have you guys help me. I'm going to try this one on my own. I'll share my thoughts out loud with you and you can follow along as I read from the overhead. (*Displays the title of the text on the overhead, then continues.*) I know that the way Cisneros writes is very different from what I'm used to, so I may have to work a little bit on this piece to really comprehend it. One thing that sometimes helps me understand at a deep level is to pose questions *before* I start reading and then to stop and wonder about other questions *during* my reading. Because I'll have these questions in the back of my mind, I'll constantly be searching for answers as I'm reading. I want to see if that helps me keep my mind on this story and understand it as fully as I'd like.

Notice that Pat didn't begin by introducing the strategy: "Today we are going to learn about questioning." Rather, she talked about her own need to make meaning of what she was about to read. *She kept the focus on her desire to understand and wanted to see if questioning would help her do that.* It may only seem like a slight difference in your language, but it is an important one in terms of how children understand your lesson. Fountas and Pinnell (2006) write, "The goal is not naming a strategy, but applying it to the reading of text. Students can learn to repeat the names of strategies without learning a single thing about how to read proficiently, and you will have engaged them in a meaning-less (and possibly confusing) exercise" (353).

Pat continued by posing a few questions immediately after reading the title. Then she read the story aloud, pausing to think aloud about her questions. As she read on, she periodically stopped to confirm that a question was answered, to rearrange her thinking, or to pose a new question. Afterward, the students had time with partners to discuss what they noticed Pat doing and then shared out with the whole group.

The next day Pat did a shared demonstration lesson. The complete lesson follows.

Lesson Idea #1:

Involving Students in Using Questions to Aid Comprehension

Pat: Yesterday I modeled for you how I worked at understanding the story "My Lucy Friend Who Smells Like Corn." What were some of the ways I helped myself get the most out of that story?

Vanessa: Like . . . you wondered why that girl smelled like corn and then you tried to find the answer as you read.

Phuong: Yeah, and you were trying to figure out if the girl liked that friend because she had so many sisters . . . 'cause . . . umm . . .

Kevin: I know, because you were thinking she was an only child and maybe she liked that girl because she had such a big family.

Pat: So the questions I had in my mind, all the things I was wondering about— like, "Is she an only child?" Or "Why does she like Lucy so much?"— helped me keep my mind focused on that story. Is that right?

Rhonda: The questions helped you get what the story was about.

Zach: Yeah, but we said yesterday that you didn't just use those questions. You also used some connections. Remember you said that you grew up in a big family and that kinda stuff.

Pat: You're right, Zach. When we read, we use *all* kinds of ways to help us understand. We have lots of thoughts—about things the story reminds us of, or questions we are wondering about, or images we form in our heads. I know that many of you use all those strategies as you read to keep your mind focused. We're going to try something together now. Today I want all of you to read an article with me, but this time it will be a nonfiction piece. I want you to decide if *having questions in your mind* helps you under-stand nonfiction. (*I write on the whiteboard "How does having questions in your* *mind help you understand nonfiction?" and repeat this question as our focus of the day. Then I put the first page of the article on the overhead. The students can see the picture of three adorable animals, the title, and a picture caption, but the text of the first page is covered over.)* We're going to do our best today to understand this article titled "Who Are These Masked Bandits?"

Several students: Oh, they're so cute! What are they? Are they baby raccoons?

Pat: I see that some of you have questions already. Let's read this picture caption too. (*They read together.*) "Uncover the amazing survival story behind these mysterious creatures." Now with just that much information—the title, the picture, and that sentence—turn to your partner and brainstorm some questions you might have.

The students spent a few minutes talking about their wonderings. Then each pair of students wrote one question on a sticky note to post on the chart (see photos). The students followed along as Pat read the article. She stopped occasionally to let the students talk about the answers to questions on the chart or other thoughts they were having. On the second and third pages of the text, she stopped at preplanned points in the article to allow the students to generate more questions *during* the reading.

Notice the column headings on the charts in the photos: Questions Before, Questions During, Found the Answer, Inferred the Answer, Need More Information. By comparing the two charts, you can surmise how the lesson continued.

Once the article and the chart work were completed, Pat gave time for digesting the importance of the strategy. The students did another turn and talk and then shared out with the whole group. Their assignment was to discuss

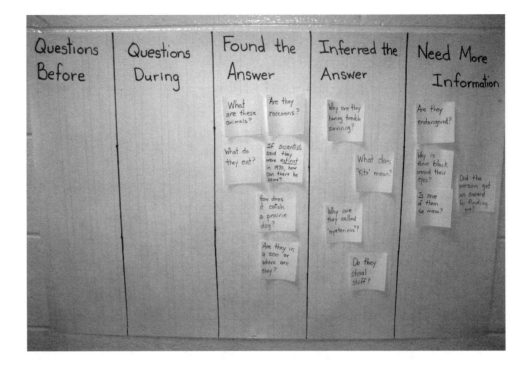

responses to the question "How did having questions in your mind help you understand this article?" A few students were honest in admitting that when we do things as a whole class sometimes their minds wander, but having the questions kept them paying attention.

Also, during the share time Pat asked, "Is questioning something you might try on your own? Why or why not?" Keep in mind that many students will tell you what they think you want to hear. They may say that the strategy of questioning is a great idea and they may try it someday, but you will not know that for sure unless you watch the students and hold individual conferences with them about their reading.

Granted, a few lessons on this topic are not enough for many children to be able to begin self-initiating this particular strategy. What you have seen here is only a piece of the big picture of the gradual release model. As you'll read later in this chapter, the teacher remains alert for which students need more focused attention and guided practice with the strategy.

Visualizing

We hesitate to even use the name of a strategy in a subheading, as we have with "Questioning" and "Visualizing," because we know full well that one strategy rarely operates alone. When you visualize, or make mental images as you read, you usually are making that picture based on some *prior knowledge* you have with that topic, or you are *inferring* based on some past experience. For example, if you read the chaos scene in *Water for Elephants* by Sara Gruen (2007), when all the animals escape and stampede, your individual picture would be personalized by your own knowledge and experiences of circuses, circus animals, and how you envision the characters of Jacob and Marlena. You can't help but use other strategies as you create that image in your mind's eye.

Still, as a teacher, you may choose to spotlight visualizing in some lessons to show students how to help themselves stay engaged while they are reading and understand the characters, setting, plot, poem, or nonfiction information being presented in a text. Lessons focusing on visualizing are especially important for struggling readers who don't realize that these pictures formed in the mind are a normal part of thinking while reading. Again, remember that the reason we are making a strategy visible for students is so they use this particular strategy to make meaning as they read or to untangle information when they are confused.

Most young children are able to visualize quite naturally. Pat experiences this often because she is a storyteller. She knows that during the telling of a story called "Tinderbox," when she describes three enormous dogs who are guarding chests of copper, silver, and gold, the children show her with their faces that they are right there in the story picturing "one dog with eyes as big as saucers, another with eyes as big as dinner plates, and a third with eyes as big as cartwheels!" They often illustrate one of the scenes on their thank-you notes after her visit, and she's always amazed at the detail.

We should definitely capitalize on this ability to visualize. Eventually the texts children read will not have corresponding pictures and they will need to make those images with their own minds. For many children this will be easy, but for others they won't make the transfer from picture books to easy chapter books that have less picture support. It's important for children to realize early on that *the words alone* can transform into a mind picture—that their own imaginations must take over the job that the illustrator used to do for them.

Terry Thompson says that "an inability to visualize effectively can wreak havoc on the process of making meaning" (2008, 71). Thompson helps us understand that as our imaginations bring texts to life, the pictures are more like movies than still life. "The images we create while we read should change and shift with the story. True visualization isn't static. It involves incorporating any movement that's taking place; making characters' actions and expressions change; calling up tastes, smells, and tactile feelings; and including sounds—all the while adjusting these images to the twists and turns of the plot as it moves forward" (Thompson 2008, 72).

Modeled Lessons for Visualizing

We both start with poetry when teaching how visualizing can help readers comprehend. There are so many poems to choose from, and we can quickly find those appropriate to any K–4 grade. Poems are often short, saying a lot in very few words. They are easy to display on an interactive whiteboard, an overhead projector, or a chart.

While the students in one second grade were immersed in a poetry unit—choral reading; having fun with rhyme, rhythm, alliteration, and tongue twisters; memorizing and performing some of the poems; and learning about the tools that poets use—Pat helped the teacher, Tania Dedham, with comprehension lessons focusing on visualizing. Here is how one of those lessons went.

Lesson Idea #2:
Visualizing with Poetry to Aid Comprehension

Pat: Boys and girls, we've been reading lots of poems from the poetry books we all brought in to share with each other. You've been having fun with a lot of the poems and learning about the tools and techniques poets use to write poems. You've even written some great poems of your own! Today we're going to talk about understanding what a poem is about. Sometimes we can read all the words of a poem, but we're not quite sure what it's about.

Theo: Yeah, I skip some of those if they seem too hard.

Pat: Well, I thought I'd model for you today what I do to get the most understanding that I can out of a poem. I discovered that it helps me to use the poet's words to make pictures in my mind. Watch how I do that and then we'll talk. (*Pat displays Siv Cedering's poem "When It Is Snowing" on the overhead. She reads it aloud two times and then she thinks aloud.*)

> ***When It Is Snowing***
> **Siv Cedering**
>
> *When it is snowing*
> *the blue jay*
> *is the only piece of*
> *sky*
> *in my*
> *backyard.*

Pat: I'm picturing my own backyard right after a big snowstorm. It's early morning and I'm the first one awake. I go into our sunroom, which has lots of glass windows, and I see snow everywhere in the backyard. Snow is on the deck, the ground, the branches of the trees, and the pile of wood. There's not one footprint in it yet. It's just whiteness everywhere. Then I see the sky and there is not one speck of blue up there; it's totally grey. I'm thinking it may continue to snow all day long. I'm wondering when we'll ever see the sun and blue sky again. And then, all of a sudden, I see a blue jay.

He lands on the deck railing. He looks so blue! It's amazing to see it against the white snow of the whole backyard. I think that's what this poet meant when he wrote, "the blue jay is the only piece of sky." A bird isn't really a piece of sky. But on this day, with all that white snow and that very grey cloudy sky, he *is* the only piece of sky in my backyard.

Pat lets the children turn and talk for a moment with a partner. She asks them to talk about what they were noticing and thinking about when she was sharing her mental picture with them. Then they share their ideas with the whole group.

Nikki: I started making some of my own pictures when you were talking.
Belial: Yeah, me too.
Pat: Well, that's good to know you are ready to start visualizing on your own. How do you think that picture helped me understand that poem?
Warner: You might've got all mixed up thinking that the bird was in the sky, but then your picture had him down closer to the white snow.
Pat: Yes, I needed the bird to be right there in my backyard, just like in the words of the poem.
Erick: You kinda figured out how the bird could be like the sky . . . 'cause of the picture you had in your head.
Nikki: Why didn't the author just put a picture there next to her poem? She could. Lots of the poems have pictures with them.
Pat: She certainly could have gotten an illustrator to do that, but I wanted to show you what my brain could do to understand a poem if all I had was the words. What do you think, boys and girls, are you all ready to try one? I'll put up another poem and you can talk with a partner about some of the pictures you are creating from the words of the poem. When you talk about your picture with your partner, you can decide if those pictures are helping you understand the poem.

As with most strategy lessons, Pat realized that the students would need practice with visualizing before they would begin to use this strategy to actually aid their comprehension. This first lesson wasn't enough for them to internalize the strategy. For a few days she and Tania took turns sharing poems with the students. They purposefully picked poems that might cause a bit of confusion, hoping that as the children discussed their mental images they would be able to negotiate the meaning together.

One such poem, "Umbrellas" by Maxine Kumin, incorporates a metaphor. The speaker of the poem notices that when she looks out her office or apartment window and looks down upon the city on a rainy day, all the umbrellas look like flowers opening up. None of that is stated outright, and the children have to work together to figure out lines such as, "Wag their stems and tangle" and "Plaid ones cross at corners." Each student had a copy of the poem typed up in the center of a paper with plenty of room to write on either side. As Pat and Tania listened in to partner conversations and read the notations, they made note of which students needed more practice in small groups.

Shared Demonstrations and Guided Practice with Visualizing

Pat and Tania did a variety of shared demonstrations for the whole class and some with small groups. They also held guided reading sessions for select groups of students. A brief explanation of those follows:

- ❀ They used parts of *Song and Dance Man* by Karen Ackerman (1988). The story is of a grandpa who used to dance on the vaudeville stage. They covered the book with brown paper and didn't show the illustrations. After reading it through once, they returned to a small section when the grandpa took his grandkids up to the attic. They read a few pages that included descriptions, such as "faded posters of Grandpa when he was young hang on the walls" and "we see a dusty brown, leather-trimmed trunk in the corner." They also read the page where the characters examine all the contents of the trunk. The students then shared the visual images they created in their minds. Pat and Tania helped the students understand that it is the words of the text along with one's background knowledge that determines the mental image.

- ❀ *Andrew's Loose Tooth* by Robert Munsch (1998) is another picture book that worked well. The story is of a boy whose tooth won't come out, so several family members as well as a dentist and a tooth fairy try to get it out. Again Pat and Tania covered the pictures. They assigned a role to each pair of students. "Listen for when your person (mom, dad, dentist, etc.) enters the story. Later you will draw a picture of the image you got when you heard that part of the story." Although it is normal for each person's picture to differ, Pat found the two different pictures of the tooth fairy quite interesting. One child drew a more traditional tooth fairy, whereas the other child's image more closely matched the words of the text: "The Tooth Fairy roared up right away on a large motorcycle." A discussion followed around the fact that background knowledge helps form your mental image, but listening and interpreting the words of the author is just as important.

- ❀ They also used a few nonfiction passages. One such passage (found in Appendix 10) was an answer to the *Highlights* magazine question of the month, "How do snakes open their mouths so wide?" Although the explanation is only a few paragraphs long, Pat and the children worked their way through the words, creating images to help them understand. They used two chopsticks to help demonstrate how the snake's jaw is attached much further back than human jaws. A rubber band also supported the picture of the stretchy ligament that held the jaw bones together.

- ❀ Tania and Pat each held several guided reading sessions with students who needed some intensive support. They used several of the chapters from *Owl at Home* by Arnold Lobel (1975) because each chapter could stand alone. They also used some more poems typed up with room on the sides for making notes.

❀ They used another nonfiction article from *Highlights* with a small guided reading group. This article answered the question "How come the moon seems to follow you when you move?" (A copy of this article is in Appendix 11.)

❀ During independent reading time Pat and Tania asked students to mark a place in their books that they felt would cause a reader to create a visual image. Several children read these during share time. After a student read a passage, the other children discussed their visualizations.

❀ Another time they sent the children off on a search through the poetry books to find a poem with some confusing lines. They asked the children to read the poem to a partner to see if together they could create images that would help them negotiate the meaning of the poem.

The preceding examples are a sampling of ideas for a spotlighted study of how the strategy of visualizing supports readers in making meaning of texts. The teacher should remain alert for opportunities to make the connection for the students between using the strategy and comprehension. One goal should be for the students to feel the strategy working for them. They will only take ownership of this strategy, or any strategy for that matter, and incorporate it into their reading process system if they feel it has value for them.

Studying Other Teachers at Work

Spend a few minutes reflecting on the questioning and visualizing lesson ideas. When Pat shares videos of these lessons or lessons like these in staff development workshops, she asks the participants, "What factors did the lessons have in common? What stood out for you as something that made the lesson effective?" Most groups notice these characteristics:

❀ The texts chosen were interesting to students of this age.
❀ The texts were large enough for everyone to see.
❀ The teacher read the text as the students followed along. This allowed the students to focus on the meaning of the piece as well as the particular strategy being learned, rather than on figuring out the words.
❀ Because the teacher used the think-aloud technique, she was very explicit in her modeling. She was able to *show*, not just *tell*.
❀ The teacher talked about how the strategy helped her comprehend what she read, rather than just teaching it for the strategy's sake.
❀ Students were often engaged in conversations.

❀ The teacher set up authentic opportunities for students to use the strategy while she was still available for support.

❀ The teacher used visuals and made charts when appropriate; children drew pictures.

❀ The teacher allowed children to practice with a partner while she watched and took notes; the teacher observed in order to discover which students needed more support and guided practice.

❀ The teacher provided opportunities for the children to verbalize how the strategy helps them comprehend.

How to Move Students to Independence

Recently Pat was invited to work for a day with the elementary teachers from three South Carolina schools. One question that she was asked to address was, "How do you get students to move from guided reading practice to using the strategies independently?" In other words, the teachers felt that they had completed enough instruction on certain strategies, therefore they should be seeing evidence of students using those strategies to help them comprehend. And yet, while some students did, some did not.

This started Pat thinking about many of the books offering strategy instruction lessons. Do you ever notice that the examples and student artifacts are from the kids who grasp the strategy and begin to use it? We never hear about the students who sat through all the same modeled lessons and shared demonstrations, and even a guided reading lesson or two on the topic, and *still* don't "get it." In other words, these children were still not effectively using comprehension strategies to help them understand what they were reading. Pat suspected that these were the students the South Carolina teachers were asking about.

As she pondered their question, she realized that neither she nor any literacy consultant for that matter could answer the question for them. Only each teacher could discover the answer based on his or her own experiences, teaching, and students. In order for each teacher to do this, Pat came up with six reflection questions that could facilitate each participant in finding his or her answer:

1. Was my modeling explicit enough?
2. What happened during the shared demonstrations? Who talked?
3. How much guided practice was given to the students having the most difficulty?
4. What assessments do I have in place for checking which students are effectively using the strategies and which are not?
5. How appropriate were the materials used during the guided practice strategy instruction?
6. Did I change my language to facilitate transfer?

The first question deserving attention relates to your modeling and shared demonstration contexts. Was your teaching explicit and focused? Or were you trying to do too much? Did you really demonstrate how the strategy of activating schema (or making connections or questioning, etc.) helped you comprehend or solve problems as you read? Is there another way you could have said it? The students need to get the message that this strategy could help them at another time, while reading another text. If they view your demonstrations as activities to watch but are not engaged in them, then they will never take on the strategic action. Cambourne (1988) describes engagement as seeing one's self as a "potential doer" of the action.

As you reflect on your shared demonstrations, think about who did the talking (question 2). We sometimes feel a lesson was successful if there was lots of talk and interaction. But if the talkers were the average and above average students all through the shared demonstration, we can't assume that everyone achieved the same level of understanding. It would be wise to follow a whole-group shared demonstration with small-group lessons involving the quieter or less able students.

Next, question 3 asks us to reflect on *how much and to whom?* Remember, guided reading practice is instruction tailored to the students who need work on a particular strategy, skill, or reading behavior. Under the guise of "being fair," teachers sometimes make the mistake of thinking that all students need the same number of guided practice lessons. In truth, some students may be fine immediately after seeing your modeled lesson. Others, however, may need several lessons on that topic. We suggest offering more guided reading lessons to students who are not grasping the concept. Keep your instruction focused until you begin to see evidence that the students understand and are using the strategy, skill, or behavior.

Our rule of thumb is this: There is no formula for strategy teaching. We can't say, "Well, one modeled lesson, two shared demonstrations, and three guided practices ought to do it!" We have to watch the students.

The idea of keeping a watchful eye on the students leads us to question 4, about the types of observations and assessments a teacher uses while the strategy instruction is going on (see sidebar on the next page). We can't wait until we are bringing a particular strategy unit to a close before we notice a child has a problem. We need to be observant all through the strategy instruction. Some teachers use individualized conferences, others take anecdotal notes while the students practice with partners, and still others have an assessment component as part of their guided reading lesson. Teachers need to take time to reflect on the artifacts that students are creating by noticing what the students are writing on sticky notes or in the margins of an article. Harvey and Goudvis remind us, "By looking carefully at our kids' work and listening to their words and thoughts, we derive authentic understanding of how they are doing and what they have learned or not learned" (2007, 39).

Question 5 asks, "How appropriate were the materials used in the guided practice strategy instruction?" If the texts were too difficult, then the students

What assessments do we have in place for checking which students are making use of the strategies and which are not?

- Individual conferences
- Texts that can be written on
- Sticky notes
- Listening in on group conversations
- Oral or written responses

would expend too much energy solving words and not enough on practicing the integration of the new strategy with the other strategies they've previously learned. Besides providing a "just-right" level of text, think about whether the text matched the strategy being discussed. For example, if you are working on visualizing, then the text should have parts that call out to the reader to make visual images. Or if you are teaching about activating background knowledge before reading, then be sure the text is on a topic about which the students have some background knowledge.

The last reflection question reminds us to consider the language we use throughout the teaching contexts. During *modeling* our language is very explicit; our words are carefully chosen to get our point across. As we move into *shared demonstrations*, conversations develop around the text and around the strategy being discussed. The teacher's language guides and facilitates understanding. During *guided practice* the teacher's language is more of a reminding type as he or she prompts and nudges students to try a specific strategy or behavior. Finally, when students are reading *independently*, the teacher uses language to either reinforce students in their attempts or help a child make connections to past anchor lessons. Figure 8.3 takes you through the specific language that a teacher may use while teaching about questioning. Notice how the teacher's language changes as he or she backs off on support.

Closing Thoughts

The examples of lessons in this section were from second- and third-grade classrooms. These can easily be adapted up or down the grade-level spectrum. Our intent was not to demonstrate lessons on each strategy; that's been done in many other books (see sidebar on page 141). We chose to share only a few lessons on questioning and visualizing to serve as examples so that teachers could reflect on what makes a strategy lesson effective.

Learning how to comprehend is not something that is only taught in upper elementary grades; reading to understand starts with the very youngest readers. Teaching in ways that help students take on various strategies and build a reading process system is what comprehension instruction is all about. Debbie Miller's book *Reading with Meaning* (2002) made teachers of primary grades aware of how this could be done. Miller believes that all children can benefit from being in a class where the teacher makes his or her thinking visible to children. "I make sure my think-alouds are genuine, my language precise, my responses thoughtful" (54).

Stages of Gradual Release	Teacher Actions	Teacher Language
Modeling	Teacher: • Initiates • Thinks aloud • Tells students how it helps him or her	• I'm going to read this article about _____ because I want to learn _____. • One thing that helps me understand the information as I read is to ask questions before I start and while I'm reading. Watch me. • These questions kept my mind from wandering. • I understood the article because _____.
Shared Demonstration	Teacher: • Still initiates • Invites students to participate • Makes a list of questions with students • Finds answers with students and discusses throughout the reading • Asks the students how it helped them • Creates anchor chart when applicable	• What questions do you have? Let's make a list. • Have we found any answers to our questions? • How did that question help us understand this part? • Are we understanding and remembering the information because of our questions? • Retell what the article was about to your partner. • Explain how having questions in your mind kept you engaged with this article.
Guided Practice	Teacher: • Sets up opportunity for small-group practice • Reiterates what the class has been working on • Refers to anchor charts • Listens and observes • Supports students who still need teacher assistance	• We're going to practice having questions in our minds before we start to read to see if it helps us keep our mind focused on the information. • Use the stickies to _____. • Mark a place where you found an answer. • Add a sticky if a question pops into your head as you are reading.
Independence	Teacher: • Does *not* initiate • Leaves anchor charts displayed for students to reference • Observes through individual conferences • Reinforces the students who are using the strategy • Watches for the children who do not comprehend • May have to go back to sharing the task with students who do not comprehend	• Those questions you asked helped you today (reinforces child who mentions the strategy). • This part really confused you. What could you do to help yourself? • Do you remember what we did on the _____ article to help us understand it better? Could you try that here?

Figure 8.3 Teacher Language Changes Through Stages of Gradual Release

We believe that all children, from the very start of learning to read, should stay actively focused on meaning making. For some average readers and for all struggling readers, this needs to be explicitly modeled and supported. We want all students to learn to think as they read.

Ellin Keene (2008) tells an interesting story in her newest book, *To Understand*. She questioned a college professor who gave her a B on a paper. She thought she had met all the criteria for an A, but the professor said her paper lacked "original thought." Keene realized that no one in her schooling had actually taught her how to have "original thoughts." For us, that's what teaching for comprehension means with elementary students. Let's teach kids to have original thoughts about what they read. Let's show them how it's their job to create the meaning, to have ideas, and to make inferences and responses to what they read. The meaning of any text does not exist in the black marks on the paper but is created by combining the words on the page with the thoughts of the reader (Rosenblatt 1994). Comprehension is thought—and that is definitely the bottom line when it comes to teaching reading.

CHAPTER 9

Spotlight on Inferring and Summarizing

Have you ever heard the story *Tailypo,* in which a creature comes into an old man's house in the middle of the night looking for his tail? When Pat tells this famous folktale to third graders, they always have an intense discussion afterwards about what the creature was. One child, using the words from the story "two pointed furry ears" and "fiery red eyes," will suggest a fox or a rabbit. Another will remind us that it had to be small enough to slip through the cracks in the log cabin. Some other children will zero in on the end of the tale when the creature "ripped everything to shreds. And now there's nothing left of the old man or his cabin, except for a chimney standing there," and they will insist that the creature had to have the claws of a bobcat or wolverine. Together the students usually conclude that the creature is an imaginary one, composed of various features from several animals.

What Pat loves about these discussions and many others like them is that the children are inferring, reading between the lines of text, without even realizing that they are doing so. Would it be smart to stop such a lively discussion to define inferring for them? We doubt it. It's important for the teacher to know that they are continuing to make meaning of the story long after the telling is finished, but it is not important for the students to stop their thinking processes to determine what strategy or operation their brains are busy performing. When we keep the focus on meaning making, children will draw upon the strategy of inferring as well as many other strategies. In the preceding example, the children were also visualizing (making mental images of that creature) and activating their background knowledge (thinking of all the features of animals they knew). In fact, they were integrating their strategies so well it would be difficult to separate them.

The beauty of storytelling is that the children have to create their own images, depending on the words of the story alone with no picture support. Pat uses no book, shows no pictures, and does not use any props when she storytells. Granted, not every teacher is a storyteller, but tales like *Tailypo* can be found in picture book form (Joanna Galdone [1984] has an excellent version of this story, *Tailypo: A Ghost Story*) or in collections, such as *More Scary Stories to Tell in the Dark* by Alvin Schwartz (1986). You could always cover the illustrations as you read aloud. The point is to allow discussions to spring naturally from the ideas, confusions, connections, or questions that the students have.

In Chapter 8 we focused on comprehension and how to go about teaching strategies in a way that children would take them on and use them independent of the teacher's suggestion. We will continue along those same lines of thinking in this chapter as we spotlight information and lessons on inferring and summarizing.

There was no particular reason for choosing questioning and visualizing in the last chapter over any other strategy. We easily could have shared lessons on making connections or activating schema. Our intent was to support teachers in designing strategy lessons, not to create a hierarchy of strategy order. It was not our intention to say that any one strategy is more valuable than another to teach; ultimately all the strategies interlock and overlap to form an integrated reading process system. However, we chose inferring and summarizing to focus on in this chapter for a few reasons.

Inferring, as we've seen in the *Tailypo* example, is when a reader combines the words of the author with background knowledge to draw some conclusions. Summarizing, on the other hand, is encapsulating a lot of information that one has read into some main points. Both of these are vital parts of the reading process system.

Inferring is one strategy that we find often causes confusion for some teachers; it can be difficult to define and teachers can be unsure of how to teach for it. By giving inferring a fair amount of attention in this chapter, we hope to clear up some of that confusion as well as to emphasize how closely connected inferring is to comprehension. So much of what we do as we read involves inferring.

We chose to highlight summarizing in this chapter because so many teachers link this strategy with content areas. Determining what's important enough to remember and coming up with main ideas of passages are often taught in upper elementary grades but are occasionally neglected in primary grades.

The act of summarizing always seems like such a school thing to do. Students are asked to summarize for a book report, or summarize what they learned in a science or social studies unit, or summarize a famous person's life as they do a biographical report. Even finding the main idea of a passage on standardized tests is a form of summarizing. The fact that summarizing is used so much in school (and probably more so as students move through the grades) is reason enough to teach students how to do it. But we also use summarizing as a part of our everyday literate lives. For example, imagine that a friend asked for a book recommendation. You might suggest that she read *March* by Geraldine Brooks. Of course, she'll ask what it is about. And you say, "Well, do you remember how *Little Women* had a mother and several daughters as characters, but the dad was away at war? That's Mr. March. Brooks made up the story of what Mr. March was doing while away in the Civil War. The author did an amazing job. She's an incredible writer." You can probably think of similar examples of summarizing in everyday life.

Children naturally use summarizing when answering questions such as "How was your Thanksgiving break?" They would answer by summarizing the highlights of their vacation rather than telling every detail.

We have several aims in this chapter:

- ❀ Raise teachers' awareness about the concept of inferring
- ❀ Point out and give examples of the many opportunities for inferring that appear in books, even for the very youngest readers
- ❀ Share our ideas about summarizing and why it is important to model explicitly
- ❀ Share a vignette of one teacher as she introduces and demonstrates summarizing to the class

Raising Awareness of Inferring

Inferential thinking is what readers do all the time to get underneath the literal or surface level of texts. When inferring, readers can appreciate subtle humor, figure out a mystery, understand a character, find meaning in metaphors, and so on. When Pat read *Life of Pi* by Yann Martel (2001), the story of a young boy who finds himself in a lifeboat with a hyena, an orangutan, a wounded zebra, and a 450-pound tiger, she had to infer what she thought each of the animals stood for. There was much more going on in this novel than what appeared on the surface.

Some teachers may think inferring is predicting, but we believe it includes more than just predicting. To us, inferring is the large umbrella topic, with predicting falling underneath. Fountas and Pinnell (2001) say that readers who infer "go beyond the literal meaning of a text to derive what is not there but is implied" (317). Owocki (2003) says that when readers infer they "round out and fill in what the author has written, giving the piece a personal texture and making it whole from their own perspectives" (46). And then there's Colin, a first grader in Debbie Miller's class, who says that "inferring is thinking in your head to help you understand, when the story doesn't let you in on it" (Miller 2002, 117). No matter which definition you prefer, you'll agree that readers who infer take the words of the author and combine them with their activated schema to draw conclusions about the story or the information presented in a text.

Several teachers at our school use the visual shown in Figure 9.1 to show children what readers do in their heads when inferring.

Of course, the goal for students is not that they learn a definition of inferring, but rather that they do it while reading. Children actually come to school already knowing how to infer. We can read this sentence to any class of students—"The children put on their mittens and scarves and went out in the snow to play"—then ask them, "What season is it?" and they always know it is winter. That's inferring. Or we can put on a mad face and say, "What if your mom looked like this? How would she be feeling?" Correct again. That's inferring too. Teachers need to realize that children already have the concept of inferring and the ability to do it without ever knowing a term for it. Building on this existing strategy aids their comprehension when learning to read.

Figure 9.1
Inferring

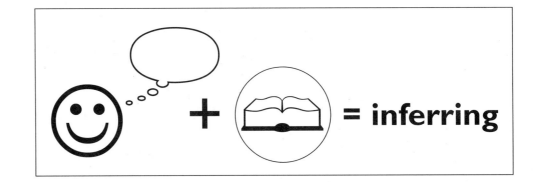

We have changed how we introduce inferring to students over the years. A few years ago we might have said, "Today we are going to learn about inferring. Inferring is reading between the lines to get at a deeper meaning of the text. It's something good readers use and you can learn how to use it too." But we've changed our thinking about how to introduce strategies (as we discussed in the previous chapter.) Now we begin with meaning making rather than with naming and defining a strategy. We start with a modeled demonstration, thinking aloud about a piece of text. We keep the focus of the lesson on comprehending and then have the students notice how we went about acquiring meaning. Based on what they come up with, we may or may not use the term *inferring*, but we will certainly get across the concept of what it means when readers infer. An example of a lesson Pat has done follows.

Lesson Idea #3:

Making Inferences to Aid Comprehension

Pat: Boys and girls, today I have a poem to share with you. (*Pat displays it on the overhead projector.*) I'll read it two times and then I'll think aloud. I'm trying to get the full meaning behind this poem and understand it the best I can. After I think out loud, I want you to turn to a partner and talk about some of the ways you noticed that I was helping myself understand it.

> ***Forget-me-not***
> **Ralph Fletcher**
>
> *I left one flower*
> *on Grandma's coffin:*
> *a forget-me-not*
> *as if I could.*

Pat: (*After reading the poem two times.*) I think this is about somebody dying because I know what a coffin is. (*She circles the word* coffin.) A coffin is one of those boxes that they bury people in. I think someone's grandmother died. (*She underlines "Grandma's."*) I'm not sure if the "I" in the poem is a male or female, but I think it's a child. Yeah, I think it's a kid, maybe a boy, who wants to give his grandma something. He decides to put a flower there on her coffin, not a rose or a daisy, but a forget-me-not. (*She circles* forget-me-not.) I think he chose that flower because he really loved her and he never wants to forget her. He's probably even thinking, "as if I could ever forget her." I remember how sad I felt when my grandmother died. I think I know how this kid is feeling.

Pat then lets the children turn and talk to a partner about what they thought she was doing to help herself understand this poem. They usually say things like, "You used what you knew," "You made connections to how you would have felt," "You took guesses about who the narrator was and tried to back it up with a reason," and so on. When one student alludes to the fact that Pat put a lot more thought into it than what was actually written on the page, that's when she might go into what inferring means. She would talk about what reading between the lines does for a reader—how proficient readers talk back to the text and elaborate with thoughts of their own all the time.

Pat frequently follows a modeled demonstration with a shared one to give the students an opportunity to try their own hand (or brain) at inferring. Szymusiak and Sibberson (2003) give great suggestions for doing shared demonstrations with the poems from Rebecca Dotlich's *When Riddles Come Rumbling* (2001) or with the retelling of fairy tales from different characters' points of view, as in *Once Upon a Fairy Tale* (Starbright Foundation 2001). These authors stress with their students that they need to back up their inferences with evidence from the text.

Pat asked her husband Rick (who always includes a poem in her birthday and Valentine's Day cards) to write a riddle poem like the ones in the Dotlich text, since that book is now out of print. Feel free to use the following poem with your class. You can find a copy in Appendix 12.

I'm sometimes new
Yet always old
I shine like the sun
But I'm really cold.

I'm round like a ball
But I don't spin
So you can see my face
Again and again.

Though I'm up really high
A cow once jumped over
When astronauts came
They had a rover.
By Rick Johnson

When Pat uses this poem in a shared demonstration, she displays it on the overhead projector in addition to giving the students a copy. She has the children read the poem with a partner, circle words or phrases that they use to figure out the riddle, and write their thoughts in the margins. They then share their ideas in a whole-group setting.

Opportunities for Inferring Abound

When working with a group of teachers, we like to ask them to think about all the ways a reader might infer while reading fiction or nonfiction. As teachers brainstorm a list, they begin to see how large the idea of inferring actually is. The spectrum of all that fits under the heading of inferring is often eye-opening for the teachers. The following is the list that one group of teachers came up with. We have elaborated on their list by defining each item and adding an example under each.

Setting: Books often have a description of a place or time period that readers have to infer. For example, in *Minnow and Rose* by Judy Young (2009), students can figure out the time period of the text not only from the clothing the characters are wearing in the pictures but also from the words. When Native American Minnow describes her age as "ten seasons of berry picking" and Rose is "covered in dust kicked up by the oxen" as she watches the "covered wagons form a circle," students infer that the story is not taking place in present day.

Character's personality: In many fiction books the author doesn't give a description of the main character's personality, yet the reader can infer a lot from how a character acts, how he or she reacts to certain situations, what he or she says, and how he or she says it. For example, in an old favorite, *Guess Who My Favorite Person Is* by Byrd Baylor (1985), a little girl plays a guessing game with a stranger she meets in the field. By the way she plays the game, how she talks to the stranger, and the answers she gives during the game, we infer that she is bossy, imaginative, sensitive to her surroundings, and quite intelligent. A favorite author of ours, Kevin Henkes, develops marvelous characters in his books. Even first graders can determine that, in *Chester's Way* (Henkes 1991), Chester and Wilson are cautious, neat, and always prepared, in contrast to Lilly, who is more on the daring, wild side.

Feelings or thoughts of a character: In *Freedom Summer* by Deborah Wiles (2001), the people of a southern town opt to fill the community swimming pool with tar rather than desegregate. Students need to infer how the two friends, one black and one white, feel as they sit on the diving board "staring at the tops of the silver ladders sticking up from the tar."

Author's perspective: Sometimes readers can determine the stance an author is taking on a particular topic that is a central theme of a book. For example, in *Fast Food! Gulp! Gulp!* by Bernard Waber (2005), the author writes about a fast-food cook who finally quits and goes off to open a healthy food restaurant for "folks taking time to enjoy the scenery." Readers can infer the author's feelings towards the modern practice of eating on the run.

Poem's meaning: Poems always say so much in so few words. Students of all ages can learn to infer meanings in a poem by a poet's choice of words and phrases. In *The Blacker the Berry*, poet Joyce Carol Thomas (2008) presents a series of poems that celebrate the many dazzling shades of brown, bronze, and black. Children infer the meanings of sentences such as "I refuse to walk too long in shadows" or "I am midnight and berries."

Theme: Children can be supported as they figure out the underlying theme of a picture book, as with *The Dot* (2003) or *Ish* (2004) by Peter Reynolds. Keep track of the picture books you read over the next few weeks and see if any have a theme of honesty, loyalty to friends or to a cause, hope, love, belief in one's self, overcoming challenges, or accepting and appreciating diversity. You will be surprised at the many opportunities for inferring that you discover.

The problem: Narrative stories usually include a problem that needs to be solved. Often the problem is not stated outright but must be inferred by the reader. Readers must find evidence in several parts of the text to realize the main problem of the story. Get students talking at a young age about what Gustavo's problem is in *The Best Mariachi in the World* by J. D. Smith (2008) or Jeremy's problem in *How I Became a Pirate* by Melinda Long (2003).

The narrator: Picture books, novels, and poems sometimes use the word *I* to refer to the narrator without ever telling you exactly who the *I* is. Readers need to infer to figure that out. What's interesting with first-person narration is that the *I* can be a person or an object. In picture books, the reader can infer who the *I* is not only with the words but also with the pictures. In *The Trip Back Home* by Janet S. Wong (2000), we hear the narrator saying, "I fed the hungry pigs," "I rolled the rice," and "I threw the sticky balls." We also see in an illustration a little girl about six years old. Later, when students are reading chapter books, they will not have the added support of the illustrations. For examples of authors who often use first-person narrative, see the picture books of Eve Bunting and Byrd Baylor.

Character's point of view: Various characters in books often have different points of view toward a person or issue presented in a story. For example, in Kate DiCamillo's (2007) beautiful story *Great Joy*, Frances and her mom each have a different point of view about the homeless organ grinder who stands on their corner.

Meaning of new vocabulary: Many of the stories you choose for your interactive read-alouds may have vocabulary words that are unfamiliar to your students. Children can infer the meanings of these words by using the context of the sentence or story line or by information they discover in the illustrations. In the nonfiction book called *Ladybugs* by Hartley and Macro (2006), even kindergartners can infer the meanings of the boldface words *vibrations, huddle,* and *aphids.*

Figurative language: Colloquial sayings, some quite far-fetched and others not often used in present-day conversations, frequently appear in texts for young children. In Daniel Pinkwater's *The Big Orange Splot* (1977), the people of the town think that Mr. Plumbean "lost his marbles and slipped his hawser!" Readers catch on to these meanings as the townspeople continue to point out that Plumbean "has bees in his bonnet, bats in his belfry, and knots in his noodle!"

Humor: There are many books that are laugh-out-loud funny to K–4 students, but others that contain more subtle humor. Students may need support or nudging to infer the humor in *Alice the Fairy* by David Shannon (2005). How does Alice use her magic wand to turn oatmeal into cake, her white dress into a red one, and Daddy's cookies into hers?

The teachers who brainstormed this list also included sarcasm, irony, allusions, symbolism, and inferring the significance of a text, but we find that most of these literary elements are usually found in texts read by much older readers.

Examples of Ways We Teach Children to Infer

Once teachers realize all that inferring encompasses, they can stay alert for opportunities to nudge their students to infer. Remember that students can learn to infer at the word level (inferring the meaning of new or unusual vocabulary), the text level (predicting what might happen, or inferring something about the setting, characters, or plot), and beyond the text level (theme, author's perspective, and so on).

Many readers of this text may have tried out a lesson idea from Debbie Miller, Cris Tovani, Steph Harvey, or any of the other authors who make great suggestions in their professional books on comprehension strategy teaching. We have certainly tried out several. After a while, though, the idea of inferring and how to nudge students to use this strategy to help them comprehend became second nature for us, and we began to teach it here, there, and everywhere. Opportunities just seemed to arise all the time. In the following section we list some of the books we have used in lessons as we supported students in making meaning of texts by inferring.

Books in Which Students Have to Infer Meanings of Words

William Steig is a great author to use when looking for a book that uses high-level vocabulary in stories for young children. In *The Toy Brother* (1996), older brother Yorick considers his little brother Charles to be a real pain. But when Yorick accidentally shrinks himself down to a few inches high, he realizes his brother has some unique qualities. Children listening to this tale are able to infer possible meanings for the words *miniscule, dolt, relishing, gratifying, antidote, consume, flask, flabbergasted, stature, retch,* and *bowled over.* Here are some other books we've used for the purpose of teaching how to infer the meanings of words:

- ❀ *Rotten Richie and the Ultimate Dare* by Patricia Polacco (2006)
- ❀ *Crocodilians* by Anne Gordon (2001)
- ❀ *Tacky the Penquin* by Helen Lester (1990)

- ✤ *Spinky Sulks* by William Steig (1990)
- ✤ *Nocturne* by Jane Yolen (1997)
- ✤ *Buster Goes to Cowboy Camp* by Denise Fleming (2008)
- ✤ *More Parts* by Tedd Arnold (2003)
- ✤ *Hello, Harvest Moon* by Ralph Fletcher (2003)

We also like Terry Thompson's (2008) suggestion to have kids infer the feelings of characters by labeling faces in comic strips with stickers—"content," "pleased," "fuming"—to expand vocabulary. In *Adventures in Graphica,* Thompson (2008) describes how important it is to have kids realize synonyms for words. He noticed that some of the ELL students at his school got questions wrong on standardized tests because of their limited English vocabulary. Even though the children knew the character in the passage was feeling down, the ELLs didn't recognize that the choice *gloomy* was the correct box to fill in.

Books That Lend Themselves Well to Predicting

Many teachers have a knack for finding an appropriate stopping point in a text to allow the students to turn and talk to a partner about their predictions. Primary students love to make predictions. They infer what will happen next by using their knowledge of what has happened so far in the story along with their background knowledge.

We have used Robert Munsch's *Stephanie's Ponytail* (2007) with primary students. Stephanie is the fashion leader in the class. When she wears her hair in a ponytail, all the kids do their hair that way the next day. Every different hairstyle is copied a day later. One day Stephanie announces that the next day she plans to shave her head. Perfect prediction point!

Another favorite of ours is *The Z Was Zapped* by Chris Van Allsburg (1987). Even though it's an ABC book, students of all ages have fun predicting what is meant by each picture and what the next line might be. For example, the letter *P* has a crow sitting on top of it nibbling on the letter. The next page says, "The P was repeatedly Pecked." After you read the first few examples, for A, B, and C, the kids catch on and then you have twenty-three other inferring opportunities.

Emily Gravett (2006) wrote the clever book *Wolves*. In it, a rabbit sits reading a book about wolves and learns all about what these predators would love to do to rabbits. The pictures, meanwhile, show a wolf getting closer and closer. Gravett gives us a great point at which the students can predict an ending. And then the author gives us not one, but two, possible endings—in case the reader doesn't like the first, more predictable, ending!

Here are some other books we have used for predicting:

- ✤ *Suddenly* by Colin McNaughton (1998)
- ✤ *Princess Smartypants* by Babette Cole (2005)
- ✤ *Duck at the Door* by Jackie Urbanovic (2007)

- *The Sweetest Fig* by Chris Van Allsburg (1979)
- *Widow's Broom* by Chris Van Allsburg (1992)
- *Owen* by Kevin Henkes (2006)

Another way to give practice in predicting is to offer the children opportunities during shared reading with a Big Book. A favorite of ours is *The Little Yellow Chicken* (Cowley 1992). Little Yellow Chicken plans a party and keeps asking friends for help, but they never will. Of course, when the party is ready to begin, the friends are all at the door asking to come in. Little Chicken calls her grandmother, Little Red Hen, to ask for advice. Because they know the story of the Little Red Hen, students try predicting what her advice will be and whether or not the chicken will follow that advice.

Books in Which Students Need to Read the Pictures as Well as the Words

Katie says that her first graders are always inferring with pictures, seeing much more than she notices. While reading *You'll Soon Grow into Them, Titch* by Pat Hutchins (1992), the students noticed many hints in the pictures about the passage of time—the tree outside the window changes, the plants grow, the mother's knitting gets longer and her stomach gets bigger (because she's pregnant), and so on. Another time, while reading *Great Joy* by Kate DiCamillo (2007), a book we mentioned earlier, one student asked if the little girl in the story had a father. The students debated. One child said, "Just because he wasn't a character in the book doesn't mean Frances doesn't have a father." Then another student noticed a small picture of a man in a military uniform sitting on a dresser in one of the illustrations. The children inferred that the dad must be away at war.

The following are other texts that have much more going on in the pictures than in the words of the text:

- *Tough Boris* by Mem Fox (1998)
- *Courage* by Bernard Waber (2002)
- *Annie and the Wild Animals* by Jan Brett (1989)
- *Two Bad Ants* by Chris Van Allsburg (1988)
- *A Country Far Away* by Nigel Gray (1999)
- *Changes* by Anthony Browne (2008)
- *Cowboy and Octopus* by Jon Scieszka (2007)
- *Robot Zot!* by Jon Scieszka (2009)

Of course, any wordless book offers plenty of opportunity for inferring among the students as they negotiate the story together. There are also some books with very little text (almost wordless) so that the reader must draw conclusions from the illustrations. We recommend reading *31 Uses for a Mom* by Harriet Ziefert (2003) near Mother's Day. Each illustration has a picture of a mom doing something with a one-word caption. How can a mom be a "ruler," a "doctor," a "bank," or a "tweezer"? The pictures hold the answers.

Here are other books with very little text:

- *This Is My Hair* by Todd Parr (1999)
- *The Peace Book* by Todd Parr (2009)
- *Ring! Yo?* by Chris Raschka (2000)
- *Yo! Yes?* by Chris Raschka (1993)
- *Hook* by Ed Young (2009)
- *The Mysteries of Harris Burdick* by Chris Van Allsburg (1996)
- *One of Those Days* by Amy Krouse Rosenthal (2004)

Books with Surprise or Twist Endings

When a pig accidentally knocks on a Wolf's door, he has to use his brain to outsmart the wolf in order to keep from being eaten in *My Lucky Day* by Keiko Kasza (2005). Kids catch on easily enough as the pig gets a free meal after suggesting that the wolf fatten him up before cooking him. But it is the ending that adds a twist to this trickster tale. The reader must do a bit of inferring at the end to realize that the whole episode was no accident!

Chris Van Allsburg is a master of twist endings. Any of his books work well in third- or fourth-grade classes, and we'd even use a few with second graders. Our favorite is *The Garden of Abdul Gasazi* (1979). Students have a great discussion at the end as to whether or not the retired magician Gasazi really did turn the dog into a duck.

Here are other texts with twist or surprise endings:

- *Paper Bag Princess* by Robert Munsch (1992)
- *Duck at the Door* by Jackie Urbanovic (2007)
- *Tadpole's Promise* by Jeanne Willis (2005)
- *Otis* by Janie Bynum (2003)
- *Probuditi!* by Chris Van Allsburg (2006)
- *Wolf's Coming!* by Joe Kulka (2007)

Books with Subtle Humor to Explore with Primary Students

Has this ever happened in your classroom? A few students pick up on the humor in the text you are reading aloud, and right behind their giggles is a wave of laughter from the rest of the students. But did they all "get it"? Teachers need to spend a few minutes nudging the understanding of that humor so that all children can honestly participate in the fun. Even though comedians tell us that if we have to explain a joke, then maybe it wasn't very funny to begin with, in these situations we disagree. We want primary students to appreciate the humor. The texts were written for them, and the author was probably hoping for that type of response. But some children may lack the background knowledge needed to pick up on the humor or just miss making a connection that was important. By helping in one situation, you are supporting their ability to learn to pick up on the humor on their own in future texts.

One book we've used is *Diary of a Worm* by Doreen Cronin (2003). Because the story is told from the worm's point of view, kids have to figure out what some of the diary entries mean, such as, "Hopscotch is a very dangerous game." Or "Fishing season started today. We all dug deeper."

The following are other books that contain subtle humor:

* *Diary of a Fly* by Doreen Cronin (2007)
* *A Porcupine Named Fluffy* by Helen Lester (1989)
* *Number One* by Joy Cowley (1982)
* *The Table Where Rich People Sit* by Byrd Baylor (1998)
* *Edwina the Emu* by Sheena Knowles (1997)
* *Dooby Dooby Moo* by Doreen Cronin (2006)
* *I Wanna Iguana* by Karen Kaufman Orloff (2004)
* *Cowboy and Octopus* by Jon Scieszka (2007)
* *Giggle, Giggle, Quack* by Doreen Cronin (2002)

Books in Which Readers Can Search for a Change in a Character

As children grow as readers, they will someday experience fantastic chapter books in which the protagonist changes as the story develops, such as *The Giver* by Lois Lowry (2002), *Downriver* by Will Hobbs (1995), or *Olive's Ocean* by Kevin Henkes (2005). As a reading teacher for over twenty-five years, Pat loved being in on those discussions where older elementary students talked about how and why a character changed. Because Pat sees that opportunity in all children's futures, she knows that it is beneficial in the early grades to support students to infer by watching characters develop and change as a story moves along.

In *The Recess Queen* by Alexis O'Neill (2002), first graders can recognize and verbalize how Jean changes from the beginning to the end of the story. They also notice Grace gaining confidence in her performing ability in *Amazing Grace* by Mary Hoffman (1991) and Lilly changing her mind about her baby brother in *Julius, The Baby of the World* by Kevin Henkes (1995).

Pat recently read a few of the graphic novels for primary students. She could certainly understand the allure for the group of second-grade girls in Mrs. Stillman's class who followed Babymouse religiously. In *Babymouse: Queen of the World* (Holm 2005), she is desperate to befriend the popular Felicia Furrypaws, even if it means giving up her loyal friend, Wilson the Weasel. But by the end Babymouse has a change of heart and realizes what true friendship really means.

The following are other books in which a character changes:

* *The Quiltmaker's Gift* by Jeff Brumbeau (2001)
* *Horace and Morris, but Mostly Dolores* by James Howe (2003)

- *Don't Need Friends* by Carolyn Crimi (2001)
- *Lucy and the Bully* by Claire Alexander (2008)
- Short stories "Boar Out There," "Spaghetti," and "Shells" in *Every Living Thing* by Cynthia Rylant (1988)
- *Jessica* by Kevin Henkes (1998)
- *Me First* by Helen Lester (1995)

Books That Spin Off from a Well-Known Tale

When students read or hear a fractured fairy tale, they compare the new text with the original. This comparing involves inferring as the students notice how the characters differ from the original, figure out why a character says a particular line, or tune in to a different point of view. They laugh at the wolves in *The Three Little Wolves and the Big Bad Pig* by Eugene Trivizas (1997) because of the role reversals. It's funny that the wolves are soft and furry and play croquet and that the pig comes prowling down the road and uses sledgehammers and dynamite to destroy their houses. The ending of this one is also a bit of a surprise.

Most teachers know about Jon Scieszka's books—*The Frog Prince, Continued* (1994), *The True Story of the Three Little Pigs!* (1996), and *The Stinky Cheese Man and Other Fairly Stupid Tales* (1992)—but here are a few other titles that we've used:

- *Somebody and the Three Blairs* by Marilyn Tolhurst (1994)
- *The Little Red Hen (Makes a Pizza)* by Philemon Sturges (2002)
- *Kate and the Beanstalk* by Mary Pope Osborne (2005)
- *The Gingerbread Cowboy* by Janet Squires (2006)
- *The Gingerbread Girl* by Lisa Campbell Ernst (2006)
- *Tackylocks and the Three Bears* by Helen Lester (2004)
- *Goldie and the Three Bears* by Diane Stanley (2007)

Books to Help Primary Students Delve into Theme

A book that is similar in theme to *The Big Orange Splot* (Pinkwater 1977) is *The Araboolies of Liberty Street* by Sam Swope (2001). Both texts have the theme of valuing individual uniqueness and realizing that we all don't have to be carbon copies of our neighbors. Even young children can figure this out, though they may not say it in exactly that way.

Pat remembers once reading *The Wretched Stone* by Chris Van Allsburg (1991) to a fourth-grade class. In this story, a group of sailors find an unusual looking stone. Each day they stare at the stone for longer and longer amounts of time, rarely speaking until the illustrations show that their faces have become the faces of apes. After reading the story, Pat asked the students if they thought the author was trying to send them a message in this book and if so, what that message might be. It took some interesting negotiating, but the students finally came up with the fact that the wretched stone might stand for a TV. Perhaps, the students concluded, the author is telling us we will turn into "monkeys" or "couch potatoes" or "stupid people" if we watch too much TV. Another group of students argued that the author probably didn't just mean TV, but also computer screens and video games too. That started another heated debate with several students saying, "No, Van Allsburg didn't mean video games because those are really good for your reflexes." And on it went!

It would only be fair to mention another time when nudging students toward finding a theme didn't work. Pat was reading aloud *Edward the Emu* (Knowles 1998) to Katie's first graders. The story is about an Emu who tires of being an emu and assumes that life must be greener on the other side of the hill or, in Edward's case, in another animal's cage at the zoo. Of course, Edward discovers in the end that being an emu is actually the best life for him. This theme had been easily discovered by second and third graders who listened to this book on other occasions. We should mention here that Pat's intent for this reading was not to teach about inferring at all; Katie was actually just videotaping her to show how a person can read aloud with expression, intonation changes, and hand gestures to help our ELL students.

Pat should have stuck with the original purpose, but when she finished reading to the first graders she threw a question out there: "Do you think the author was trying to tell us something here?" The conversation among the students got so crazy, Pat found herself *pushing them* in a certain direction rather than guiding or nudging. She knew she was trying to lead them too heavily in the direction of what she thought the theme was, so finally she just quit and let it run its course. Their final decision of what message they thought the author was sending was: If you didn't like being who you were, you should go to the hairdresser to change your hair color and then wear lots of make-up and different clothes! The lesson Pat learned was that inferring a theme is not an easy task. Being that it was the beginning of the year, she realized that, for these students, learning to infer a theme would take a lot more modeling and shared demonstrations.

Other books we've used to infer the theme of a book include the following:

* *Voices in the Park* by Anthony Browne (2001)
* *Bee Frog* by Martin Waddell (2007)
* *Koala Lou* by Mem Fox (1994)
* *Crow Boy* by Taro Yashima (1976)
* *Zoo* by Anthony Browne (2002)
* *Tacky in Trouble* by Helen Lester (2005)
* *Something Might Happen* by Helen Lester (2003)
* Any book of fables

Nonfiction Texts That Require Inferring
Though the preceding examples are all with fiction texts, we also look for inferring opportunities in nonfiction texts. The most common way to infer with nonfiction children's literature is with word meanings. There are usually

bolded words or interesting vocabulary that the students can figure out from the text or illustrations. In Dianna Hutts Aston's (2007) beautiful book *A Seed Is Sleepy,* readers can infer how they think a seed can be *secretive, fruitful, naked, adventurous, inventive,* and *generous* before they read the author's reasons.

Another way students have to infer in nonfiction texts is by using the illustrations to predict. For example, in Frank Serafini's Looking Closely series, he uses close-up photographs of objects in a variety of habitats along with some wondering questions to get readers to predict.

Here are other nonfiction texts we have used for inferring:

- ❊ *Bat Loves the Night* by Nicola Davies (2008)
- ❊ *An Egg Is Quiet* by Dianna Hutts Aston (2006)
- ❊ *Looking Closely Through the Forest* by Frank Serafini (2008)
- ❊ *Looking Closely Along the Shore* by Frank Serafini (2008)
- ❊ *Tigress* by Helen Cowcher (1997)
- ❊ *Antarctica* by Helen Cowcher (1997)
- ❊ *A Drop of Water* by Walter Wick (1997)
- ❊ *Little Lost Bat* by Sandra Markle (2009)
- ❊ *Stars Beneath Your Bed: The Surprising Story of Dust* by April Pulley Sayre (2005)

❊ ❊ ❊

Most of the preceding examples were used in lessons that we did as shared demonstrations or interactive read-alouds. But many of your students will need your continued support during guided reading lessons. Our job is to help students add their own thoughts to the text in order to push their understandings a little deeper. There are numerous possibilities in the beginning leveled texts that we use for small-group instruction in grades K–2. Fountas and Pinnell agree, stating, "There is some demand for inference in every level of text, and we can intentionally foster growth of this kind of strategic action in our teaching" (2006, 56).

In many books from the Rigby PM series, there are opportunities for inferring. For example, students can infer information about the characters in *New Glasses for Max* (Smith 2001), *Chug the Tractor* (Giles 1997), *Pepper's Adventure* (Randell 1995), *Baby Bear's New Name* (Randell 2003), and *The Little Work Plane* (Smith 2000). In many early level texts, there is often a lot more going on in the pictures than what the words in the text actually say.

A group of second graders were reading *Crocodilians* by Anne Gordon (2001) from the Literacy 2000 series (Rigby) in a guided reading session with Pat. As they read, Pat asked them to use sticky notes to mark places where they figured out what a word or phrase meant by looking at the illustrations. The students created this list: *undetected, lunge, snouts, tail walk, high walk, webbed hind feet, ancestors,* and *waste from factories.*

In *Guided Reading in Grades 3–6,* Schulman (2006) includes several one-page stories or articles that are perfect for small-group instruction. You are allowed to duplicate these pages for this purpose. We have found that many of those articles offer inferring opportunities for third- and fourth-grade readers. For example, students can infer the author's perspective in "When Wild Animals Become Pets" or "Lunch or Junk?"—an article about school lunches.

The preceding examples are intended to get teachers to realize the multiple inferring opportunities that arise with just about any text. But keep in mind that the best time to work with students on inferring is when it comes up naturally because of a question or confusion that the students themselves bring up. For example, one year Pat was reading aloud Naylor's (2000) *Shiloh* to a third-grade class. She came to the following passage, one of her favorite scenes in the book.

> *By the time I reach the pen, Dad's caught up with me, and he's got the flashlight turned toward the noise. The beam searches out the pine trees, the fencing, the lean-to . . . And then I see this big German shepherd, mean as nails, hunched over Shiloh there on the ground. The shepherd's got blood on his mouth and jaws, and as Dad takes another step forward, it leaps over the fence, same way it got in and takes off through the woods.*
>
> *I unfasten the wire next to the pine tree, legs like rubber, hardly holding me up. I kneel down by Shiloh. He's got blood on his side, his ear, a big open gash on one leg, and he don't move. Not an inch.*
>
> *I bend over, my forehead against him, my hand on his head. He's dead, I know it! I'm screaming inside. Then I feel his body sort of shiver, and his mouth's moving just a little, like he's trying to get his tongue out to lick my hand. And I'm bent over there in the beam of Dad's flashlight, bawling, and I don't even care.*

Several of the students immediately started talking about how sad they were because the dog died. Other students argued back, "No, he's not dead." Pat and the students carefully returned to the words of the text to infer and look for evidence one way or the other.

Guidelines for Teaching How Inferring Can Aid Comprehension

Whether or not students ever say the word *infer* does not really matter to us. More important is that teachers begin to realize how often a reader needs to infer as he or she reads. Inferring is the heartbeat of comprehension. It is fused together with almost every other strategy. Children need to learn that readers *think* as they read—and that thinking can go far beyond what the words on the page actually say. Below are some tips to reflect on as you think about teaching the children in your classroom to infer.

✤ Start early. There is no grade level at which the teaching of inferring begins. All children can learn to think about texts in this way.

✿ Look for inferring opportunities everywhere. We have suggested various titles in this chapter, but you will find similar examples in the books you are already reading.

✿ Send the message to your students that this is what readers really do. When you give time for discussing a character's feelings, a poem's meaning, an author's intent, and so on, you are showing how much you value original inferential thought.

✿ Nudge children to go beyond the literal level. Sometimes just posing a question or saying "Hmm" at the right moment will invoke the kind of discussion in which children dig deeper to create meaning of texts.

✿ Choose texts that lend themselves to children having inferential thoughts. As we mentioned in our interactive read-aloud chapter, choose books that have issues that are worth discussing.

✿ With nonfiction, take time to help kids figure out the meaning of new or interesting vocabulary or to infer what stance the author is taking. Then help children critically assess if they agree or disagree with the perspective of the author.

Summarizing

As with any strategy, before we focus on teaching summarizing, we like to be sure that it is something that readers do in real life.

Imagine this scenario. You recently returned from a week at the beach without your children and a friend asks, "How was it?" You answer, "Great! We walked on the beach every morning and saw several incredible sunsets in the evenings. There was lots of eating out, swimming in the ocean, and lying around reading books. One day we had a sailboat ride on the bay. All in all, a relaxing vacation."

Notice that you did not tell every single thing that happened that week, but gave the highlights and general feel of the whole vacation. People summarize like this all the time.

No one ever taught us to summarize when we went to school. When we were assigned report topics, we went directly to the library encyclopedias and copied facts verbatim. Then we organized the facts into paragraphs and turned in our report. If you had really good handwriting, you usually got an A!

Today, we actually know how to model the kind of thinking the brain does as we summarize. In order to summarize, a reader deletes unimportant information, keeps crucial information, and puts some parts into his or her own words, sometimes combining two or more ideas into one.

When a reader summarizes he or she:
- Deletes unimportant information
- Highlights important words or phrases
- Puts ideas in his or her own words

Students need to hear you think aloud and see you do these things:
- Cross out extra and/or repeated words
- Circle important words and phrases
- Write in the margins

Therefore, as you model, students need to see you *cross out* unnecessary information, *highlight* important facts, and *rewrite* the information into your own words (see sidebar on page 174).

Let's take another peek into a classroom where reading specialist Mary Schulman has pulled out one particular strategy, summarizing, to spotlight with the students.

Lesson Idea #4: Summing It Up

Figure 9.2
Mary Schulman's
Summarizing Chart

Mary: (*Visiting a fourth-grade class.*) Your teacher invited me here today to talk to you about some ways I know to help you comprehend nonfiction texts. Sometimes there is so much information presented in a nonfiction book or article that we have to find ways of shortening it so our brain can hold what's most important. We call this summarizing or paraphrasing. Other people might say "getting the main idea or gist of the whole piece" or "what are the most important points worth remembering?" (*Shows Figure 9.2 on the overhead projector as she talks.*) When I summarize I *delete* some things that don't seem all that important; I *highlight* key words or phrases that seem most important; and I put some ideas in *my own words.* (*She writes the words* delete, *high-light,* and my own words *on the overhead as she talks. Then she puts the beginning of an article with its title and picture on the overhead.*) I'm going to think out loud today and show you how I make those decisions—about what to keep, what to get rid of, and what to write in the margins. I'm going to use the first part of this article on iguanas, called "Ya Wanna Know Iguanas?" (Ranger Rick 2008). I have an interest in any kind of lizard; I think they are cool animals! So I want to see how much I can learn about these iguanas.

As Mary continues her demonstration, she reads the first page of the article aloud. Then she goes through a second time talking about what she is circling, deleting, and writing in the margins and why she is choosing to do so. (See the article with her markings in Figure 9.3.)

When the demonstration is completed, Mary thinks aloud as she writes the following summary in front of the students.

Figure 9.3
"Ya Wanna Know Iguanas?" and Mary Schulman's Notes

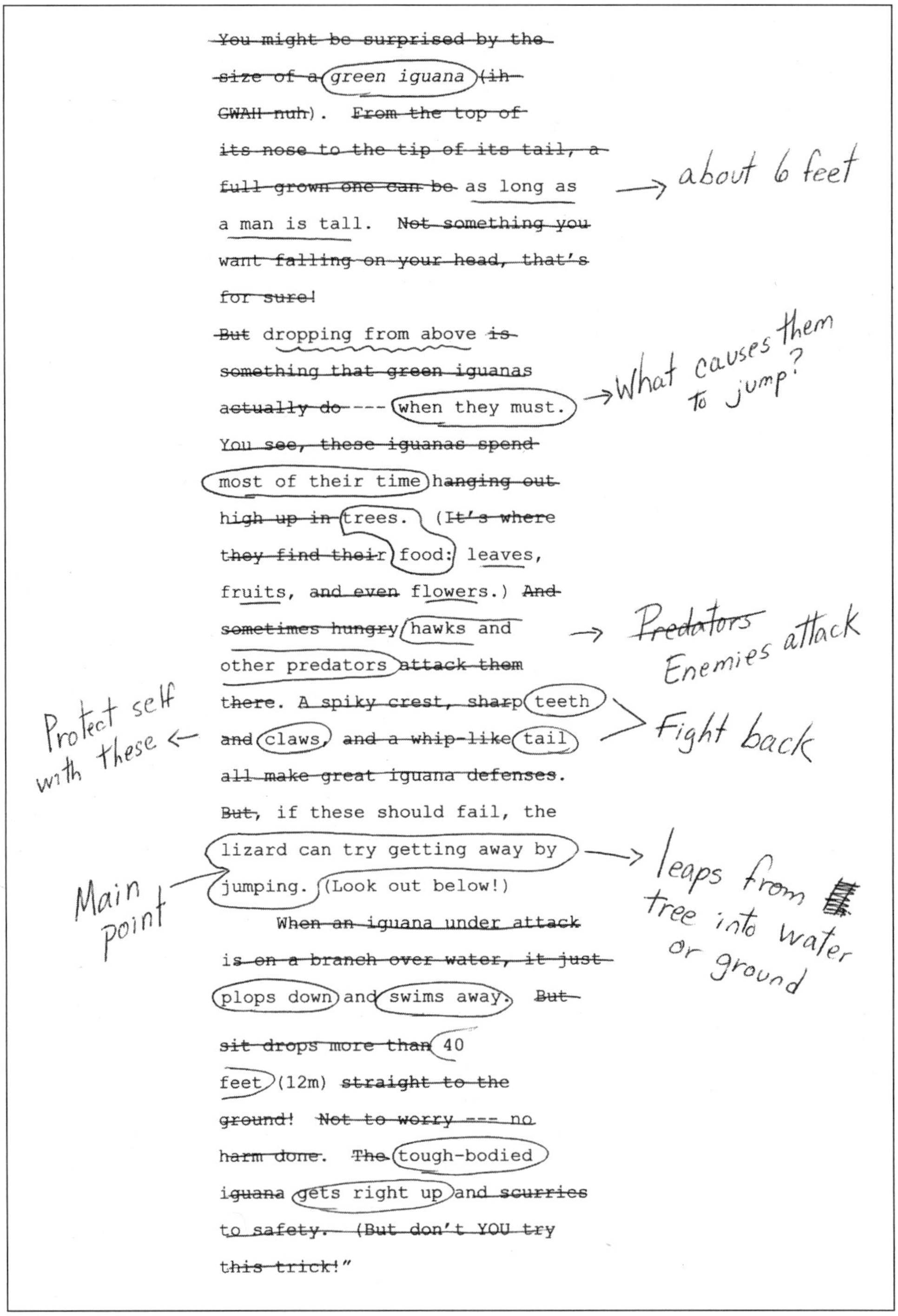

~~You might be surprised by the size of a~~ green iguana ~~(ih-GWAH-nuh)~~. ~~From the top of its nose to the tip of its tail, a full-grown one can be~~ as long as a man is tall. ~~Not something you want falling on your head, that's for sure!~~

~~But~~ dropping from above ~~is something that green iguanas actually do~~ --- when they must. ~~You see, these iguanas spend~~ most of their time h~~anging out high up in~~ trees. (~~It's where they find their~~ food: leaves, fruits, ~~and even~~ flowers.) ~~And sometimes hungry~~ hawks and other predators ~~attack them there~~. ~~A spiky crest, sharp~~ teeth ~~and~~ claws, ~~and a whip-like~~ tail ~~all make great iguana defenses~~. ~~But,~~ if these should fail, the lizard can try getting away by jumping. (Look out below!)

~~When an iguana under attack is on a branch over water, it just~~ plops down and swims away. ~~But sit drops more than~~ 40 feet (12m) ~~straight to the ground!~~ ~~Not to worry --- no harm done~~. ~~The~~ tough-bodied ~~iguana~~ gets right up and ~~scurries to safety. (But don't YOU try this trick!~~"

Green iguanas, some 6 feet long, can often be found up in trees because they eat leaves, flowers, and fruit. When an enemy attacks, they protect themselves with claws, teeth, spikes, or a whipping tail. If those don't work, they jump out of the tree and land unharmed.

During the lesson a variety of points came up. First, the students noticed how the fifteen sentences in the article were reduced to three in the summary. They checked the summary together to see if all the major points were included. The students and teacher also talked about how authors often throw in funny parts, like "But don't you try this trick!" These parts enliven the article, but would not be necessary in a summary. Another point they discussed was how you need to combine a few ideas into one sentence, as in the first sentence in Mary's sample summary.

Mary used the second section of this article to do a shared demonstration the next day. This time the children were involved in making the decisions about what to cross out, what to highlight, and what to put in their own words. The discussion that ensued that day led to the collaborative writing of a second summary.

The rest of this article is composed of pictures with a paragraph of information following each photo. With partners, the students were asked to pick one of the boxed paragraphs and write a one-sentence summary. The classroom teacher and Mary both circulated among the students, listening in on their conversations about how to create their one-sentence summaries. The notes the teachers took helped them plan future lessons.

❀ ❀ ❀

No matter which primary grade Katie is teaching, she often chooses to end a science or social studies unit by having the students summarize what they've learned. To Katie and her students, summaries don't always have to be written. When her second graders finished their unit on the desert—which included many interactive read-alouds, inquiry projects with partners, visits and slide shows from people who had been to the desert, and some online research—they decided to turn their classroom into a desert scene. First they brainstormed the list of what they thought was most important about their desert study, and from there decided what they needed to make and how they would make it. The room itself was transformed into the students' summary of what they had learned. On the next page you can view a picture of the classroom designed as a desert as well as one of the classroom at the end of a rainforest study.

By the time students are in third grade, they inevitably will be asked on a standardized test, "What is the main idea of this passage?" It's not okay for us to wait until third grade to include the concept of summarizing in our instruction. There are plenty of ways in kindergarten, first, and second grades to address this:

❀ Help students practice one type of summarizing by planning book reviews, teaching students to tell the main idea, but not to give away the ending.

❀ Use summarizing at the close of a social studies or science unit. Ask, "What were the most important things we learned about Native Americans [or community living, the water cycle, animal adaptations, etc.]?" Students can

then record this information in a community writing experience or do an art project similar to the desert scene mentioned earlier.

❋ Ask children to draw a picture of the big idea after a read-aloud.

❋ As a class, write a letter to parents summarizing the events of a field trip or other shared experiences.

Closing Thoughts

Teachers who are willing to broaden their vision of how reading works need concrete examples of what instruction entails when it is meant to support children building a reading process system. Our aim in this chapter, along with the two preceding chapters, was to give as much of a peek into classrooms as we could to show what strategy teaching looks like, particularly for children who struggle. In Chapter 7 we began with the very earliest strategies that young readers need to acquire. Then in Chapters 8 and 9 we demonstrated how comprehension teaching can begin early and continue through the grades.

In the next chapter we will connect instruction to assessment. If we want teachers to teach with reading process in mind, then we must also address observing and assessing their readers from this same theoretical understanding.

CHAPTER 10

Assessment:
Looking Closely at Readers

In order to know how our readers are progressing, we must be careful observers, constantly making decisions about how to use the information we gather to inform our instruction. We agree with Regie Routman when she says, "In our test-obsessed culture, we must return sanity to classroom teaching. Formative, ongoing assessments—by teachers and students based on daily work—need to be the mainstay" (2007, 77). The results of a standardized test or the number or level from a computerized end-of-book test will not help us in our day-to-day teaching. While we acknowledge that standardized tests do have a place within education (although we believe a much smaller place than what they currently occupy), we don't believe that this type of data is enough to support our daily instruction. Therefore, this chapter focuses on the kind of assessment that is inseparable from teaching. Our topics include:

- ❋ The importance of authentic, ongoing, and informative assessment
- ❋ How we use *informal* (conferences, observations, and anecdotal notes) and *formal* (running records, benchmark assessments, and Observation Survey tasks [Clay 2007]) assessment tools to gather information
- ❋ What ongoing assessment looks like in a classroom
- ❋ How we analyze the information we gather to find out how a child is progressing in constructing a system of strategic actions
- ❋ How we use assessment data to inform our teaching
- ❋ Several methods of documenting and organizing the information collected and how we share this information with all the teachers working with a child

Authentic, Ongoing, and Informative Assessment

We believe that assessment must be authentic, ongoing, and informative in order for teachers to effectively use it while instructing children. When we are reading, writing, and talking with children throughout the day, we continually look for what readers can do and what they can almost do and then make note of those literacy behaviors. It is within the context of meaningful literacy work, including meaningful assessment, that a child's reading process system is developed.

We use the information we collect to tell us which students are struggling and in what areas, as well as which students are ready to move on to greater challenges. This is an ongoing, recursive practice that requires close observation of behaviors in order to accelerate children's development of a network of strategies. As Fountas and Pinnell say, "You cannot see into children's minds, but their behaviors can guide your teaching decisions" (2009, 51).

We need to keep track of all our readers' progress, but struggling readers need selective attention and close observation. We must be intensely aware not only that they are struggling but also of what is contributing to their struggle. For many of the other children in our class, the need to be as vigilant is considerably less. But the struggling readers, as we explained in Chapter 2, are not developing a reading process system to help them solve words and understand texts. Thus, our assessments must be designed to provide us with knowledge of what they need in order to continue constructing that system of strategies: "Our goal as teachers is . . . [to] help them build systems that resemble the systems of effective, flexible proficient readers" (Fountas and Pinnell 2009, 60).

So how do we know if a child is constructing a system? We recommend that teachers take note of how children are problem solving words and be on the look out for the behaviors children use to navigate text and work through difficult parts. Clay (2001) advises, "To look only at letters and words, or how comprehension questions are answered, is to ignore the problems faced by the reader to sequentially 'solve the parts within the wholes' to get the precise message" (79). Although there is not one established list of behaviors to check off, there are certain factors that do indicate whether or not a child is beginning to construct a functioning system. A child who is successfully developing a reading process system demonstrates these behaviors:

- Is no longer confused about directionality and voice/print matching
- Makes substitutions based on meaning, structure, and visual information, indicating that multiple sources of information are being used to problem solve words
- Uses strategies flexibly and automatically (refer to Figure 2.1 and Appendix 1)
- Returns to the text to reread and check for understanding
- Shows evidence of self-monitoring
- Self-corrects many of the errors
- Increases fluency and rate of reading

Keeping these behaviors in mind helps us stay focused on what's most important for our K–4 students. We want all students to become flexible problem-solvers who have a variety of strategies and behaviors available to them in order to grow and develop as readers.

Assessment Tools

Throughout the day and throughout the year, we use a variety of assessment tools to collect information on readers. Informal tools include anecdotal notes taken during individual reading conferences or while observing students engaged in literacy activities, such as shared or guided reading and community or individual writing times. Formal tools include benchmark assessments, running records, and adapted tests from Clay's (2007) Observation Survey tasks (for beginning readers).

Conferences

Every time we sit down next to a child who is reading or writing, we have an opportunity to assess his or her progress and help him or her construct a reading process system. Conferring with children is a major part of every reading workshop. A conference is basically a conversation between the teacher and a student. The teacher looks for what the child can do independently, what he or she can almost do, and what he or she is not yet able to do. From this, the teacher determines what the child needs to learn next as a reader.

During the conference the child may read part or all of a book while the teacher takes notes. The conference is filled with authentic conversation about the book and about what the reader is doing. Through this observation and talk the teacher learns much more information than from comprehension questions like those in basal textbooks or in popular computerized reading programs. Some of the information we are looking for while having a reading conference follows:

- Is the child comprehending and to what extent?
- What strategic actions are being used?
- How are the strategic actions helping the reader understand what he or she is reading?
- How does the reading sound? Is it smooth or choppy? Is it well paced and phrased? Does the child attend to punctuation?
- What does the child do when stuck on a word? What sources of information is the child using or neglecting to use?
- Is the child enjoying the book?
- What is his or her attitude toward reading?

This is not an all-inclusive list. The point is to keep in mind what you know about developing a reading process system. You will notice in the examples in this chapter that the teacher works to discover the child's processing abilities rather than just list items (words or letter sounds) that the child missed.

Other Anecdotal Note-Taking Opportunities

Having an individual conference during reading workshop isn't the only time we take notes on students' literacy behaviors. Observing students throughout the day while they are writing, reading from the classroom library, interacting with texts during math, science, or social studies, and using literacy during creative play can give us vital information. Taking notes is also part of every guided reading lesson. Reflecting on our anecdotal notes allows us to see patterns and behaviors that change over time.

Running Records

In addition to the informal assessment tools of conferring and observing children throughout the course of the day, we often use formal assessment tools. One of those tools is the running record. In Katie's school we rely heavily on running record information and are continually looking for ways to help all teachers improve their ability to take and analyze running records. When we combine running record information with what we learn during a conference or while observing a student, we can better meet the needs of that specific child.

Clay defines a running record as "a tool for recording and then interpreting how children work on texts" (2001, 45). A running record gives us insights into which strategic behaviors are being used or not used as well as information about what level text is appropriate for a child. To take a running record, you use a coding system to record on paper what a child says and does while reading.

If you are a teacher who administers the Developmental Reading Assessment 2 (DRA2) (Beaver and Carter 2006), then you are familiar with running records. We view running records as an essential piece of our ongoing reading assessment and instruction cycle, not only as a part of the DRA2. Learning how to take a running record requires training and is beyond the scope of this book, but the books listed on page 68 are helpful resources on learning to take running records. In Chapter 4, we shared information on how to look at running record errors and self-corrections to see if a child was using meaning, structure, and visual information to solve words. Refer to pages 67–68.

Developmental Reading Assessment 2

Besides running records, other formal assessment tools include benchmark reading tests such as the Developmental Reading Assessment 2 (Beaver and Carter 2006) or the Fountas and Pinnell Benchmark Assessment System (Fountas and Pinnell 2007). Teachers typically use these tools at the beginning, middle, and end of the year.

Our county requires us to administer the DRA2 to children in grades K–5 at the beginning and end of each school year. This test gives teachers information on the child's instructional level, comprehension, and fluency. With the beginning levels, the child reads aloud a leveled book from the kit while the teacher takes a running record. A child reading at higher levels reads a selected passage aloud as the teacher takes a running record, and then the child finishes the book silently. Upon completion the child is asked to retell the book. The teacher also asks questions that check on the concepts about print at the early levels, moving into more advanced questions about inferring and making connections at higher levels. The information is then scored with a rubric that assesses accuracy, fluency, comprehension, and strategy use.

The DRA2 is a useful tool at the beginning of the year. A teacher is able to assess each child in a one-on-one testing situation to determine a good starting point as well as a focus for instruction. Although we are not required to administer the DRA2 midyear, teachers at our school often choose to do so with children whose progress we are most concerned about. It is helpful to see how these children do on the formal DRA2 in comparison to the running records from our ongoing assessments. Doing this assessment in January gives us time to fine-tune our instruction and/or develop intervention plans for those children who are not making adequate progress.

Our county uses the DRA2 data as a standardized assessment and the results are officially reported. Therefore all teachers must be correctly trained; our central language arts office provides this training for every teacher. However, any individual school or whole school system can purchase the DRA2 kit.

Beginning Reader Assessments

Other formal tools used in our district for children who are in kindergarten or first grade, and for selected second- and third-grade students, are adapted from Clay's (2007) Observation Survey tasks. When students are emergent readers, the information attained from these tests is very useful to teachers. The tasks that we use include Letter Identification, Hearing and Recording Sounds in Words, Writing Vocabulary (all from Clay), and High-Frequency Word Assessment (adapted from Clay). All of these were described in Chapter 7 on page 109.

A Classroom Assessment View

Let's take a look at a few children from a typical primary-grade classroom. It is reading workshop time and the children are reading independently. Katie grabs her assessment notebook (more on this later) and sits down next to Angel for a quick check.

Angel is an eager learner who likes to keep big stacks of books beside him during reading workshop. Katie asks him to choose a book and read it to her. He opens one and immediately starts making up an elaborate story to go with the pictures. He holds the book correctly and turns the pages after telling her about each picture. He is not looking at the print on each page.

From this brief interaction, Katie can tell a lot about Angel as a reader. He knows that books are read from left page to right page. He knows that books tell a story and that the pictures can help you with the story. However, Angel pays little attention to the print on the page, even though he knows most of his letters, some sounds, and has a few words he recognizes on sight. After just a few minutes observing him interacting with a text and quickly recording what she is seeing, Katie can determine her next instructional focus for Angel. He needs to be taught how to look at print and use what he knows to figure out the text.

Next, Katie sits down beside Bella and asks her to choose a book from her book box. She picks a Henry and Mudge book that she says is easy for her. Using her finger to point under each word, she reads the text accurately. However, her reading sounds very word-by-word. She also stops after every page and looks at Katie for confirmation. After listening to her read just a few pages, Katie knows what her next teaching point will be. Bella's use of her finger is slowing down her reading; she needs fluency work. She also needs to build confidence as a reader and become less dependent on Katie for confirmation. Listening to her read a few pages informs Katie's teaching and helps guide future instruction.

Katie then signals to Alex to join her at an empty table. Alex is a student she saw in a guided reading group on the previous day. During that session, Alex was asked to join the group of children who were not making any attempts at unknown words, but always waited for someone to tell them the word. Katie's teaching point in the guided reading lesson had been about what readers can try when they are stuck on a word.

Katie now asks Alex to read the book to her while she takes a running record. This is only the second time Alex has read this text. Katie wants to check what he can do independently, that is, what he took away from yesterday's lesson. He begins to read and comes to a tricky word on the second page. Katie does not prompt him, because no teaching or prompting is allowed during a running record. She waits to see what he is going to do. He looks at Katie, looks back at the book, and then starts making the sound of the first letter in the word. Katie is happy to see that he is using some visual information to begin to problem solve. He is getting his mouth ready for the first sound. However, he is not using meaning to figure out the unknown word. His reading looks like this:

Child:	<u>Mother</u>	<u>bird</u>	<u>is</u>	<u>in</u>	<u>the</u>	<u>n . . . n . . .</u>
Text:	Mother	bird	is	in	the	nest.

After a short wait time, Katie gives him the word. Alex continues reading, responding in a similar way three more times. Katie waits until he finishes, then goes back and uses this information as her teaching point. Though Alex has shown evidence of attempting to use first letter information to help him, he also needs to learn to reread, check the picture, think about the story, and put in a word that makes sense. Katie notes that Alex will need more guided reading lessons on word solving strategies.

Notice how these assessments with Angel, Bella, and Alex took place within the reading workshop, an authentic setting. They were brief interactions that gave Katie an abundance of information to bring into future teaching situations. The more we know about what students' strengths are and what they struggle with, the more closely we can match our instruction to what each child needs to learn next.

Analyzing the Information from a Reading Process Standpoint

In order for our teaching and assessment to remain inseparable, we constantly keep the network of strategies in our minds as we assess (see Figure 2.1). If we believe that each reader builds a reading process system and that our job is to support each reader in developing this system, then we must assess through this lens. Therefore, we ask ourselves questions like the following:

- ❁ Can the child *predict* at the word level?
- ❁ How does the child *search and gather* information to solve a word?
- ❁ Does the child *link* or make analogies from an unknown word to a new word?
- ❁ After predicting, can the child *check and confirm* that the word looks right, sounds right, and makes sense?
- ❁ Is the child *self-monitoring* for voice/print match?
- ❁ Is the child *self-monitoring* for meaning?
- ❁ Is the child *flexible* while problem solving, making several attempts at an unknown word?
- ❁ Can the child *activate prior knowledge* before, during, and after reading?
- ❁ Is there evidence that the child can *make connections* between texts or to personal experiences?
- ❁ Can the child *pose questions* or *make mental images* to help stay engaged with text?
- ❁ Can the child *infer* information from the text?
- ❁ Does the child read in a *fluent* manner? Does he or she use the punctuation to help? Does the child slow down to solve a problem and then resume a good pace?
- ❁ Can the child *predict* at the text level?
- ❁ Can the child *distinguish between important and nonessential information*, particularly in nonfiction texts?
- ❁ To what extent is the child able to *critique* or *evaluate* a text?

The information we collect in this way is much more helpful than a grade-level number or reading accuracy rate. We realize it would be difficult to keep every one of those questions in mind at all times. Different questions pertain to different situations. The more teachers layer their knowledge about how reading works, the easier it becomes to assess through the lens of reading process understanding, whether you are using formal or informal assessments.

The information you learn about your students by assessing in this manner will help you plan instruction that is appropriate, timely, and specific.

To help us improve in our ability to assess students while keeping these questions in mind, we have found that analyzing several running records from one child with colleagues is particularly beneficial. A small allotment of time can be given for this at each team meeting. Together teachers can notice patterns in a child's strategy use and behaviors. By examining running records over time, teachers can be "monitoring changes in how the reader works on the text, what the reader is noticing, what is easy, what is confusing, and what needs the teacher's attention" (Clay 2001, 46). An example of what happened at a recent team meeting follows.

Six teachers, a reading specialist, and the assistant principal gathered around a table for a team meeting. Each person had copies of one child's running records, which had been taken over the past few weeks. The teacher who took the running records shared a bit of background information on the child, then proceeded to share a little bit about each of the four running records. After the teacher shared, the group began to discuss what they noticed, specifically looking for patterns in the child's strategy use. They made sure to connect all of their observations back to the data collected on the running record forms. One teacher pointed out that when the child was stuck he paused and then put in a word that either made sense or matched visually. Another teacher wondered if the child ever went back and reread. As the group looked back over the running records, they noticed that there was little evidence of rereading on all four running records. Although he used meaning or visual information on unknown words, he did not go back to gather more information or to check and confirm his substitutions. The group decided that teaching him how to use rereading should be the next instructional focus.

The teachers agree that this practice helps them improve as analyzers of all children's processing abilities, even if that child is not from their own classroom.

Informing Our Teaching

As we continually collect data, we are simultaneously planning our instruction for the whole class, small groups, and one-on-one teaching. Instruction takes place through the various components of a comprehensive literacy framework (see Chapter 5). When our assessments indicate that the majority of the class needs a particular skill or strategy, we can model this during an interactive read-aloud, shared reading, or community writing. However, when our assessments indicate that only a few children need practice with a specific skill or strategy, then guided reading or individual conferences might be a better time and place for that lesson. The more support a child needs in developing his or her reading process system, the more small-group or one-on-one instruction will occur. Also, the more the child is struggling with reading, the closer we look at that child.

The following are the stories of two struggling readers, one in first grade and one in second. Notice how we gathered information from a variety of assessment tools and then planned our instructional goals based on that information.

Edward

Edward was a first grader in Katie's class who was learning to speak English as his third language. He was in his second year at an English-speaking school. Edward did not pass the beginning text (level A) on the DRA2 at the start of the year in first grade. He did not have voice/print match although he was able to handle the book correctly and turn the pages from left to right. He was able to identify seven out of fifty-four letters on the Letter Identification test, and got one out of thirty-seven sounds and letters correct on the Hearing and Recording Sounds in Words test. Katie noticed that he had difficulty following along during shared reading and that his eyes often wandered from the text.

Over the first few weeks of first grade Katie's beginning reading work with Edward showed her that he was able to hold on to a pattern in a book immediately after she modeled, but was not able to read the text independently at a later time. As the class used the name chart frequently in the first two months of first grade, Edward learned to connect a "hook" with letters. For example, he would say "Quinn" when pointing to a Q, "Uthman" for a U, and so on. During community writing time, he could contribute a letter as long as it was given a hook to a student's name. He also used the name chart as a reference during reading and writing workshop.

Edward had difficulty attending during read-aloud and community writing time and often rolled around on the floor or asked to use the restroom. His writing consisted of detailed drawings of race cars. He occasionally wrote a letter or two on his page, but these often did not connect with the story. He did not write any words on his stories, although he was able to tell about his picture and create a story orally in his limited English.

Katie sat down with Kent, an ELL teacher, a few weeks into the school year, and they discussed Edward's strengths and weaknesses. They agreed that his progress was slow and that he was lacking key beginning reading skills and strategies. They decided a "double dose" of reading instruction was necessary to help accelerate Edward's progress. Katie would meet with Edward one-on-one daily, as would Kent, who previously had only been meeting with him in a small group. They also decided that they needed to make a list of goals for Edward and continue to check back with each other to see how they were meeting those goals. It was important that they both focus on the same goals and make sure their language and prompting were aligned.

Notice the language they used to write their goals as *clear expectations* for Edward. They believed that he would be able to attain these goals and that they would be able to teach him. They gave themselves four to six weeks to concentrate on the following goals.

Edward will:

❀ Have solid voice/print match and directionality under control
❀ Increase his knowledge of letters and sounds and be able to use the information when reading and writing
❀ Be able to write several high-frequency words and be able to locate those known words in continuous texts
❀ Write the beginning sounds in words and label pictures
❀ Pass the DRA2 level 3 text in reading
❀ Participate in and attend to whole-group instruction

Hannah

Hannah, a second grader, was a native English speaker with strong oral language skills. She was a quick learner when information was presented to her orally, but said she did not like to read. While many things in school came easily for her, she struggled with reading. She had quite a few expert avoidance moves—often wandering through the room chatting with friends looking for the perfect spot to sit, slowly organizing her books in her book box instead of reading, and so on. Hannah passed the DRA2 level 10 at the start of the school year; she was able to identify all letters of the alphabet in the Letter Identification Test, and had a large number of known high-frequency words that she recognized quickly and could write. She scored a 32 out of 37 on the Hearing and Recording Sounds in Words test; she mostly used letter/sound relationships to solve words.

When reading, Hannah read quickly and made frequent errors. She did not go back to self-correct or reread to problem solve. She tried to finish books quickly and did not slow down to make sure she was getting the meaning of the story.

Hannah loved to write long stories about herself and her friends, although many of her stories had repeating words and phrases such as "I like my friends. I like my dog. I like the park." She could read what she wrote, because she tended to use only her known words in her writing. She did not take risks in her writing or reading.

Hannah enjoyed listening to read-alouds and participated fully in both interactive read-aloud and shared reading discussions. She was able to comprehend and analyze texts that were read to her at a far higher level than the texts she could read independently.

Hannah had a lot going for her, but was definitely struggling with developing a functioning reading process system. Katie needed to draw upon Hannah's strengths and link them with the new learning she was being challenged with. After looking closely at the assessment information she collected, including the DRA2, running records over several weeks, and anecdotal notes from numerous conferences, Katie came up with the following goals.

Hannah will:

❋ Develop stamina and be able to sustain independent reading for up to twenty minutes
❋ Reread to problem solve, self-correct, and check and confirm
❋ Use known words to self-monitor and self-correct
❋ Make connections between what she is reading and personal experiences, realizing that reading is something she can enjoy
❋ Choose books that interest her and give her something to talk about, respond to, and gain information from

Focusing on these specific goals over a period of four weeks allowed Katie to make sure her teacher language and instructional focuses were designed to both support and accelerate Hannah's literacy learning.

❋ ❋ ❋

We realize that it would be difficult to get this detailed for every child in your room, but we would argue that it is essential to look this closely at your struggling readers. In the past, when teaching struggling readers, our tendency was to bounce all over, trying to do too much all at once, because we knew the child needed so much. But now, when we take the time to look at what a child can do and write down a few specific goals, we stay focused. Our teaching is no longer hit or miss. This practice contributes to the progress these children, like Edward and Hannah, are now making.

Documenting and Organizing Assessment Information

Once you have collected all of this assessment information, what do you do with it? Katie will admit that years ago when she first started teaching, she knew she had to take detailed notes on each student. But she wasn't really sure what to write or how to organize all those notes. She tried many different organizational tools—most of which ended with stacks of sticky notes, address labels, and various assorted forms and notebooks in a mess, and it was impossible to find what she needed. Although she tweaks her assessment organizational methods each year, she finally found a general structure that works for her.

As we describe how Katie currently organizes her assessment information, as well as ways to share information with specialists who are working with her students, don't feel that you need to follow any of these ideas exactly. Everyone has unique needs and priorities. You will need to find a system that works for

Figure 10.1
Class Grid

Class Grid for **Reading ~ Sept. 17**

Abirla ·using V info., focus on meaning	Bobby ·1:1 ·not matching beg. letters	Jasmine ·good 1:1 ·reads wd. x wd. ·looking / checking	Dalia ·L→R ·unaware of 1:1, starting to touch words	José ·just starting to get 1:1 ·may forget patterns
Lily ·needs 1:1 ·sliding over words ·uses pictures	Quent ·fluent & smooth ·good self- correction	Charles ·very wd. by wd. ·fluency! read in phrases	Toby ·has 1:1 ·can locate words after rdg. text	Amir ·learning to check 1st letter
Rose ·very concerned about accuracy ·needs to think about story	Antony ·needs repeating pattern ·1:1 & L→R	Suzette ·uses pictures well ·has 1:1 match ·prefers nonfict.	Joseline ·no 1:1 ·good L→R ·uses V at times	Marcus ·focus on M ·very V
Evette ·strong back- ground knowl. ·using M,S,V	Michael ·uses 1st letter V info. ·needs to look for word chunks	Mohammad ·using pictures & M ·needs to look at V info.	Anthony ·rereads when M is lost ·beginning to SM & SC	Yolanda ·SC often ·uses M,S,V
Salud ·high interest ·uses V info. ·focus on M				

you and your organizational style. Don't be afraid to experiment, change, and adapt to make it your own.

Katie's assessment data is housed in a large, three-ring binder, as well as on several clipboards. The binder ensures that everything is organized and in one place, whereas the clipboards allow her note-taking forms to be portable.

One form that allows Katie to look at her entire class at a glance was introduced to her by her colleague Ann Mabry. This weekly form is a one-page class grid with a box for each child. (See Figure 10.1 for an example of a completed form and Appendix 13 for a blank copy.) Katie types a child's name in each box and saves this on her computer so she can easily print it out when she needs it. At the top, she has a place to write the subject (Reading, Writing, Math) and the date. Throughout the week, she takes a look at the whole class—writing down one or two strengths and one or two needs for each child. Filling in this form allows Katie to reflect briefly on each child. Looking over the completed form allows her to see common areas of strengths and needs in the class. She keeps it on a clipboard, handy for jotting down quick notes throughout the day.

Katie uses this completed form to plan her whole-group instruction for the upcoming week and to plan small-group guided reading lessons. After she has used the class grid to plan out lessons for the week, she files it in her assessment notebook in case she needs to refer back to it. She then puts a blank form on a clipboard for the upcoming week.

Figure 10.2
Class List Form

Monthly Class List for Reading - February

Names											
Abirla	2/1 GR	2/2 RR	2/2 GR	2/3 GR	2/4 GR	2/5 C	2/5 GR	2/8 GR	2/9 RR	2/9 GR	2/10 GR
Bobby	2/1 GR	2/2 C	2/3 GR	2/3 RR	2/4 GR	2/5 GR	2/8 GR	2/10 GR			
Jasmine	2/1 GR	2/2 GR	2/3 RR	2/3 GR	2/4 GR	2/5 RR	2/5 GR	2/8 C	2/8 GR	2/9 GR	2/10 GR
Dalia	2/1 GR	2/2 C	2/3 GR	2/4 RR	2/4 GR	2/5 GR	2/8 GR	2/10 GR			
José	2/1 GR	2/2 GR	2/3 RR	2/3 GR	2/4 GR	2/5 GR	2/8 GR	2/9 RR	2/9 GR	2/10 GR	
Lily	2/1 GR	2/3 GR	2/4 GR	2/5 RR	2/5 GR	2/8 GR	2/9 C	2/10 GR			
Quent	2/2 GR	2/4 GR	2/9 GR								
Charles	2/2 GR	2/4 GR	2/9 GR								
Toby	2/1 GR	2/2 RR	2/2 GR	2/3 GR	2/4 GR	2/8 GR	2/9 GR	2/10 GR			
Amir	2/1 GR	2/2 GR	2/3 GR	2/4 GR	2/8 GR	2/9 RR	2/9 GR	2/10 GR			
Rose	2/2 GR	2/4 GR	2/9 GR								
Antony	2/1 GR	2/3 GR	2/4 RR	2/4 GR	2/5 GR	2/8 GR	2/9 C	2/10 GR			
Suzette	2/2 GR	2/4 GR	2/9 GR								
Joseline	2/1 GR	2/2 GR	2/3 RR	2/3 GR	2/4 GR	2/8 GR	2/9 GR	2/10 GR			
Marcus	2/1 GR	2/2 GR	2/3 RR	2/3 GR	2/4 GR	2/8 GR	2/9 GR	2/10 GR			
Evette	2/1 GR	2/3 GR	2/5 GR	2/8 GR	2/10 GR						
Michael	2/1 GR	2/3 GR	2/5 GR	2/8 C	2/9 GR	2/10 GR					
Mohammad	2/1 GR	2/3 GR	2/4 GR	2/5 RR	2/5 GR	2/8 GR	2/9 C	2/10 GR			
Anthony	2/1 GR	2/2 GR	2/4 RR	2/4 GR	2/5 GR	2/8 GR	2/9 RR	2/9 GR	2/10 GR		
Yolanda	2/1 GR	2/3 GR	2/5 GR	2/8 GR	2/10 GR	2/11 C					
Salud	2/1 GR	2/3 GR	2/5 GR	2/8 GR	2/10 GR						

RR—Running Record   C—Conference   GR—Guided Reading

Katie began using one central notebook to house her assessment data a few years ago, after attending a session by Gail Boushey and Joan Moser, "The Sisters," at the National Council of Teachers of English conference. They gave her some great ideas for organizing her assessment notebook, and she adapted their ideas to work for her in her classroom. Boushey and Moser have since published a book about this called *The CAFE Book* (2009), if you would like to read more about how they set up their assessment system. Katie uses a large, three-inch binder to keep everything in one place. Each section is marked with tabs, so she can easily find what she is looking for.

The following sections are tabbed in Katie's assessment notebook:

- Completed class grid forms. These are useful to look back to see how the class is progressing.
- A class list for each month, with boxes to record the dates when she meets with a student. The meeting may be for taking a running record, a guided reading group, or an individual conference. This allows Katie to see if there are any kids she has overlooked or who are in need of a conference. She simply writes the date and the initial of what kind of meeting they had (RR for running record, GR for guided reading group, C for conference). See Figure 10.2 for an example of a completed class list form and Appendix 14 for a blank version.
- Completed guided reading planning sheets (explained below). Katie keeps these forms to refer back to and to track student progress in her guided reading groups.
- Individual student forms. Each student has a tab in the notebook where Katie files individual goal sheets and anecdotal notes throughout the year, as well as all the running records for that child. See Figure 10.3 for an example of a completed form and Appendix 15 for a blank version. An explanation of how Katie uses these forms follows.

The individual student forms are where Katie records all of her anecdotal notes and keeps track of the reading focus for instruction she sets with each child. This focus changes periodically as the child takes on using the strategy or behavior that they have been working on. For example, the form may say "Readers go back and reread when something doesn't make sense." Under the focus are two columns. Each time Katie meets with a child, she records what she notices the child doing or almost doing in the first column. For example, if one day a child was able to go back and reread with heavy prompting, but not independently, she could record that. In the second column she records other things she notices the child will need to learn next. For example, she may notice that he or she needs work on fluency. While that isn't her current focus, recording it will help her know what to focus on in upcoming conferences and guided reading groups. Choosing a focus for instruction for each child allows Katie to make her teaching more effectively match the needs of every child in her class.

The individual student forms are also a great way to collaborate with other teachers. When one of Katie's students is working in a pull-out or push-in situation with an ELL, special education, or other resource teacher, they choose a focus for instruction together and then they both record information after working with that student on a shared form. Having all of the anecdotal notes in one place allows them each to continue where the other teacher left off, keeping the focus and the language the same.

Katie found this extremely helpful when working with Gina Elliot, an ELL teacher, who collaborated with her in teaching several students. These students made tremendous progress that year, and Katie believes that was due in large part to the constant communication between her and Gina. If Katie noticed in

Figure 10.3
Individual Student Form

Individual Student Form

Name: __Anthony__   Dates: __10/5 – 10/19__

Focus for Instruction: __Using 1st letter (single__
__line of text)__
__1:1 match on multiple lines of text__

Date	What is the child doing or almost doing?	What's next?
10/5	<u>Where Are We</u>? (3) ·sliding finger - make sure he's looking	10/6 Do running record Check - "does it match?"
10/7	<u>Playing</u> ·using pattern ·no SM unless asked	Work on confirming 1:1 match as his job
10/9	<u>Looking Down</u> ·using meaning and structure - check ✓	·RR ·Check ✓ ·Use known words to monitor & SC
10/13	<u>Lily and the Leaf Boats</u> - excellent monitoring	10/14 Running Record ·1:1 ·Using knowns!
10/19	<u>Zac and Chirpy</u> - RR here ° "<u>You</u> have to come check" ✓	Next focus: Checking and Confirming

Gina's anecdotal notes that she had introduced a new book the previous day, Katie could start her lesson with a quick running record and then build on the lesson focus Gina had already started. Having this shared form saved them time on getting together to share their thoughts. It was all there on the form. Though teachers always have the best intentions of planning meeting times with the specialists who work with their students, in reality, it's often difficult to find the time.

    This consistency is so important for our readers who struggle. Many of them are pulled out of the classroom for various intervention groups, so if the teachers are not working together and sharing common goals along with a common language, the children often do not benefit from this additional

Figure 10.4
Guided Reading
Planning Sheet

Guided Reading Planning Sheet	
Date: 2/5 Group: Jasmine, José, Amir	
Running Record: Jasmine - Tiger, Tiger	
New Book—Title/Level/Genre: The Van (3) fiction	
Introduction	**Planning notes**
M: meaning statement, question to activate background knowledge, new concepts, character names **S:** awkward language structures, literary language, irregular verb forms **V:** predict and locate, unusual text layout, new punctuation	·character names ·How will they all fit? ·Where do you think they are going?
Focus for Strategy Instruction **(before, during, and after reading)** searching/gathering, predicting, activating schema, checking/confirming, maintaining fluency, self-monitoring, linking, making connections, visualizing, summarizing, questioning, inferring, evaluating, synthesizing	Monitoring & Checking ·use initial letters ·known words to SC
After Reading	
Ideas to Keep in Mind During Discussion of Text	Where are they going?
Word Work examples of visual information (letters, clusters, endings, prefixes, irregular spellings, etc.)	Build / Mix/ Fix (here, is, the, in)
Students	Observations
Jasmine	·very wd. by wd. ·using 1st letter w/ prompt
José	·lots of guessing, but using 1st letter = M!
Amir	·using 1st letter & meaning! ·strong! ·good predictions

instruction. Using a common anecdotal recording sheet helps both teachers stick with a teaching focus and build on one another's instruction.

You'll notice in the bulleted list on page 193 that Katie keeps the *completed* guided reading planning sheets in her assessment notebook. However, these are first kept in a separate, small folder that is handy for her as she works with groups. In that folder, she keeps a planning sheet for each group she is meeting with that week and copies of the books they will use for that guided reading lesson. On the sheet, there is room at the bottom for Katie to jot down quick notes and observations as she works with a group. See Figure 10.4 for an example of a completed form and Appendix 16 for a blank version.

Katie also may choose to write notes in her assessment notebook as she meets with groups, especially if she is focusing on a specific child. Remember, each student has a tab in the notebook, so she can easily flip to that section. Before she files any of the guided reading planning sheets in her assessment notebook, she makes sure to look over her notes and add any pertinent information to the individual student forms. Katie's guided reading folder is shown in the photo.

While this is a complete picture of Katie's assessment notebook, feel free to use all, part, or none of the above. Check with your colleagues as to what assessment systems work for them. Also, there are sections in several of the professional books we have mentioned that explain a variety of organizational tools. The important thing is to keep track of your children's learning in a way that is manageable for you.

A Tightly Woven Fabric

Assessment that is truly woven into the instructional framework of the day is the most useful kind. The image that comes to mind is of one of those potholders we used to make as children. Remember how you would put all the stretchy loops vertically over the plastic frame? And then you would weave the others, under, over, under, over. To us, that is the picture of assessment done authentically as children are engaged in their daily reading and writing activities. It is assessment that is used to inform the constant focused instruction that children need to support them as they build a reading process system.

For struggling readers, the weaving together of assessment and instruction is of utmost importance. For them, every moment counts. We can't have them wasting time on things that frustrate or confuse them, or on practicing items in isolation without connections to real reading. We don't just teach for solving a specific word or reading a specific book, but for accelerating the child's reading process system. With each time you instruct a struggling reader, you must build his or her processing power. Ongoing, authentic, informative assessment is what makes that happen.

A strong record-keeping system will allow you to be more prepared when meeting with parents or guardians about a particular child's progress. In the next chapter, we address some of the most frequently asked questions from families regarding literacy acquisition.

CHAPTER 11

Sharing Information
with Families

Over the years we have all gotten questions from parents about the teaching of reading and writing. Some questions show their concern or worries: "How's my child doing?" "Will my child have to repeat a grade if her reading doesn't improve?" Other questions might feel like a personal attack on your teaching methods: "Why aren't you doing more of such and such?" "Why don't you correct all his spelling errors on those stories he writes?" And then there are even questions like the one a friend of ours was asked: "Is it okay that I make my child read the book backward because that's the only way I can tell if she really knows all the words?" No matter the query, it is our job as teachers of young readers to answer parents the best we can.

Many teachers ward off a lot of these questions by finding ways to communicate with their students' families right from the beginning of the school year to help expand their understandings of how reading works, explain classroom practices that support all readers, and inform them about expectations of what will come home throughout the school year.

At the beginning of each year, we carefully draft a welcome letter to our new families. We want them to know right from the start how important it is for us to work together and to be partners in their child's education. A copy of the letter that Katie sent home at the start of one school year is in Appendix 17.

The majority of parents are not educators and therefore they rely on us to inform them of how children best learn to read. Many remember how they were taught or identify with suggestions from radio, TV, or magazine ads. Some parents or guardians are anxious about the educational system and fear that their child might not get what he or she needs to succeed. We believe that it is our job not only to teach the children in our classrooms each year but also to help families understand how they can best help their children at home. This chapter addresses some of the most common questions and concerns that we have heard over many years of teaching. It is our hope that you can use these answers as you educate the families you work with, as well as the chatty adult who finds you at the gym or the local swimming pool.

We've written the questions as we have heard them asked by family members. Following each question is a response phrased in the way we might talk to our families. The sections following each response, "The Home/School Connection," expand on the responses and in some instances include instructional suggestions that might be appropriate when working with that child.

Question 1: *"It seems like my child just memorizes the books he brings home. Last night he even told me he could read it with his eyes closed. Is this okay?"*

That's not unusual for beginning readers. I had a child the other day who told me the same thing. But right away I answered him *in my serious voice,* "Oh, but that's not really reading though. Readers look at the words and think about the story." We don't want children to get the wrong impression about reading. We want the children to understand that readers do not need to memorize books. They will learn how to figure out what the print says and think about what it means. You could try asking your child to touch under the words as he reads. That will help keep his eyes on the text.

It also sounds like your child might be ready for some books where the pattern changes, stories that aren't so easy to memorize. We don't want to keep him too long in books that follow a consistent pattern. It's good if he always has a bit of reading work to do. I'll take a look at what's in his book box tomorrow. It's possible he's picking books to bring home that are too easy for him. He may have some others in his box that would be better for him to bring home to practice reading with you.

The Home/School Connection: In whatever way you can, send children the message that reading is like a puzzle—you have to work at figuring it out; you have to make the story make sense. A reader does this by using everything he or she knows—background knowledge of the world, previous experiences, knowledge of language, the pictures, the words, and the letters. We always want to be sure the students are doing some reading work, even on beginning texts. That's why we might make some original books with emergent readers—so we can make little changes in the patterns. This forces the child to have to pay attention to the print and self-monitor what he or she is reading. The child needs to know that looking and checking are part of a reader's job. Refer to the self-monitoring section of Chapter 7.

Remember that those early level 1 and 2 texts (the texts students are prone to memorize) are for getting voice/print match under control. These books have patterns and are simple enough for the children to memorize as they read them repeatedly. As soon as you see evidence of one-to-one matching under control, move them into books where they will need to put their emerging system of strategies together and check and confirm what they are reading.

Question 2:

"What do I say or do when my child gets stuck on a word? I want to help. Do I just give her the word? Or say 'sound it out'?"

The first advice I'd give is to stay relaxed. Don't panic when she gets stuck. If you stay calm, your child will know that figuring out words is part of the normal process of reading. We do want children to use their knowledge of letters and sounds, but we want them to do that in combination with meaning and structural knowledge. In other words, we encourage them to always think about what would make sense in that sentence, what would sound right, and what would look right. There are just too many words in English that you can't sound out by using phonics, like *said, thought,* and *knife.* Give them a little support by saying, "Hmm, what would make sense there?" or point to the picture. Sometimes going back and rereading the sentence from the beginning helps the child keep the meaning in her head, so you could just tap the start of the sentence and say, "Try that part again."

In the classroom your child is learning to use some symbols to help her remember what to try when she is stuck on a word. I'll send home an index card with those symbols on it (see Appendix 4) and you can have that handy when your child reads to you.

Another thing to think about is how your child is reacting when you give suggestions of what she could try. Some beginning readers get very frustrated when working with parents; they want to do everything perfectly for you. If she is experiencing too much frustration or is getting angry, just tell her the word she's struggling with. I'd rather the experience you have with her while reading at home be a very enjoyable one. Don't worry about the teaching or the prompting. I'll take care of that in the classroom. I will also check her book box to make sure the books she is bringing home aren't too hard. Having her occasionally problem solve a word is okay, but if there are too many hard words, I'd rather you just read the book to her.

The Home/School Connection: Little by little we want to educate parents to understand that proficient readers solve words by using meaning, structure, and visual information (see Chapter 4). Most parents only know the prompt "sound it out," so take every opportunity you can to teach them about how students are learning to use a balance of all the sources of information. Invite parents into your classroom to watch you read with students. They'll pick up on your mannerisms, your prompts, and your attitude just by watching.

Another idea is to work with a reading teacher to offer a session for parents on how to listen to their child read and what to say when he or she is stuck. We also have a bookmark (with strategy language listed on it) that we sometimes send home in the child's book (see Appendix 18). The goal when teaching children to solve words is to have them use meaning (the context of the sentence or what would make sense), structural knowledge (what would sound right), and visual knowledge (their knowledge of letters and sounds).

Question 3:   *"My child still doesn't know all his letters and sounds. What can I do to help him at home?"*

I think it's very important to have a partnership between home and school, so I'm glad you asked about helping him. There are certainly things you can do at home as he is learning to read. But before we talk about letters and sounds, remember that not every child progresses at the same rate. Although some children in the class may know more letters and sounds or already be reading longer books, I treat every child as a reader in my room. Even though he only knows some of his letters and sounds, he is still reading books and writing every day at school. The good news is that he can begin to learn to read without knowing all his letters and sounds first. The best thing you can do is to read aloud to him every night. Ask him to share the books he brings home, and then choose another book for you to read to him. Talk about the books and enjoy that time together.

There are also some alphabet games you can play with him. But these should be in addition to reading together every night! The alphabet games should be quick and fun. A free website, www.starfall.com, has letter and sound work that children enjoy. You can also make or buy cards with letters of the alphabet and pictures on them. You and your child can play a matching game where you match the *C* card with the cat picture. I would be happy to send home some more ABC games with your child. We use magnetic letters in the classroom. You can find these at drugstores or toy stores and then keep them on the refrigerator for your child to play with.

Keeping a family journal is another thing that will help build your child's letter/sound knowledge. You can get a notebook and write notes to each other. Some of what he writes may be in pictures. Remember to accept what your child writes—don't expect correct spelling. If he can write *HS* for *house*, that is great! Help him say words slowly and write the sounds he hears. Any other type of daily writing is great too—shopping lists, notes to his siblings, reminder notes, and so on. Writing is one of the best ways to develop letter and sound knowledge.

The Home/School Connection: Parents often think that their child needs to know all of his or her letters and sounds before he or she can learn to read or write. It's important to inform parents that in the classroom, we don't hold children back from beginning reading and writing experiences because they have limited letter knowledge. We want to make sure we are sending lots of books home to have families read together so they are not spending all of their time learning letters and sounds in lieu of reading and enjoying stories together.

For your work with letters and sounds, lots of daily reading and writing (not copying or handwriting practice) needs to happen in the classroom. Refer to Chapter 7 for more information on this topic.

Another thing we do with those very few children who are having a difficult time learning letters and sounds is to make an individual ABC book (see photo). Though many children in kindergarten may have individual alphabet books, in first and second grade we only make them for children who still cannot identify all the letters of the alphabet. We occasionally make two alphabet books so the child has one to keep at home.

After a letter identification assessment, we record the letters known to that child and make a personalized book with a page for each of his or her known letters in alphabetical order, leaving the pages for unknown letters blank. Each page will have the uppercase and lower-case version of the letter along with a picture. The picture should be one that the child has linked to that letter. As the child learns more letters, we add them on the blank pages.

As Clay (2005b) describes, "The alphabet book is merely a record of what is known with spaces for what is 'yet to be learned.' That gives the child a sense of the size of the task and a feeling of control over his own progress" (37). You can make these books with the child and then send them home for the child to share with his or her family.

Question 4: *"My child seems to know a word one day, but then she forgets it the next day. Should I put all the words on cards and drill her on them?"*

There are some children who see a word once and remember it forever. Unfortunately that is not the case with most kids. When students are learning to recognize new words in print, they need to have many, many experiences with those words. For example, your child may recognize the word *here* in one book because she knows the pattern of that book well and it's a very familiar text for her. But when that word appears in another book, she may not auto-matically know it—perhaps it appears in a different place, or has a capital at the beginning, or is written with a different font. The high-frequency words, like *can, the, go, come, look,* and so on, will keep coming up in all of the beginning books we use with her.

The more she sees a new word in a variety of settings and the more times she problem solves that word in texts, the more she will come to know that word. It's better for her to get that repeated practice of the high-frequency words in actual books rather than putting those words on cards and doing flash card practice. Flash card practice may lead your child to believe that reading is only about accurately calling the words. We wouldn't want her getting so focused on saying the words correctly that she loses the sense of the story. We stress that reading is making meaning of the story or book she is reading.

In addition, your child is using a lot of these high-frequency words as she writes during writing workshop. She is learning to use the word wall, a class-room reference display that contains many of these same words. All of this will quicken her eventual automatic recognition of these words.

The Home/School Connection: For most children, it takes many encoun-ters with a word to fully know that word. And for struggling readers you may have to multiply that number of encounters by ten or more. Learning a word so that it is known absolutely does not usually happen overnight. Clay uses the expression "levels of knowing" to help us understand the process children go through learning new words. We have adapted the hierarchy Clay (2005b) presents to show how the child moves through these levels:

* First encounters the word
* Learned the word only recently
* Successfully can problem solve the word in some texts
* Can easily write the word, but can be easily thrown and not recognize the word (different fonts, written in capitals, and so on)
* Recognizes it in most contexts (the word is well known)
* Fully known in variant forms

It's our job to keep exposing the children to high-frequency words. We can use them in community writing and bring children's attention to them. They will come up in morning message as well as appear frequently in the texts the students are reading.

If the parent asking Question 4 is not referring to high-frequency words but rather to words that the child got from using the picture (for example, *helicopter*), then your answer will be different. In such a case, you will have to explain how the child used his or her meaning, structural, and visual information to figure out that word. When reading beginning-level texts, a child can often read a word, like *helicopter*, correctly because he or she used the picture and the first letter. That's a good thing. However, expecting children to identify these words in isolation on flashcards would be way out of that child's reach.

Question 5: *"You talk about teaching my child 'strategies.' What is a 'strategy'?"*

Reading strategies are hard to describe because they are the things that are happening in your brain as you read. We can't see a strategy happening, but they are essential to our understanding as we read. Let me give you an example. When I read an article in a magazine or newspaper about a new restaurant opening I start thinking of all the questions I have. "When will it open?" "What kind of food will they have?" "How expensive will it be?" Or if I'm reading a travel magazine, I might be reminded of a similar vacation I've been on. Your brain is always thinking as you are reading. These questions you are thinking about, the pictures you are getting in your head, and the connections you are making are some of the strategies that readers use to help them understand what they are reading. You see, reading isn't just saying the words correctly. It's much more than that. It's all of the thinking that goes on in the head of the reader.

When your strategies are working, you will stop when something doesn't make sense, sound right, or look right, and then go back and fix it. This is what we teach your child, since we want him to know that reading is thinking and making meaning.

The Home/School Connection: Many parents only think of what's *visible* about reading, such as the letters, sounds, and words. It is our job to teach them about what's *invisible* in reading. That's where strategies come in (see

Chapter 2). For many of us who have thought of reading as a list of skills to be taught, this is a new way of thinking. Understanding the strategies from the chart in Figure 2.1, how they overlap, and how the whole system works in an integrated way has been a major focus of this book. You can't see the strategies actually happening in the head of the child, but you can notice evidence in his or her behaviors. This is one of the hardest things to get parents to grasp, and they may not get it from your "quick answer." You'll need to communicate with families throughout the year, let them come in and observe your teaching, and share the progress their child is making in terms of strategies and behaviors. When you talk to parents about what their child needs to learn (how to self-monitor, how to predict a word that makes sense, how to use phonics information while they are reading, how to infer for deeper understanding, and so on), they will begin to better understand reading as a process rather than a collection of letters, sounds, and words.

Question 6:

"I remember learning a bunch of rules, like 'when two vowels go walking, the first one does the talking.' Why aren't you teaching my child the phonics rules? Shouldn't she learn all the phonics rules and sight words first, and then learn about comprehension when she gets in the upper grades?"

Phonics *is* integrated throughout our day, although we don't teach phonics rules in isolation. Research shows that because there are so many exceptions to the rules, it isn't effective to teach most of these to children. For example, the popular rule "when two vowels go walking, the first one does the talking" only works about 45 percent of the time. We teach children that reading is making meaning, so we want to keep our focus there, rather than on memorizing phonics rules. If a child is reading along and then stops to try to remember a rule to solve a word, the meaning is often lost.

We do have word work woven into various parts of our reading and writing workshop—during shared reading and writing, community writing, morning message, and so on. We teach children to look for patterns in words and notice things for themselves. Rather than having us give them a rule, we want the children to generate what they are noticing about how words work.

Comprehension is taught hand-in-hand with word solving, since making meaning is what reading is all about. If a reader can call the words but doesn't understand what he or she is reading, then the child is not really reading. Comprehension is not something that starts in third or fourth grade. We do lots of comprehension teaching beginning right in kindergarten.

The Home/School Connection: In Stephen B. Kucer's book *Dimensions of Literacy* (2005), he refers to Clymer's list of phonics generalizations and the percentage of how many words actually follow each rule. You would be surprised at how few rules are applicable more than 50 percent of the time. We don't see teaching these rules as a useful part of our instruction. We prefer to teach flexibility, especially since so many of the phonics rules are not fully applicable. We want students to know that many letters make several sounds and, likewise, that sounds can be represented by several different letters. Therefore, readers should be flexible with the phonics information they acquire.

Frank Smith (2005) says that phonics make sense to people who can already read. To struggling readers, a list of rules to memorize sometimes confuses them and takes away the focus from meaning making. Children need to learn to use meaning and structure, along with their phonics knowledge, whenever they are solving words. Refer to Chapters 4 and 7 for more information about teaching phonics and how it is integrated throughout daily instruction in a comprehensive literacy approach.

Question 7:

"My child is bringing home books that are too easy. He can read from his big brother's beginning chapter books. Why are you wasting his time with those baby books?"

The books I send home with children *should* be easy. These are books that I have introduced in small-group sessions and he has read with my support. He should feel very comfortable reading those books to you. I want him to be able to show off his good reading by sharing books that he can read independently. Reading books multiple times helps build self-confidence and fluency. I don't want your child to get discouraged or frustrated by giving him books that are too hard.

It's exciting that he is so eager to read and is picking up his brother's books! Many children want to jump into chapter books and attempt to read their older siblings books. Although it may look like he can read the books his big brother is reading, we want to make sure he understands what he is reading. Perhaps those harder books would be good for you to read aloud to your child after he shares the books he can read all by himself. We don't want to push children too fast since that can lead to frustration. Sometimes a child can call many of the words in a book but isn't able to understand what the book is about. That means the book isn't a good match.

Longer chapter books like the Harry Potter series are wonderful as family read-alouds; you can model good reading and have lots of conversations about what is happening in the story. We want to make sure the reading your child does at home is comfortable and encouraging. The instruction we do at school will continue to move your child into more difficult books—but he still needs lots of practice on books that are just right for him at home. I will take a look at the next book he chooses to bring home. Although I want them easy and just right, I agree with you that they shouldn't be too easy.

The Home/School Connection: Marie Clay says this about home/school practice: "Send easy books home for independent practice. A child who is on the way to independence needs to read often from many different books selected to be easy for him to 'go it alone.' It is the quantity of successful reading that builds the assured independence of the competent reader" (2005, 98). It is our job to communicate this message with families. We do not want our efforts at school to be thwarted by undue pressures at home. Many parents think that the harder the book is, the better. We know that this could discourage children, especially our struggling readers, and send a message that it's not okay for them to be where they are in their reading progression. We want to encourage independence at school and at home, and this often requires us to educate our families about the importance of reading within the zone of proximal development (see Chapter 3).

On the other hand, it is possible that a child has moved past the books he or she is taking home, and they really *are* too easy. Occasionally, children can grow by leaps and bounds, making huge growth in a short amount of time, and this has escaped your attention. It happens to all of us. If a parent inquires about this, it would be wise to do two things. One, do a quick reassessment using benchmark books and make sure you are giving the child appropriate texts in guided reading sessions. Two, take a few minutes to clear out his book box, taking out the books that are way too easy.

Question 8: *"What level is my child reading on? Is she in the high, middle, or low reading group?"*

I determine the guided reading groups each week by my ongoing assessments. Our groups change weekly, depending on the needs of each student. Because these groups are so flexible, they don't have set names and aren't considered high, middle, or low like when we were in school. Each child has different strengths and areas to work on, and I want to make sure each child is with other children who need to focus on the same thing. That information helps me decide how to group the children and what level book to use. Because these needs change, our groups change weekly.

I use levels to help me choose appropriate books for instruction, but I don't identify your child by what level book she is reading or what reading group she participates in. I feel it can be detrimental for a child to focus on the level of books. When a child thinks of herself as a number, it can turn reading into a competition. I want to keep the focus on your child as a reader; in other words, I want to focus on what she does when she is stuck and how I can help her learn more ways to solve her own problems while reading. Let's talk about what strategies your child is using and what's next for her in her growth as a reader. (At this point, you can talk about that particular student with the parent.)

The Home/School Connection: Teachers and parents can get caught up in the leveling craze that seems to dominate some schools. It turns into a competition of sorts, and the focus often turns to moving children up in levels rather than making sure they are developing a functioning reading process system. To us, the levels are for our use as teachers as a guideline for choosing texts. We never want the children to identify themselves by what reading level they are on. It makes us very sad to hear children say, "I'm an 8" or "I can only read red and blue books." Is this really how we want children to think of themselves as readers? It is our job as teachers to take the focus off of the levels.

Books are marked in a variety of ways, by the publisher or by the teacher, and we do realize that children and parents are aware of the numbers, letters, or colors. However, we make it very clear from the beginning that those symbols are for our use in organizing the books in our classroom.

Modeling how readers talk about themselves in the classroom and not referring to children by level will help them learn to ignore the level and instead focus on what kinds of books and authors they like. For example, Katie is a reader who likes realistic fiction books by authors like Anita Shreve and Ann Patchett. She also enjoys reading nonfiction biography and memoirs about people who do sports like cycling, running, and hiking. Isn't this how we want our students to describe themselves as readers? We'd rather hear a child say "I'm a reader who likes nonfiction books about animals and poetry, and I also love Mo Willems" than "I'm a reader who reads level 12 books."

When your guided reading groups are flexibly grouped based on student needs and the focus for instruction, you will not have a low, middle, and high group. In fact, your class probably won't divide into three distinct groups at all. You don't have to give the groups names. Simply calling the names of the kids you want to meet with is a quick and easy way to gather the group together. Of course, your groups may have some of the same kids in them over time, but not using a group name will help alleviate the issue of labeling kids.

Question 9:

"I know my third grader is way behind in reading. What are you doing to help him catch up?"

There are so many things we do in our classroom that are designed to improve children's reading. Let me mention a few. Right now I'm working hard at building your child's confidence. He began the school year feeling like a failure in reading; he's very aware that he is not where the other kids are. Up until now, he's been walking around with books that are way too hard for him, pretending to read them. I had a good discussion with all the kids during the first week of school about how we weren't going to have any "fake reading" in this room. I told them it was my job to help them all learn to read and enjoy books that are just right for them. I make sure that he has lots of books that are easy for him. I want him to know what it feels like to be a fluent reader, so practicing in books that are easy for him is a good way to feel confident.

I also give him books that contain a bit of a challenge for him, but these are done several times a week in a small group with me. I teach these students ways to solve their problems when they get stuck. Several of them have been used to just letting someone else give them the word, and they have to realize that they need to be active problem solvers. When he successfully figures out a word or rereads to make a sentence or phrase sound better, I compliment him. He is beginning to gain confidence and feel proud that he is adding to his collection of strategies that help him solve problems independently. Occasionally I meet with him one-on-one to zero in on his specific needs.

I look for opportunities for your child to shine. For example, he is very good at understanding and responding to the books I read aloud in class. Sometimes I let him lead a discussion group with several students who want to talk about the read-aloud text further.

We have writing workshop daily in my classroom. A lot of what he is learning during writing time will also help him with his reading because reading and writing are so closely related.

In addition to my work with him, I have an instructional assistant that he reads to once a week. He loves having that one-to-one attention of an adult who always tells him how great he sounds. He's also part of a group of students who go to the kindergarten room once a week. He reads his familiar books to a buddy there and that seems to be helping to build his confidence too.

I don't want you to worry about your child. I'm aware of his issues with reading and I'm working hard to support him. You can continue at home reading aloud to him each night. He loves the _____ books (name something that you know interests this child). I can loan you some of mine or help you find some in the school library. Let that reading time with you be a pleasurable experience. He'll really grow by having those memorable experiences reading books with you at home.

The Home/School Connection: Of course, the preceding answer would need to be adapted based on the student in question. For example, if that child is receiving any support from another teacher in addition to your work with him, you would want to explain that. We wanted to give you some general areas that you might like to address, which is why we mentioned building confidence as a reader, matching the child with "just-right" books, guided reading sessions to focus on specific needs, and how writing supports reading.

If the parent asking this question doesn't know anything about how you build community in your classroom, you may want to add some ideas from that area. The parent wants assurance that the child is not being teased because of where he is as a reader. You can talk about how you build that respect among your students from day one—that everyone in the class has different strengths and weaknesses, how it would feel to be teased, and how we are all in this class to support one another and cheer our classmates on.

You may want to encourage the parent to get some books on tape or CD for this child; public libraries usually carry good selections. Most struggling readers are capable of discussing books with their peers that they have heard read to them. Just because they can't read at a certain level doesn't mean we should deprive them of the joys of what is in those great books! Parents can help build a literacy background for that child. When the other kids are talking about the latest Harry Potter or Magic Tree House book, he can join in the conversation. Another good suggestion might be for this child to be introduced to some of the great graphic novels that are popular now. Many reluctant readers are getting hooked on reading with graphic novels.

In some instances you will find that parents are having a struggling third grader read out loud to them when it might be better for the child to read silently. If the child is at a developmental point where reading silently is more comfortable, he or she can become frustrated when asked to read aloud at home. The child becomes far too focused on *how he or she sounds* to the parent and loses the meaning of the story. Be sure to let parents know that silent reading and discussing the story after certain sections would be okay.

Question 10: *"I'm thinking of giving my child prizes for every book she reads. Won't that motivate her to read more?"*

You know, I really believe that reading is a reward in and of itself. It's great that you want to encourage her to read more. Giving prizes might motivate her to read more at first, but it's so important that she find enjoyment in reading for its own sake, and prizes can't guarantee that. When we offer kids pizza, stickers, or other prizes for reading a certain number of books, we can actually send a message that reading is something unpleasant so we have to resort to prizes to get them to read. I want children to be motivated to read because they enjoy books and reading, not because they might get a prize if they read. Also, when kids are counting the number of books they read in a race to see who can read the most, they often choose books that are way below the difficulty of what they should be reading. They sacrifice quality for quantity.

When you take your child to the library or a bookstore, spend some time finding books she enjoys. Ask her what she wants to learn more about or what kind of books she likes to read. Make a special time each evening for you and your daughter to sit down and read together. Our goal is to have children get intrinsic pleasure from reading rather than only reading for extrinsic rewards. A great deal of research shows that incentive programs may actually be detrimental and cause children to like reading even less.

The Home/School Connection: We want children to love reading. Taking the focus off of reading and putting it on the quantity of books read, points, or rewards tells children that we want them to read for our sake, not for theirs, or in order to get something. In Alfie Kohn's research on extrinsic rewards he says, "Children are likely to become enthusiastic, lifelong learners as a result of being provided with an engaging curriculum; a safe, caring community in which to discover and create; and a significant degree of choice about what (and how and why) they are learning. Rewards—like punishments—are

unnecessary when these things are present, and are ultimately destructive in any case" (Kohn 1994).

If we want children to enjoy reading, we need to make sure that they take ownership in choosing engaging and appropriate books to read. It is up to us as teachers to create a climate in our classrooms where children are asking, "What can I learn?" rather than "What do I get?" This is especially difficult if you work in a system that uses rewards and extrinsic motivators. There are many incentive programs out there that encourage keeping track of points for the number of books read in order to win prizes (toys, pizza, stickers, food coupons, etc.). We need to voice our concerns about these and question why we are being asked to use them in our classrooms. We need to make sure our rooms are full of interesting, relevant reading material and that kids are matched with books they can read. If children have access to a wide variety of reading material, they will choose to read for the sheer pleasure of enjoying a good book.

Some popular computerized reading programs award kids points for answering questions correctly. The questions are very literal. For example, after reading a book on the life of Henry Ford, one question asked, "What year did Henry Ford get married?" These types of questions encourage memorization in place of understanding, analysis, synthesis, and other higher level thinking skills. They also limit children, because many teachers will only allow children to read books that have accompanying quizzes and are on the right color level.

Frank Smith says that reading "provides its own rewards. Becoming a reader is a satisfying activity. What encourages children to read, and thus learn to read, isn't some promise of satisfaction in the future, or an 'extrinsic reward' like praise, high marks, a special treat, or the avoidance of derision or punishment, but being able to read. Watch children engrossed in a book from which they are learning about reading, and there will be no need to ask where the fundamental satisfaction lies" (2005, 13).

Question 11: *"My child is always telling me about the books you read aloud. Where can I find them to borrow or buy? I know my child would enjoy getting these books for a birthday gift."*

Our read-aloud time is a highly valued and meaningful time in our classroom. I love that your child comes home and talks about the books we read! That's exactly what I hope will happen when I share a good book. Most of the books I get are from our school library, the public library, or from the local bookstore. I also order a lot of books from Amazon.com to keep in our classroom library.

In my weekly newsletter, I always list the books we have read aloud that week. You can find these books by searching online at Amazon.com or by asking at your local library. Make sure and ask your child what his favorites are, too. When you read these books aloud to your child a second or third time, his comprehension of that text will deepen. A book is always a great gift, and time spent reading together is an even greater gift!

The Home/School Connection: As we wrote in Chapters 5 and 6, reading aloud is a key component of literacy instruction. We want to promote reading outside of school as much as we can, and sharing the books we read aloud in the classroom is the perfect way to do this. Children love hearing their favorites read over and over, and families often want to know what kinds of books to buy or check out from the library.

Katie sends home a weekly newsletter called the *Keier Flyer*. It's a short, one- or two-page newsletter to summarize our week. (See Appendix 19 for a copy of the *Keier Flyer*.) She has the kids contribute to the writing, and they compose much of it together on the interactive whiteboard. She includes pictures of classroom activities, community writing projects, and thoughts on their week. One thing that appears in each edition is a list of the books she read aloud that week. Family members can ask about the books, inspiring good dinner table conversation, and also have a list of wonderful titles to look for at the library or to purchase for their child.

Question 12: *"I check my child's backpack every night, but there aren't many papers coming home. Where are the worksheets and workbooks that I remember doing in school?"*

I appreciate that you are checking your child's backpack and wanting to know what we are doing at school each day. Thank you! However, I'm afraid you won't find that information from papers sent home. I give very few worksheets because the majority of our learning is done interactively—with the whole class, in small groups, or with partners. We spend the majority of our time on authentic tasks such as reading books, writing original stories, and collaborating on projects together. I find that worksheets take very little thought, aren't what real readers and writers do, and don't meet the needs of every child. Most worksheets are simply "busy work" to keep the children occupied while the teacher is working with other kids. I would rather the kids be reading and writing during this time.

Talking about our learning is a much better way for me to check for understanding than asking kids to complete a worksheet. Most worksheets focus on skills in isolation, and do not have the children reading and thinking.

The best way to learn about what your child did at school is to ask her! Have a conversation about the new things she learned, questions she has, and what she is excited about. If she tells you "nothing," look at the *Keier Flyer* (mention your newsletter here) and start your conversation with something mentioned there. And, as always, feel free to stop by our classroom and take a look at the walls—they tell the story of our learning each week.

The Home/School Connection: In Chapter 5, we described a comprehensive literacy approach. Worksheets simply don't fit into this type of classroom environment. We feel that worksheets are not a good use of time in school—time when kids could be reading, writing, or talking about their learning. Worksheets are not authentic, meaningful, or differentiated enough. They may keep kids busy, but for our most struggling readers, they need more than to be "kept busy." Our time is too precious to waste on activities that are not what real readers and writers do. You will often have parents who question this and who want to see lots of papers coming home each week. We've found that communicating with these parents frequently and clearly is essential. Weekly newsletters and frequent invitations to visit our classroom to see the community writing projects, book boxes, writing folders, and all the tracks of our thinking hanging up on charts in the classroom help parents see the learning that is taking place. They will soon come to understand that stacks of crumpled up worksheets are not nearly as meaningful as what goes on in our classroom.

There is a wonderful poem by Donna Whyte that Katie sends home at the beginning of the year. It answers the question, "What's in your backpack?" in a creative, meaningful way. You can find the poem at www.gkestner.com/YouAskWhat.pdf.

Question 13: *"We don't speak English in our home. I want my child to learn English, but I don't know how to help him with his reading. What can I do?"*

It is so wonderful for a child to become fluent in two or more languages! Continuing to help him with reading and writing in your home language will actually support his learning of English. So feel free to read to him, talk about books, or just tell him stories of your own growing-up experiences in your language. If you don't have any books at home in your first language, check our school library or your local library. They may have some for you to borrow.

As for the English books he is bringing home from the classroom to read to you each night, you can talk about the story in your home language before he reads it by looking at the pictures together. Then have him read the book in English. Any book your child brings home is a book he's already read with me, so he should do fairly well with it. After your child reads it to you, converse in your own language. Try a few of these questions to get a conversation going: "What was your favorite part of this book?" "What did this story remind you of?" "Would you have done something different if you were that character?" (See Appendix 20 for an English and Spanish bookmark with these and other questions.)

The most important thing is that your child knows that you are interested in his learning. Praise him or compliment him. Tell him you are proud of how hard he is working in school. Ask him about projects he is working on during the school day and about the topics that interest him the most.

Perhaps you'd like to sign up for our "Partners in Print" program (a Pacific Learning program). It's for any parent who wants to learn more about working with your child at home. It's offered in Spanish and English, and the workshops are once a month after school. (If your school has a program like this and if the parent is interested, help him or her to join the group. Then be sure to send reminders home of upcoming meeting dates.)

The Home/School Connection: As the teacher, be sure you are checking the books that your ELL students are bringing home to reread to parents. These should be texts that you have introduced in guided reading or ones the child has read with a friend. You don't want the child working at a frustration level when reading books without an English-speaking adult present. Practice at home should be comfortable and enjoyable.

Find ways to communicate with your non-English-speaking parents whenever you can. Many school districts have translation opportunities. Let those parents know you value their home language and traditions. Students should continue learning their home language simultaneously with learning English. The important thing is for these parents to know that there are ways they *can* help their child's literacy learning even if they do not speak English themselves. Offer books on tape in English for the families to borrow. When we have done this, we learn from the child that the whole family sat around and listened to the book. Ask your PTA to look into being sure your school library has some books for these children in their home language.

One year, Pat and the first-grade teachers offered a nighttime program for parents about how to have conversations about the books the children were bringing home each night. They found translators for their top four languages—Spanish, Korean, Vietnamese, and Urdu. (If your school district doesn't provide translators for events like these, you can often find translators within your community. Be resourceful!) On the night of the workshop, each language group sat with their translator. During the first part of the program, Pat presented information on what parents could say or do before, during, and after reading. She would stop periodically for translations. The second part of the program had a first-grade teacher who modeled reading and talking with a child about a book. Each language group had their own teacher/child team. Through their translator, the parents were able to ask very specific questions of the first-grade teacher in a small-group setting. This is just one example of a school reaching out to the parents of their ELL students.

Lastly, if you are in a school where the faculty is new to working with ELL students, you might want to consider reading one of these two books: *Becoming One Community: Reading and Writing with English Language Learners* by Fay and Whaley (2004) or *"The Words Came Down!": English Language Learners Read, Write, and Talk Across the Curriculum, K–2* by Parker and Pardini (2006).

Question 14: *"What are you doing to prepare my child to take the state tests? I'm worried that since she struggles with reading, she won't pass the tests. Shouldn't you be doing more test preparation?"*

Our state tests are an important piece of third through fifth grade, and I understand your concern. I definitely want the kids to do well, and I want to teach them how to take the tests in a smart way. However, I don't agree with spending months on test preparation. I am spending lots of time helping your daughter become a strong reader. That's what really matters, because she will have to read the tests in order to do well. I am teaching test-taking skills within the context of our daily reading workshop. For example, when we are reading poetry, I use "test language" such as *stanza, couplet, rhyming patterns,* and *free verse.* A few weeks before the test, we will do some concentrated focus lessons on specific test-taking skills.

My main job is to help your daughter become a strategic reader. In this way, she will be able to navigate the test language and be able to take the state tests and do well. I don't want test preparation exercises to replace the quality reading and writing experiences that we do every day in the classroom.

The Home/School Connection: "In order to be effective test takers, students must first be effective readers" (Greene and Melton 2007, 15). We completely agree with this statement. If we spend all of our time teaching kids how to take tests and neglect teaching them how to be strategic readers, then we are doing a huge disservice to the children we teach. There is so much more to being a proficient reader than a passing standardized test score. We need to spend the majority of our time with children teaching them how to read. Test preparation can be effectively integrated into a daily reading workshop if standardized tests are viewed as a specific genre, just like nonfiction or poetry. We can use the language, format, and structure of tests as mini-lessons during our reading workshop.

In their wonderful book called *Test Talk,* Amy Greene and Glennon Melton (2007) show us how teachers can teach test genre through their daily reading workshops while maintaining best-practice teaching. *Test Talk* includes sections on finding the main idea, identifying author's intent, and inferring, with very specific classroom lessons.

In this era of testing, teachers need to take a stand for keeping the teaching of literacy at the heart of our day—not test preparation. You do not need to purchase expensive workbooks or test prep software. Teaching children how to be good test takers can be done on the same material they are reading each day in reading workshop without giving up the essential elements in a comprehensive literacy approach.

Question 15: *"How do I know that my child understands what he is reading? What should I do when he finishes a book?"*

While your child is reading, you can tell if he understands if he laughs at the funny parts, spontaneously talks about what the characters are doing, or connects to an experience of his own. Encourage these natural responses, because they give you hints into what your child is thinking as he is reading. Along the same lines, if a child frowns or pauses or reads the punctuation wrong, these are hints that he is losing the overall meaning of the story. You'll want to slow him down and encourage him to reread those parts and maybe talk about what's happening in the book.

The best way to tell if your child understands what he has read is by talking to him. You don't need to check on him by asking a series of specific questions about the characters or setting; just talk naturally about the book. Try starting a conversation with something general like "So what did you think of that book?" or "What was your favorite part?" or "Did it remind you of anything?"

When I finish reading a good book, I want to tell someone about it. I often call up a friend or my mom and talk about the parts I liked and the parts I keep thinking about. Give your child an opportunity to do the same. Be a good listener, and let your child share about the books he is reading.

I have a bookmark with some conversation starters, if you'd like some ideas (see Appendix 20, with questions in English and Spanish). I'll send one home with your child and you can use that to help you with your conversations.

The Home/School Connection: Many parents remember when they were in school and were required to answer questions about books they read, or do a book report, a diorama, or some other elaborate project. Some of them have a hard time when we tell them that talking about a book is one of the best ways to check for understanding and to foster a love of reading. I remember dreading the book reports that inevitably followed every book I read in elementary school. I loved reading but hated doing all the "stuff" that was assigned after I read. I really just wanted to talk to someone about the book, and then read another book!

We want kids to do what comes naturally after reading—and that is talking about what they have read. Perhaps you have started book clubs in your classroom or have reading buddies. No matter how you structure it, making time for children to talk about what they are reading is essential. Some good resources for setting up primary book clubs and reading buddies are *Growing Readers* and *Reading for Real*, both by Kathy Collins (2004, 2008). Limit the book project assignments and use your class time for reading and talking about books. If we want our students to become lifelong learners, we need to give them many opportunities early on to experience what readers do in the "real world." I've never been part of a book group that completed a diorama before our next meeting, and I would not ask children to do that either.

Question 16:

"I know my child is struggling. Should I take her to one of those learning centers or buy a kit to teach her how to read?"

I understand your concern and your desire to have her reading problems solved quickly. But please know that I am working with your child every day on exactly what she needs. Every child learns at a different pace and in different ways. Although many of those advertised programs promise that your child will be reading on grade level at the end of their sessions, that usually doesn't happen. Perhaps your child will be able to pass the test they give to exit the program, but I want much more than that for her. I want her to build the strategies that help her solve problems independently when she becomes stuck while reading. Often when children leave these programs where they've practiced skills in isolation, they are unable to transfer these skills to the classroom when reading real books.

A computerized reading program or a kit that focuses on phonics is an expensive option that often doesn't work. In fact, many of these programs work against what we are doing in the classroom. I want to help your child become a strategic reader, not learn a list of items like many of these programs teach. In class your child is learning to focus on meaning and to use strategies to help her when she reads. My advice is save your money, and don't go to a computerized learning center. If you'd like, I can help you find a qualified reading tutor who can support what we are doing in the classroom and can help your child become a stronger reader. I would be happy to meet with that tutor to share what I know about your child as a reader and writer.

The Home/School Connection: Most commercial tutoring programs and reading kits focus on item knowledge, not on helping a child construct a reading process system. Parents are looking for reassurance here—they need to know how you are helping their child in the classroom. Many are hoping they can buy something quickly to get their child up to speed. We need to communicate with families and educate them on why the advertised programs they see on the television are not what's best for their child. Refer to Question 5 on "What is a strategy?" Explain to parents how item knowledge differs from teaching children to be strategic readers.

Parents need to understand that there is not a "quick fix," despite what advertisements may say. Helping a struggling reader is a much longer process, and one that can't be done with a kit or by an untrained person. Help parents find qualified reading tutors for their children instead. Many districts keep a list of qualified tutors, and often there are several teachers in your building who would like to tutor after school. Make sure you frequently communicate with the tutor and share information to better accelerate that child's reading development. Parents who are able to afford this luxury for their children need to be supported in making good decisions. They only want what's best for their child, and it is up to us to educate parents as well as children.

Closing Thoughts

In this chapter, we've answered sixteen of the most commonly asked questions. However, we realize that there are many more possible inquiries that you may need to address. Regardless of the question, we suggest the following guidelines:

* Honor the parent's concern. It is important that you take their question seriously and they know they are being heard.
* Rephrase the question to be sure you understood the parent correctly. When you paraphrase what a parent is asking, it gives him or her the opportunity to clarify.
* Be sure you follow through on whatever answer you have given the parent. For example, if you say you will check the book box or send something home, be sure you do that in a timely manner.
* Choose your language carefully to avoid "educationese." Speak clearly and explain any acronyms or terms you may take for granted. Make sure to ask if the parents have any more questions after your explanation.
* Don't overwhelm the parent with too much information. Give them something to walk away with, and then offer a follow-up appointment to talk more.
* If the question is coming from an upset or angry parent, it's best to keep listening, paraphrase, and let the parent talk out the issue until you are sure you understand. You may need to involve another professional, such as the reading specialist or an administrator, to help you talk through and solve the problem. It's okay to say, "This is an important question, and I'd like to talk to my colleagues and get back to you on this."
* If the timing is bad (for example, if a parent stops you in the hall when you are with your class or drops in when you are teaching), it's best to acknowledge their question by saying, "I'm glad you brought this up. Let's schedule an appointment to talk more about this."

Throughout this book we have opened avenues that we hope have broadened your knowledge of reading process. In turn, you will be able to open avenues of understanding for parents. Educating our families and our community about how reading works needs to be an integral part of our job. If we want families to support children at home in ways similar to what we do in the classroom (or at least not in contrast), then we need to continually find ways to communicate valid information.

CHAPTER 12

Teachers Make
the Difference

The passport to effective reading instruction for all students is in the hands of teachers. Though every district has its curriculum guidelines, materials identified for use, and grade-level standards, it is the teacher who will carry out the daily instruction of students. More specifically, the teacher of a struggling reader will help determine whether that child succeeds or not, based on the teacher's instruction, attitude, and support. We agree wholeheartedly with many literacy professionals who believe that expanding teachers' knowledge should be a high priority.

We wonder if schools and districts are asking the right questions. They often are concerned with these questions:

* What *materials* should we buy?
* What *method of teaching reading* should we use?
* What *reading program* should we use so that all our students become literate?

Perhaps the questions they should be asking are these:

* How are the *teachers* in our building understanding reading process?
* What is the theory-in-the-head of the *teacher* of how reading works?
* How can we arrange for long-term staff development opportunities that would expose our *teachers* to updated knowledge about a reading process system that each reader needs to construct for himself or herself?

Let's stop worrying about what to buy next and instead start directing the funding toward long-term staff development for those who *can* make a difference, the classroom teachers.

No one would argue with the fact that there continues to be a significant number of struggling readers in every school district. To combat those numbers, we have proposed in this book that all teachers do several things:

* Develop expertise in the strategies that make up a reading process system
* Understand how those strategies work together as an integrated system
* Learn how to support a child who is not presently constructing such a system

Armed with more information about how reading works, we believe teachers would be better able to support struggling readers who are not building a network of strategies to help them solve words and understand texts. For us, this is a key element in the solution to eradicating the struggling reader issue.

Carol Lyons warns about what would happen if we leave the struggling reader issue unsolved. It would affect all of us. "Allowing large numbers of children to leave the primary grades with minimal skills ensures them a life of school failure, as well as probable poverty and long-term dependence on society, the consequences of which are disastrous to the well-being of the nations of the world" (2003, 188). We cannot ignore it. We can't hope some other teacher will take care of this student or that one. It is not only the reading teacher's problem, or the LD teacher's, or the ELL teacher's—the problem belongs to all of us. So we must each do our part. School administrators and teachers alike should remain vigilant about finding ways to teach all children, no matter what their strengths and weaknesses.

Making a Difference

On Donalyn Miller's blog site, called The Book Whisperer, she asks people to tell their stories about what turned them into readers. Many responders wrote that it was a teacher or parent who said the right thing at the right time or gave them the perfect book at the perfect time that had a lasting impression on them. Who wouldn't want to make a difference in a child's life, turning that child into a lifelong reader? When a child learns to read, the world is open to him or her. Being the one to open that door for a child is a fantastic feeling.

Elementary school teachers of grades K–4 often experience that great feeling of having made a difference in a child as a reader. Pat has had seven years of teaching Reading Recovery students and has seen her share of at-risk students who turn into confident, excited readers. Katie has worked in seven special needs schools and has taught numerous children to read and discover a love of reading. We are sure many of you could share your stories about parents who have said, "Thank you for turning my child on to books!" or "This year with you as his teacher has been the best ever! He loves reading!" or "She used to hate reading and now she begs me to take her to the library!" The hard fact is: *we want that for every child.* But remember, struggling readers are masters at hiding out, faking it, slipping through the cracks, and camouflaging themselves. It's our job to find them and teach them well.

Broadening Our Vision of How Reading Process Works

As we have said, what we are proposing in this text is that every single teacher who works with young readers acquire a certain level of knowledge about reading process. This could mean a change in the way reading is understood by some educators. The generally accepted theory of how reading works is that reading consists of a number of skills that can be taught in some sequential manner (the simple theory that we described in Chapter 2). The more complex theory of reading that we have presented in this book, one of a repertoire of strategies that work together in an integrated way, would be a change in thinking for some teachers.

We know that changing a predominantly accepted theory can be a long and difficult process. We remember back to more than twenty years ago when most teachers viewed writing as a list of items, such as spelling, grammar, and punctuation, to be learned, drilled, and practiced. Now, many teachers understand writing as a process, thanks to the work of Donald Graves, Lucy Calkins, Ralph Fletcher, Katie Wood Ray, and many others. Sound writing workshops are alive and well in many classrooms around the country.

Shifting the thinking about how reading works will take time, shared knowledge, and a willingness on the part of all elementary teachers to remain lifelong learners. We have certainly seen evidence of the beginnings of this shift. You will notice it too if the schools in your district are beginning to have these characteristics:

- More teachers wanting to know how to help their struggling students in the classroom
- More teachers reading about strategy teaching and developing lessons that support students to take on the strategic actions that proficient readers use
- More Reading Recovery teachers being trained in order to meet the needs of the at-risk students in first grade
- More Literacy Collaborative or other coaching situations being implemented so that all teachers, veteran or novice, can expand their knowledge of classroom environments, instructional practices, and assessment that support the development of all children as readers and writers
- More teachers providing time for students to focus on authentic reading and writing experiences

Even Marie Clay wrote that a change is underway in how we view reading process. "Although we may not yet have definitive descriptions of all the strategic activities or operations that are acquired in early literacy this kind of shift in our thinking is happening" (2005a, 13). *A shift in our thinking.* Many more teachers are starting to view reading as a process in the head of the reader and to understand that struggling readers need help in building that process.

Whenever we use the term *struggling readers* we are reminded of how P. David Pearson describes these students. At the Ohio Reading Recovery Conference in 2000, he called them "would do well if they had the resources" students. We like that statement because it gives us hope. If the students had the resources—expert teachers who focus on "acquiring knowledge and skills to make sound judgments and create environments that scaffold student learning and maximize children's opportunities to learn" (Lyons 2003, 169)—then they too could succeed.

Pat once read an interesting idea in *The Manufactured Crisis* by Berliner and Biddle (1996). The authors were comparing the standardized scores in math of eighth-grade students in the United States and Japan. Japan's scores were much higher. But the authors realized that "Japanese schools were *requir-*

ing eighth-grade students to take mathematics courses that stressed algebra, whereas such courses were typically offered to American students a year or two later" (55). So the fact that American students did poorer on the end of an eighth-grade test really had more to do with the fact that they had not had the *opportunity to learn.* That concept stuck with Pat and she began to think about it in relation to struggling readers. If we give them the *opportunity to learn* how to build a reading process system, they too can become proficient readers. In other words, quality instruction from a knowledgeable teacher matters. Struggling readers can learn to read; we just need to find ways to teach them better and give them the best *opportunities to learn.*

How Can We Make a Difference?

Frank Smith says, "Teachers must change the world a little bit at a time" (1998, 90). In the end, that was our reason for the massive undertaking of writing this book. We hope that we are changing the world for the struggling readers you teach because we have added to the *shift in your thinking* about how reading works. Below are some possibilities of how you can begin to use this new information to make a difference in your school, with the teachers you work with, and with your students.

⚙ Join a teachers-as-readers book discussion group with any one of the many professional texts we have mentioned. If you are in a school with little opportunity for staff development in the areas we've been discussing, start your own group. There will always be a few teachers who will join you. A study guide to help you facilitate a discussion of this book, along with several study guides for other books, is provided on the Web site of Stenhouse Publishers (www.stenhouse.com).

⚙ Facilitate a discussion at a faculty meeting in response to the question "What is reading process?" Try a poem, such as *Wash in the Street* in Chapter 2, to spur on a discussion of what makes up a reading process system in proficient readers.

⚙ Gently push to include discussions about instruction for struggling readers at your team meetings. You can begin with talk about ZPD (see Chapter 3) or how to prompt and model for students how to use a balance of sources of information (see Chapter 4).

⚙ Take a look at your daily schedule and make sure it allows multiple opportunities for weaving in reading process instruction (see example in Chapter 5).

⚙ Keep track of the time that your struggling students are involved in real reading and writing. Is it as much time as your more able readers are spending engaged in authentic tasks? If you struggle with this, find a colleague to talk with and share ideas.

- Reflect on your guided reading groups. Think about whether you are teaching just the book and a few new words or focusing on a strategy that will support the readers in solving their own problems (see the guided reading section of Chapter 5).

- Spend time carefully choosing your interactive read-alouds and give time for the children to engage in talk beyond the text. Use the turn-and-talk model and the questions included in Chapter 6 to start student conversations.

- Get together with other kindergarten or first-grade teachers who have beginning readers like the ones described in Chapter 7. Share ideas about what you have tried that helps these emergent readers get control of those early reading strategies and behaviors.

- Experiment with your strategy teaching introductions (as we discussed in Chapters 8 and 9) to make sure you are focusing on making meaning rather than just doing strategies for strategy sake.

- Expand your practice of assessing and observing students with reading process in mind. Find a colleague to pair with. Focus on one struggling child. Figure out what strategies the child has under control and what he or she needs next as a reader. Then write a few instructional goals, as we did for Edward and Hannah in Chapter 10.

- If possible, find someone in your building or within your school system who can offer a few sessions for your staff on running record analysis.

- Start an assessment notebook that works for you (as Katie did in Chapter 10) and then share it with your team members.

- Add more ways to communicate reading process and strategy information with parents and school administrators (see Chapter 11).

- If you find that you are the only one in your building ready to shift your thinking at this point, or if you are interested in participating in online conversations, take advantage of the many social networking sites and blogs available to teachers. The National Council of Teachers of English (NCTE) Web site (www.ncte.org) has many options (Facebook, Twitter, Nings) for online discussions on a variety of current literacy topics. You can also find many authors of current professional books, as well as educational publishers like Stenhouse, Heinemann, and Scholastic, on Twitter and Facebook. Many of these authors have wonderful blogs as well.

We hope that this book helped you broaden your understandings of how reading works so that you can make a difference in the lives of children, in the understandings of the parents you come in contact with, and in the teachers you collaborate with on a daily basis. You can be the one who catches readers before they fall.

APPENDIX

Appendix 1   Strategic Actions for Reading

In-the-Head Strategic Action	What It Means	What It Sounds Like When a Teacher Calls Upon a Child To Do the Strategic Action	What It Sounds or Looks Like When a Child Self-Initiates the Strategic Action
Predicting at the Word Level	A reader can predict a word he does not automatically recognize. (Though his substitution may not be accurate, he is still predicting a word for the unknown word by using one or more sources of information.)	• Can you think of a word that makes sense there? • What word might look right there? • Get your mouth ready for the first part of the word. • Go back and reread. Can you think of a word that would look right, sound right, and make sense there?	• The child can substitute a meaningful word for the unknown word (couch for sofa). • The child can substitute a word that makes sense and sounds right (running for jogging). • The child can substitute a word with some of the same letters (where for were).
Predicting at the Text Level	A reader can make predictions on what will come next in the text based on prior knowledge and based on what has happened in the text so far.	• What do you think will happen next? • What do think this book is going to be about? • Let's get our minds ready to read. Look at the cover, title, and pictures and think about what you might read in this book before we start. • What do you think that character is going to do?	• I think the book is going to be about . . . • The cover and title makes me think this book might be about . . . . • I think I might learn more about . . . . • I think the character might . . . . • I think I know how the story is going to end.
Checking/Confirming	A reader can check, or compare, one kind of information against another by looking at multiple sources of information (meaning, structure, visual).	• Check that again. • Does that make sense? • Does it look right? • Does it sound right? • What else could it be? • The teacher can ask the child, "It might be crocodile or alligator. How can you check that?" to prompt the child to look at the visual information.	• The child goes back and makes another attempt at solving a word. • The child says, "No, that's not right," and makes another attempt. • The child says a word that makes sense, but then sounds some of the letters and switches to another word. • The child runs his finger under a word, checking the letters and sounds as he says it slowly.
Maintaining Fluency	A reader can read smoothly, at an appropriate rate and with expression—paying attention to punctuation and phrasing.	• Read that again. Make it sound smooth. • Did that sound smooth or choppy? • How would you say it? • Put those words together. • Put your fingers around these words (ask the child to read it all together). • Remember what your voice does when you see those marks (!, ?, ". " ")?	• The child is reading at an appropriate rate and is using intonation and expression that matches the punctuation. • The reading is smooth and quick on familiar texts. • The child slows down when she is doing some reading work, then resumes fast, smooth reading. (continued)

Catching Readers Before They Fall: Supporting Readers Who Struggle, K–4 by Pat Johnson and Katie Keier. Copyright © 2010. Stenhouse Publishers.

Appendix 1 Strategic Actions for Reading (continued)

In-the-Head Strategic Action	What It Means	What It Sounds Like When a Teacher Calls Upon a Child To Do the Strategic Action	What It Sounds or Looks Like When a Child Self-Initiates the Strategic Action
			• The child reads words in groups to make it sound like normal speech. • The child notices quotation marks and makes it sound like the character talking.
Adjusting	A reader can change the rate of reading to reflect the text or challenges in the text.	• Read that again slowly. Can you figure it out now? • Make that sound like the character talking. How would he or she say it? • Wow, the language the author used was beautiful. Let's read it again slowly to really enjoy those words. • Let's use the (chart, diagram, graph, etc.) to help us understand this part (nonfiction).	• The child is reading fluently, but slows down to problem solve, then resumes a good pace. • The text has a part where the character is really excited. The child reads this quickly and then goes back to a steady rate for the rest of the page. • The child's reading reflects the action in the text. • The child's reading matches the genre.
Inferring	A reader can think beyond what is explicitly stated or shown in the text to better understand what is read.	• What do you think the character is thinking or feeling? • What does the picture tell us? • Who is the narrator? • Look at the picture. What do you think that character might be saying or thinking? • Why do you think the author wrote that? • What is the big idea, or theme, of this book?	• I think the character (feels, thinks, wants) … • The picture makes me think … • I can tell whose voice is telling the story. • I think the author wanted us to … • The big idea is …
Evaluating/Critiquing/Analyzing	A reader can think about what he has read and make judgments, reflect upon, and evaluate texts.	• Why did the author write it that way? • How can text features help us understand the information better? • Did you enjoy this text? Why or why not? • Do you agree or disagree with the author? Why or why not? • From what point of view was this written? • Did this text show an issue fairly? Why or why not? • What voices were heard? • What voices were left out? • How dependable is this information?	• I think the author wrote this book because … • I think … helps me read (poetry, nonfiction, fiction, etc.) because … • I liked this book because … • I didn't like this book because … • I agree/disagree because … • This author is definitely for/against … because … • This book was written from the point of view of … • We heard what … thought, but not what … thought. • I'm still wondering ….

Appendix 1 Strategic Actions for Reading (continued)

In-the-Head Strategic Action	What It Means	What It Sounds Like When a Teacher Calls Upon a Child To Do the Strategic Action	What It Sounds or Looks Like When a Child Self-Initiates the Strategic Action
Synthesizing	A reader can put together information from the text with her own prior knowledge to form new understandings.	• How has your thinking changed? • What do you understand better now? • What did you learn?	• Now I understand … better. • I learned … • I changed my thinking about …
Questioning	A reader can ask questions before, during, and after reading.	• What are you wondering? • What questions do you have so far? • Now that the book is finished, what questions do you have?	• I wonder … • Do you think … • I want to find out more about … • At first I wondered …but then I figured out …
Activating Schema	A reader can use his background knowledge to help him make meaning from text.	• What do you know about …? • Before we start to read, let's talk about … . • How does what we are reading connect with what you already know about … ?	• I know … • I think … • I saw on the *Discovery Channel* that … • That reminds me of … • I know how that character feels because when that happened to me, I felt …
Summarizing/Determining Importance	A reader can take information from a text and decide what the most important parts are. A reader can distinguish between essential and nonessential information. A reader can paraphrase what a whole passage, article, or story is about.	• What is this book mostly about? • What are some big things the author wanted you to remember? • What do you think is the most important thing in this book? • Can you briefly tell me about what you read?	• The most important thing is … • I think the author wants me to remember … • After I read this part, I think the main idea is … • That part is not important because …
Visualizing	A reader can make mental images before, during, and after he reads. The images come from the words and pictures in the text combined with the reader's background knowledge.	• What picture did you get in your head? • How does the picture in your head help you understand what you are reading?	• I can see … in my head while I am reading. • The picture in my head helped me understand … • I felt like I was there with the character when … • The child draws or describes in words the setting of the story beyond the actual words of the book.
Making Connections	A reader can connect the text to her own life experiences, prior knowledge, other books, or events in the world.	• What does that remind you of? • How did that connection help you understand what you read? • How do you think that character was feeling? Has that ever happened to you? • What do you know about …	• That reminds me of … • This book is like … • I know how that character is feeling because I … • I remember …

Catching Readers Before They Fall: Supporting Readers Who Struggle, K–4 by Pat Johnson and Katie Keier. Copyright © 2010. Stenhouse Publishers.

Appendix 1 Strategic Actions for Reading (continued)

In-the-Head Strategic Action	What It Means	What It Sounds Like When a Teacher Calls Upon a Child To Do the Strategic Action	What It Sounds or Looks Like When a Child Self-Initiates the Strategic Action
Linking/Making Analogies	A reader can connect new learning with what she already knows.	• What word does that look like? • Does that remind you of something you already know? • Look at this word *like*. If I change the *l* to a *b*, what word is it now? • Do you see a part you know that might help you? • What do you already know about …? How can that help you understand this book?	• It looks like … • It reminds me of … • If I know …, then I can get to … (using known words to get to unknown words)
Self-Monitoring	A reader can check himself by asking if what he is reading sounds right, looks right, and makes sense. A reader can self-monitor for comprehension, 1:1 match, fluency, and so on.	• Did you check that? • Run your finger under that. • Point to the words. • Why did you stop? • What did you notice? • Put it all together. • Were you right? • Try that again. • You made a mistake. Can you find it?	• After making an error, the child goes back and rereads, correcting the error. • The child slows down or stops, and goes back to reread the tricky part. • The child stops to talk about a confusing part in order to clarify before reading on. • The child rereads to fix a 1:1 matching error. • The child rereads with expression and proper intonation after noticing punctuation.
Searching/Gathering	A reader can search letters, words, pictures, punctuation, and other text features to gather information that helps her read and understand the text. She can use something she already knows to help her problem solve.	• Is there something about that word that can help you? • What do you see that you know? • Check the first letter/part of that word. • What would make sense there? • Does it look right? • You said … Can we say it that way? • Try that again and think about what would make sense and sound right.	• The child figures out a word in parts: *short = sh or t* and says, "Hey, there's *or*." • The child's eyes glance at the picture, then back at the word. • The child rereads after noticing end punctuation (! . ?). • The child stops at a word. This indicates she may be searching her background knowledge, the picture, or the word. • The child rereads the sentence, gathering meaning to make a second attempt at an unknown word.

Appendix 2   Individual Student ZPD Chart

ZAD What strategic behaviors can this child perform all on his or her own—in his or her *zone of actual development*?	ZPD What are some skills or strategies this child is ready to learn how to do with your modeling and assistance—in his or her *zone of proximal development*?	Out of Reach What things would you consider teaching to other children in the room, but would be *out of reach* for this child at this time?

Catching Readers Before They Fall: Supporting Readers Who Struggle, K–4 by Pat Johnson and Katie Keier. Copyright © 2010. Stenhouse Publishers.

Appendix 3   A Teacher's Language Changes When Moving from Demonstration to Independence

Teaching Phase	Teacher Language
Demonstrate	
Share the Task	
Provide Guided Practice (High Support)	
Gradually Withdraw Scaffold (Low Support)	
Give Specific Praise or Redirection	

Appendix 4   Strategy Card

Catching Readers Before They Fall: Supporting Readers Who Struggle, K–4 by Pat Johnson and Katie Keier. Copyright © 2010. Stenhouse Publishers.

Appendix 5 Morning Message Examples

Sept. 8

Dear friends,
Today is terrific Tuesday.
It is the 1st day of school.
We will learn names today.
What is your name?

Love,
Ms. Keier

Suhani Sandy
Ivan Connor
Amber Kathlyn Dang
Estefany David Mona
Ian Matthew Carlos
Diana Dallin Daniela
Brandon Jasmine Sophia
Brian

Notice how the message is used from the first day of school to build community and get to know one another's names. The teacher writes the children's names on the chart as they introduce themselves. Ordinal numbers, days of the week, and high-frequency words are also addressed.

September 22, 2009

Dear friends,

Today is terrific Tuesday! It is the 11th day of school. Our caterpillars are getting bigger. They are eating a lot of milkweed

Love,
Ms. Keier

The morning message frequently connects to content areas and new vocabulary children are learning. *Milkweed* was one of the words on our monarch word wall.

December 4, 2009

Dear Super Students,

The weather forecast is calling for snow tomorrow. Do you think it will really happen? Put a tally mark below. Have a great day!

Love,
Steve and Tricia

YES 29   NO 11

A second-/third-grade message takes a survey and integrates learning about tally marks into the morning message.

10/22/09

Good morning researchers!
Think about the country you chose to research. Find it on the map. Look at the continents map on the bottom, in the middle. Which continent is your country on?

You may work in your poetry anthologies or choose books for your book box.

Best,
Ms. Shumway

A fourth-grade message invites the children to use a map to find the country they are researching. It also directs them to the first activities of the day.

Appendix 6   Community Writing Examples

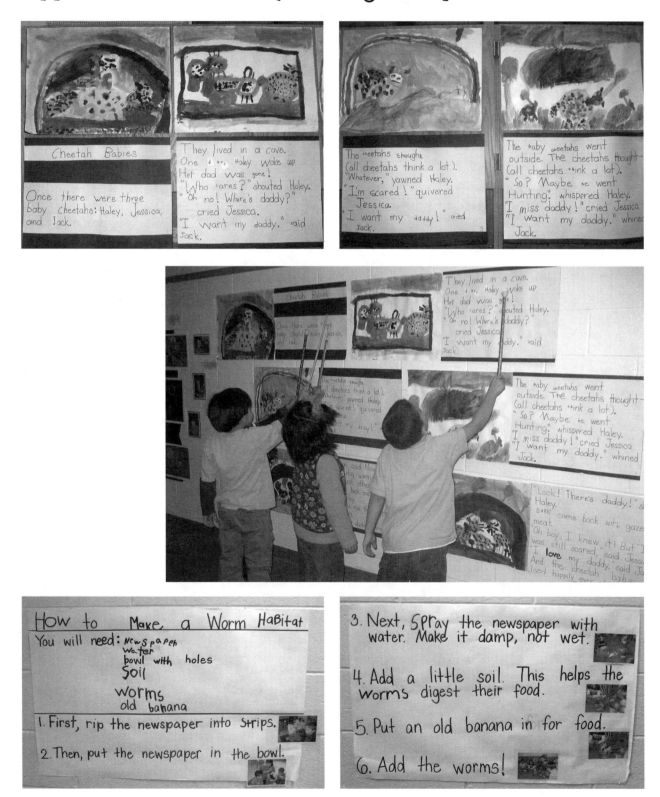

Appendix 6 Community Writing Examples (continued)

First, the Earth was clean. The truffula trees grew as big as giants! Animals lived and played happily. Until...

...The Onceler cut down the trees. He polluted the sky, land, Ponds and Earth. The Lorax yelled at him.

"I am the Lorax." I speak for the trees."

There was only one tree left! The sky was full of smog. The animals had to find a new home. The Lorax left. He was very sad.

"Good-bye World. I hope it gets clean again."

There was one truffula seed left. The Once-ler gave the seed to a Boy. The Lorax left stones that said "UNLESS" Now the word is perfectly clear!

"Unless Someone like you cares a whole awful lot, Nothing is going to get better. Its not."

Appendix 6   Community Writing Examples (continued)

Appendix 6 Community Writing Examples (continued)

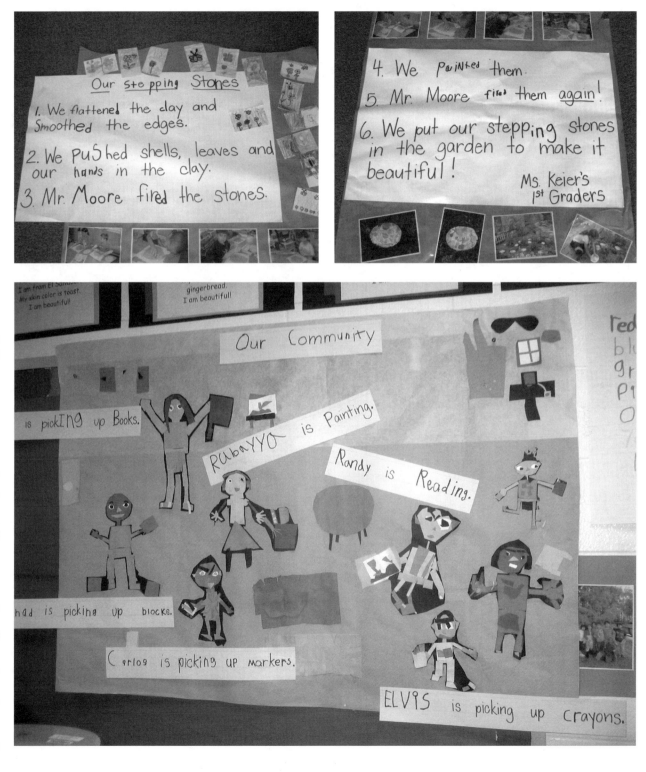

Our stepping Stones

1. We flattened the clay and Smoothed the edges.

2. We PuShed shells, leaves and our hands in the clay.

3. Mr. Moore fired the stones.

4. We Painted them.

5. Mr. Moore fired them again!

6. We put our stepping stones in the garden to make it beautiful!

Ms. Keier's 1st Graders

Our Community

is pickIng up Books.

RubaYYa is Painting.

Randy is Reading.

had is picking up blocks.

Carlos is picking up markers.

ELVIS is picking up crayons.

Appendix 7   Essential Elements of a Comprehensive Literacy Approach Planning Sheet

Lesson	Monday	Tuesday	Wednesday	Thursday	Friday
Reading To: • Read-Aloud Writing To: • Morning Message • Modeled Writing					
Reading With: • Interactive Read-Aloud • Shared Reading Writing With: • Shared Writing • Community Writing					
Reading By: • Independent Reading Writing By: • Independent Writing					

Appendix 8   A Few of Our Favorite Books for Read-Alouds

Creating a Community and Friendship

It's Mine! by Leo Lionni

The Peace Book by Todd Parr

The Kissing Hand by Audrey Penn

I Am America by Charles R. Smith

Stand Tall, Molly Lou Melon by Patty Lovell

Giraffes Can't Dance by Giles Andreae

ABC I Like Me! by Nancy Carlson

I Like Myself! by Karen Beaumont

We Are All Alike, We Are All Different by Cheltenham Elementary School

The Colors of Us by Karen Katz

Toot and Puddle series by Holly Hobbie

Big Words for Little People by Jamie Lee Curtis

I'm Gonna Like Me: Letting Off a Little Self-Esteem by Jamie Lee Curtis

The Land of Many Colors by Rita Pocock and Klamath County YMCA Preschool

Say Something by Peggy Moss

All the Colors of the Earth by Sheila Hamanaka

Whoever You Are by Mem Fox

The Skin You Live In by Michael Tyler

All the Colors We Are by Katie Kissinger

It's Okay to Be Different by Todd Parr

Skin Again by bell hooks

Mean Soup by Betsy Everitt

Scaredy Squirrel Makes a Friend by Melanie Watt

The Recess Queen by Alexis O'Neill

Have You Filled a Bucket Today? A Guide to Daily Happiness for Kids by Carol McCloud

Fun Books Your Kids Will Beg You to Read Again and Again

Skippyjon Jones series by Judy Schachner

Off We Go to Mexico! by Laurie Krebs

We're Sailing to Galapagos: A Week in the Pacific by Laurie Krebs

We're Sailing Down the Nile: A Journey Through Egypt by Laurie Krebs

The Baby Beebee Bird by Diane Redfield Massie

Little Bunny Foo Foo: Told and Sung by the Good Fairy by Paul Brett Johnson

Turkey Trouble by Wendi Silvano

Don't Let the Pigeon Drive the Bus! by Mo Willems

The Pigeon Finds a Hotdog! by Mo Willems

Knufflebunny: A Cautionary Tale by Mo Willems

Knufflebunny Too: A Case of Mistaken Identity by Mo Willems

The Pigeon Wants a Puppy! by Mo Willems

Otis by Loren Long

Chicken Soup with Rice by Maurice Sendak (music on iTunes by Carole King)

Jump Rope Magic by Afi Scruggs

Gotta Go! By Sam Swope

Robot Zot! by Jon Scieszka

No, David! by David Shannon

Mercy Watson series by Kate DiCamillo

Guess Again! by Mac Barnett

Piggie and Elephant series by Mo Willems

Diversity and Social Justice Issues

Edward the Emu by Sheena Knowles

Edwina the Emu by Sheena Knowles

It's Okay to Be Different by Todd Parr

A Castle on Viola Street by DyAnne DiSalvo

A Shelter in Our Car by Monica Gunning

Amelia and Eleanor Go for a Ride by Pam Muñoz Ryan

Angelo by David MacAulay

You and Me Together: Moms, Dads, and Kids Around the World by Barbara Kerley

Arnie and the New Kid by Nancy Carlson

Baseball Saved Us by Ken Mochizuki

The Bat Boy and His Violin by Gavin Curtis

Halmoni and the Picnic by Sook Nyul Choi

Jalapeño Bagels by Natasha Wing

Marianthe's Story: Painted Words, Spoken Memories by Aliki

Nadia's Hands by Karen English

Tomas and the Library Lady by Pat Mora

This Is My House by Arthur Dorros

We Share One World by Jane E. Hoffelt

The American Wei by Marion Hess Pomeranc

The Hello, Good-bye Window by Norman Juster

Hair for Mama by Kelly A. Tinkham

How My Parents Learned to Eat by Ina R. Friedman

Jack and Jim by Kitty Crowther

Appendix 8   A Few of Our Favorite Books for Read-Alouds (continued)

David's Drawings by Cathryn Falwell

The World Turns Round and Round by Nicki Weiss

Antonio's Card by Rigoberto Gonzalez

Babu's Song by Stephanie Stuve-Bodeen

Featherless by Juan Felipe Herrera

Puppies for Sale by Dan Clark

Playing War by Kathy Beckwith

Paths to Peace: People Who Changed the World by Jane Breskin Zalben

Talk Peace by Sam Williams

A Little Peace by Barbara Kerley

Your Move by Eve Bunting

What Does Peace Feel Like? by Vladimir Radunsky

Listen to the Wind by Greg Mortenson

If Peace Is . . . by Jane Baskwill

The Librarian of Basra by Jeanette Winter

Somewhere Today—A Book of Peace by Shelly Moore Thomas

Feathers and Fools by Mem Fox

Peace Begins with You by Katharine Scholes

The Other Side by Jacqueline Woodson

White Socks Only by Evelyn Coleman

Fly Away Home by Eve Bunting

A Day's Work by Eve Bunting

Ramadan Moon by Na'ima B. Robert

Nasreen's Secret School: A True Story from Afghanistan by Jeanette Winter

Poetry

Old Elm Speaks: Tree Poems by Kristine O'Connell George

Celebrate America in Poetry and Art by Smithsonian Institute

A Poke in the I by Paul B. Janeczko and Chris Raschka

Shape Me a Rhyme by Jane Yolen

All the Small Poems and Fourteen More by Valerie Worth

The Space Between Our Footsteps by Naomi Shihab Nye

Angels Ride Bikes and Other Fall Poems by Francisco X. Alarcon

Iguanas in the Snow and Other Winter Poems by Francisco X. Alarcon

Laughing Tomatoes and Other Spring Poems by Francisco X. Alarcon

Not a Copper Penny in Me House by Monica Gunning

Pieces: A Year in Poems and Quilts by Anna Grossnickle Hines

Hip Hop Speaks to Children: A Celebration of Poetry with a Beat by Nikki Giovanni

A Child's Calendar by John Updike

My Song Is Beautiful by Mary Ann Hoberman

Writing Mentor Texts: Books with Wonderful Words and Images to Inspire Young Writers and Good Conversation

The Best Part of Me: Children Talk About Their Bodies in Pictures and Words by Wendy Ewald

Hello, Harvest Moon by Ralph Fletcher

So Happy! by Kevin Henkes

Emerald Blue by Ann Marie Linden

All the Places to Love by Patricia Maclachlan

Snow by Cynthia Rylant

The Busy Tree by Jennifer Ward

In November by Cynthia Rylant

Water Dance by Thomas Locker

Cloud Dance by Thomas Locker

Mountain Dance by Thomas Locker

Sky Tree: Seeing Science Through Art by Thomas Locker

farfallina & marcel by Holly Keller

Pumpkin Shivaree by Rick Agran

Zero Is the Leaves on the Tree by Betsy Franco

Artful Reading by Bob Raczka

Max's Words by Kate Banks

Appendix 9   Examples of Teacher-Made Books

Appendix 9   Examples of Teacher-Made Books (continued)

I See Monarchs!

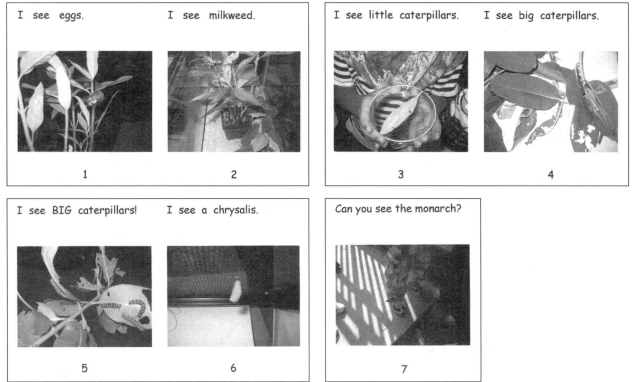

I see eggs.   I see milkweed.

1   2

I see little caterpillars.   I see big caterpillars.

3   4

I see BIG caterpillars!   I see a chrysalis.

5   6

Can you see the monarch?

7

Appendix 10 A Nonfiction Passage for a Shared Demonstration Related to Visualizing

How do snakes open their mouths so wide?

Unlike the human mouth, a snake's mouth is just right for taking in a big meal all at once.

First, the mouth is big because the jawbones are connected to the back of the skull, not the sides. When the mouth drops open, the long jaws make a big opening.

Second, the jaws can swing down far because they are not attached tightly to the skull. The jaw is linked to the end of a short bone, and the other end of the short bone is connected to the skull. The ligaments that hold these bones together are stretchy.

Finally, the two sides of the jawbone are not fused together at the chin. Instead, they are linked by another stretchy ligament that lets the two sides move apart.

So a snake's mouth can open wide partly because the jawbones can spread apart like sticks tied together with rubber bands.

From *Highlights*, March 2009, page 34. © Highlights for Children, Inc.

Appendix 11   A Nonfiction Passage for a Shared Demonstration Related to Visualizing

How come the moon seems to follow you when you move?

The moon seems to follow you because it's so far away. That idea may sound wrong. After all, how could something far away seem to follow along? To understand, start with objects that are much closer.

When you are riding in a car, close things seem to move by rapidly as you pass them. A tree or house by the road starts out ahead of you. It comes up fast, and in a few moments, it's far behind you.

Objects that are far away do not seem to move very fast. If you can see a faraway building or a mountain from a moving car, notice how long it takes for that object to pass by. Out West, you can sometimes ride toward mountains that never seem to get any closer.

The moon is more than 200,000 miles away. It is so far away that the motion of your car doesn't change its position enough for you to notice. So the moon just seems to follow you wherever you go.

Appendix 12 A Riddle Poem

I'm sometimes new
Yet always old
I shine like the sun
But I'm really cold.

I'm round like a ball
But I don't spin
So you can see my face
Again and again.

Though I'm up really high
A cow once jumped over
When astronauts came
They had a rover.

By Rick Johnson

Catching Readers Before They Fall

Appendix 13 Class Grid for _____

Appendix 14 Monthly Class List for Reading

Names												

RR—Running Record   **C—Conference**   **GR—Guided Reading**

Appendix 15 Individual Student Form

Name: _____ Dates: _____

Focus for Instruction: _____

_____

_____

Date	What is the child doing or almost doing?	What's next?

Appendix 16 Guided Reading Planning Sheet

Date: _____ Group: _____

Running Record: _____

New Book—Title/Level/Genre: _____

Introduction	Planning notes
M: meaning statement, question to activate background knowledge, new concepts, character names **S:** awkward language structures, literary language, irregular verb forms **V:** predict and locate, unusual text layout, new punctuation	
Focus for Strategy Instruction (before, during, and after reading) searching/gathering, predicting, activating schema, checking/confirming, maintaining fluency, self-monitoring, linking, making connections, visualizing, summarizing, questioning, inferring, evaluating, synthesizing	
After Reading	
Ideas to Keep in Mind During Discussion of Text	
Word Work examples of visual information (letters, clusters, endings, prefixes, irregular spellings, etc.)	
Students	Observations

Catching Readers Before They Fall: Supporting Readers Who Struggle, K–4 by Pat Johnson and Katie Keier. Copyright © 2010. Stenhouse Publishers. Adapted from original document created by: Literacy Coordinators, Pitt County Schools, North Carolina.

Appendix 17 Back to School Letter to Families

Dear Families,

I am looking forward to being your child's teacher this year! I believe that we are partners in your child's education, and I hope you will join me in making sure your child has a fabulous year! Please do not hesitate to contact me via telephone or email. Our classroom phone number (to leave a message), my cell phone number (after 7am and before 9pm please), and my email address are listed on the attached refrigerator magnet. Keeping in close communication will help support your child.

I welcome you in our classroom this year and look forward to sharing the exciting projects and learning we do in first grade. We will have several Author's and Reader's Celebrations where the children can share the writing and reading work they have done. Please join us in celebrating the wonderful work your growing readers and writers will do this year. You can look for announcements of upcoming family events in the weekly *Keier Flyer*—our class newsletter that comes home every Friday. This year, thanks to Mr. Buckley-Ess, our newsletter will be completely bilingual! English will be on one side, and Spanish on the other—and lots of great pictures of our class on both sides! I hope you enjoy seeing what we do each week.

The first grade curriculum is attached. Please let me know if you have any questions or concerns. Much of our learning is done in an inquiry-based approach, where children explore answers to their questions through reading, writing, researching, and observing the world around them. Our first big unit will be a study of monarch butterflies. We will have the eggs, caterpillars, and eventually the butterflies in our classroom. Through the magic of these insects, we will learn about seasonal changes, migration patterns, Mexico, maps, and different cultures. We will connect with a class in Mexico (where the monarchs migrate) and learn about children there and how the monarchs live in their overwintering sites. Of course, we will be doing lots of reading and writing as well as scientific observations and investigations throughout this unit.

I am looking forward to a wonderful year. It is a privilege to work with you and your child. Thank you for your support in what promises to be a fabulous first-grade year!

Sincerely,

Appendix 18 Strategy Language Bookmark

Today, _____ had a reading conference with me. Here are some of the great things your reader did today: __Pointed once under each word. __Looked at the pictures to figure out a new word. __Used the pictures *and* the sounds in the word to figure out a new word. __Reread the sentence to figure out a new word. __Reread the sentence to check on a prediction or a word. __Fixed mistakes. __Used the part he or she knew in a word to figure out a new word (in : **win**ter) __Thought about what made sense in the *story* to figure out a new word. __When reading a new word, thought about if it looked right, sounded right, and made sense in the story.	Today, _____ had a reading conference with me. Here are some of the great things your reader did today: __Pointed once under each word. __Looked at the pictures to figure out a new word. __Used the pictures *and* the sounds in the word to figure out a new word. __Reread the sentence to figure out a new word. __Reread the sentence to check on a prediction or a word. __Fixed mistakes. __Used the part he or she knew in a word to figure out a new word (in : **win**ter) __Thought about what made sense in the *story* to figure out a new word. __When reading a new word, thought about if it looked right, sounded right, and made sense in the story.	Today, _____ had a reading conference with me. Here are some of the great things your reader did today: __Pointed once under each word. __Looked at the pictures to figure out a new word. __Used the pictures *and* the sounds in the word to figure out a new word. __Reread the sentence to figure out a new word. __Reread the sentence to check on a prediction or a word. __Fixed mistakes. __Used the part he or she knew in a word to figure out a new word (in : **win**ter) __Thought about what made sense in the *story* to figure out a new word. __When reading a new word, thought about if it looked right, sounded right, and made sense in the story.

Appendix 19 Keier Flyer

The Keier Flyer
Room 210 - Bailey's Elementary School
Ms. Keier's Fabulous First-Grade News! - Volume 19
Week of March 9, 2009

Ask Me About:
** The books we read this week:
<u>Duck at the Door</u>, <u>I Saw an Ant on the Railroad Track</u>, <u>Once I Ate a Pie</u>, <u>Mammoths on the Move</u>, <u>Listen to the Wind</u>, <u>Jess Makes Hair Gel</u>

**Reading Workshop – Virginia Young Readers' books, voting on our favorite book, nonfiction text features

**Writing Workshop – writing an exciting lead (opening to our books), revising our nonfiction books with CAT - Change, Add and Take away

**Math Workshop – fact families, explaining our thinking in words and pictures, writing in our math journals, growing patterns, addition and subtraction turn around facts

**Science Workshop – scientific observations of dissolved mixtures, sticky test to determine what materials are good to make glue, making our own glue recipe, using the Predictions, Results and Conclusions charts

**Social Studies Workshop – we saw a performance in the blackbox theatre about famous Americans

We shared our predictions and created a recipe for glue. We will do the strength test tomorrow!

We made stepping stones for the butterfly garden. Mr. Moore came and showed us how to cut the clay and then do impressions of leaves, shells or our handprints. It was a lot of fun! He took them home to fire them. He will be back on the 26th for us to paint them!

Hicimos piedras especiales para nuestro jardín de mariposas. El Sr. Moore nos mostró como cortar la arcilla y hacer impresiones de hojas, conchas o nuestras manos. ¡Nos divertimos mucho! El se llevó las impresiones a su casa para hornearlas. ¡Regresarán el 26 de marzo y las pintaremos!

**Taller de Lectura – Libros de los Jóvenes de Virginia, Votamos por nuestro favorito, características de libros no-ficción

**Taller de Escritura – escribir una apertura interesante de un cuento, revisar nuestros libros de no-ficción con CAT - Cambio, Añadir, Quitar

**Taller de Matemáicas – familias de suma y resta, explicar nuestro pensamiento en palabras y dibujos, escribir en los cuadernos de matemática, patrones que crecen, tablas de suma y resta

**Taller de Ciencias – observaciones científicas de mezclas disueltas, prueba de cosas pegajosas para determinar cual material haría un buen pegamento, hacer nuestras propias recetas de pegamento, usar las gráficas de Predicciones, Resultados y Conclusiones

**Taller de Estudios Sociales – vimos una presentación en el teatro de Americanos famosos

Catching Readers Before They Fall: Supporting Readers Who Struggle, K–4 by Pat Johnson and Katie Keier. Copyright © 2010. Stenhouse Publishers.

Appendix 20 Bookmark with Conversation Starters

Reading with Your Child	Leyendo con su niño/a
Here are some questions to help you get started in conversations about books and reading. Enjoy your time!	Estas son algunas preguntas que le ayudarán a tener una conversación sobre la lectura y el libro. ¡Esperamos que disfrute esta actividad!
• What did you notice?	• ¿Qué notaste o en que pensaste al leer?
• Does this book remind you of anything?	• ¿Te recuerda de algo este libro?
• What have you been wondering as you read?	• ¿Qué te preguntabas mientras leías?
• Does this book make you think of anything else you've read?	• ¿Te hace pensar este libro en otra cosa que has leído?
• What was your favorite part?	• ¿Cuál fue tu parte favorita?
• Was there a part of the book that surprised you? Why?	• ¿Hay alguna parte del libro que te sorprendió? ¿Por qué?
• Any other thoughts on what you just read?	• ¿Tienes algo más que decir de lo que acabas de leer?
• What are you going to read next?	• ¿Qué otro libro vas a leer?

REFERENCES

Children's Books

Ackerman, Karen. 1988. *Song and Dance Man.* New York: Knopf.

Alexander, Claire. 2008. *Lucy and the Bully.* Morton Grove, IL: Albert Whitman.

Arnold, Tedd. 2003. *More Parts.* New York: Puffin.

Aston, Dianna Hutts. 2006. *An Egg Is Quiet.* San Francisco: Chronicle.

———. 2007. *A Seed Is Sleepy.* San Francisco: Chronicle.

Baylor, Byrd. 1985. *Guess Who My Favorite Person Is.* New York: Atheneum.

———. 1998. *The Table Where Rich People Sit.* New York: Aladdin.

Brett, Jan. 1989. *Annie and the Wild Animals.* Boston: Sandpiper.

Brooks, Geraldine. 2005. *March.* New York: Viking.

Browne, Anthony. 2001. *Voices in the Park.* New York: DK.

———. 2002. *Zoo.* New York: Farrar, Straus & Giroux.

———. 2008. *Changes.* New York: Walker.

Brumbeau, Jeff. 2001. *The Quiltmaker's Gift.* New York: Scholastic.

Bynum, Janie. 2003. *Otis.* New York: Voyager.

Cisneros, Sandra. 1991. *Woman Hollering Creek and Other Stories.* New York: Random House.

Cole, Babette. 2005. *Princess Smartypants.* Kirkwood, NY: Putnam.

Cowcher, Helen. 1997. *Tigress.* Chicago, IL: Milet.

———. 1997. *Antarctica.* Chicago, IL: Milet.

Cowley, Joy. 1982. *Number One.* Katonah, New York: Richard C. Owen.

———. 1992. *The Little Yellow Chicken.* Chicago, IL: Wright Group.

———. 2001. *Dan, The Flying Man.* Auckland, New Zealand: Shortland.

Crimi, Carolyn. 2001. *Don't Need Friends.* New York: Dragonfly.

Cronin, Doreen. 2001. *Click, Clack, Moo.* New York: Scholastic.

———. 2002. *Giggle, Giggle, Quack.* New York: Antheneum.

———. 2003. *Diary of a Worm.* New York: HarperCollins.

———. 2006. *Dooby Dooby Moo.* New York: Antheneum.

———. 2007. *Diary of a Fly.* New York: HarperCollins.

Davies, Nicola. 2008. *Bat Loves the Night.* New York: Walker.

DiCamillo, Kate. 2007. *Great Joy.* Cambridge, MA: Candlewick.

Dotlich, Rebecca Kai. 2001. *When Riddles Come Rumbling: Poems to Ponder.* Honesdale, PA: Boyds Mills Press.

Ernst, Lisa Campbell. 2006. *The Gingerbread Girl.* New York: Penguin.

Fleming, Denise. 1995. *In the Tall, Tall Grass.* New York: Henry Holt.

———. 2008. *Buster Goes to Cowboy Camp.* New York: Henry Holt.

Fletcher, Ralph. 2003. *Hello, Harvest Moon*. New York: Clarion.

Fox, Mem. 1994. *Koala Lou*. New York: Voyager.

———. 1998. *Tough Boris*. New York: Voyager.

Galdone, Joanna. 1984. *Tailypo: A Ghost Story*. Mooloolaba, Australia: Sandpiper.

Giles, Jenny. 1997. *Chug the Tractor*. Boston: Rigby.

Glaser, Linda. 2000. *Fabulous Frogs*. Brookfield, CT: Millbrook.

Gordon, Anne. 2001. *Crocodilians*. Auckland, New Zealand: Shortland.

Gravett, Emily. 2006. *Wolves*. New York: Simon and Schuster.

Gray, Nigel. 1999. *A Country Far Away*. Cincinnati, OH: Anderson.

Hartley, Karen, and Chris Macro. 2006. *Ladybugs*. Portsmouth, NH: Heinemann.

Henkes, Kevin. 1991. *Chester's Way*. London: Puffin.

———. 1995. *Julius, the Baby of the World*. New York: Greenwillow.

———. 1998. *Jessica*. New York: Greenwillow.

———. 2005. *Olive's Ocean*. New York: Greenwillow.

———. 2006. *Owen*. Scottsdale, AZ: Everest.

Hobbs, Will. 1995. *Downriver*. New York: Laurel Leaf.

Hoffman, Mary. 1991. *Amazing Grace*. New York: Dial.

Holm, Jennifer. 2005. *Babymouse #1: Queen of the World*. New York: Random House.

Howe, James. 2003. *Horace and Morris, but Mostly Dolores*. New York: Aladdin.

Hunt, Roderick. 1997. *Skipper's Birthday*. New York: Oxford University Press.

Hutchins, Pat. 1992. *You'll Soon Grow into Them, Titch*. New York: HarperCollins.

Kasza, Keiko. 2005. *My Lucky Day*. New York: Puffin.

Knowles, Sheena. 1997. *Edwina the Emu*. New York: HarperCollins.

———. 1998. *Edward the Emu*. New York: HarperCollins.

Kulka, Joe. 2007. *Wolf's Coming!* Minneapolis, MN: Carolrhoda.

Lester, Helen. 1989. *A Porcupine Named Fluffy*. Boston: Sandpiper.

———. 1990. *Tacky the Penguin*. Boston: Houghton Mifflin.

———. 1995. *Me First*. Boston: Sandpiper.

———. 2003. *Something Might Happen*. Boston: Houghton Mifflin.

———. 2004. *Tackylocks and the Three Bears*. Boston: Sandpiper.

———. 2005. *Tacky in Trouble*. Boston: Sandpiper.

Levenson, George. 2002. *Pumpkin Circle*. Berkley, CA: Tricycle Press.

Lobel, Arnold. 1975. *Owl at Home*. New York: Scholastic.

Long, Melinda. 2003. *How I Became a Pirate*. San Diego, CA: Harcourt.

Lowry, Lois. 2002. *The Giver*. New York: Laurel Leaf.

Markle, Sandra. 2009. *Little Lost Bat*. Watertown, MA: Charlesbridge.

McNaughton, Colin. 1998. *Suddenly!* Glasgow, Scotland: Collins Educational.

Munsch, Robert N. 1992. *Paper Bag Princess*. Toronto, Ontario: Annick.

———. 1998. *Andrew's Loose Tooth*. New York: Scholastic.

———. 2007. *Stephanie's Ponytail*. Toronto, Ontario: Annick.

Naylor, Phyllis Reynolds. 2000. *Shiloh.* New York: Aladdin.

O'Neill, Alexis. 2002. *The Recess Queen.* New York: Scholastic.

Orloff, Karen Kaufman. 2004. *I Wanna Iguana.* Kirkwood, NY: Putnam.

Osborne, Mary Pope. 2005. *Kate and the Beanstalk.* New York: Aladdin.

Packard, Mary. 2002. *Ripley's Believe It or Not.* New York: Scholastic.

Parkes, Brenda. 1997a. *Who's in the Shed?* San Francisco: Mimosa.

———. 1997b. *The Enormous Watermelon.* San Francisco: Mimosa.

Parr, Todd. 1999. *This Is My Hair.* New York: Little, Brown.

———. 2009. *The Peace Book.* New York: Little, Brown.

Pinkwater, Daniel. 1977. *The Big Orange Splot.* New York: Scholastic.

Polacco, Patricia. 2006. *Rotten Richie and the Ultimate Dare.* New York: Philomel.

Raffi. 1999. *Down by the Bay.* New York: Crown Books.

Randell, Beverley, 1995. *Pepper's Adventure.* Boston: Houghton Mifflin Harcourt.

———. 2003. *Baby Bear's New Name.* Crystal Lake, IL: Rigby Education.

Randell, Beverley, Jenny Giles, and Annette Smith. 1996. *The Shopping Mall.* Crystal Lake, IL: Rigby Education.

Raschka, Chris. 1993. *Yo! Yes?* New York: Scholastic.

———. 2000. *Ring! Yo?* New York: DK.

Reynolds, Peter. 2003. *The Dot.* Cambridge, MA: Candlewick.

———. 2004. *Ish.* Cambridge, MA: Candlewick.

Rosenthal, Amy Krouse. 2006. *One of Those Days.* Kirkwood, NY: Putnam.

Rylant, Cynthia. 1987. *Henry and Mudge, The First Book.* New York: Bradbury.

———. 1988. *Every Living Thing.* New York: Atheneum.

Sayre, April Pulley. 2005. *Stars Beneath Your Bed: The Surprising Story of Dust.* New York: Greenwillow.

Schachner, Judy. 2008. *Skippyjon Jones in the Doghouse.* London: Puffin.

Schwartz, Alvin. 1986. *More Scary Stories to Tell in the Dark.* New York: HarperCollins.

Scieszka, Jon. 1992. *The Stinky Cheese Man and Other Fairly Stupid Tales.* New York: Viking.

———. 1994. *The Frog Prince, Continued.* New York: Puffin.

———. 1996. *The True Story of the Three Little Pigs!* New York: Puffin.

———. 2007. *Cowboy and Octopus.* New York: Viking.

———. 2008. *Smash! Crash!* New York: Simon and Schuster.

———. 2009. *Robot Zot!* New York: Simon and Schuster.

Sendak, Maurice. 1988. *Where the Wild Things Are.* New York: HarperTrophy.

Serafini, Frank. 2008a. *Looking Closely Along the Shore.* Tonawanda, NY: Kids Can Press.

———. 2008b. *Looking Closely Through the Forest.* Tonawanda, NY: Kids Can Press.

Shannon, David. 2005. *Alice the Fairy.* New York: Scholastic.

———. 2006. *No, David!* New York: Hippo.

Smith, Annette. 2000. *The Little Work Plane.* Cheltenham, United Kingdom: Nelson Thornes.

————. 2001. *New Glasses for Max*. Barrington, IL: Rigby Education.

————. 2006. *The Leaf Boats*. Austin, TX: Harcourt Achieve.

Smith, J. D. 2008. *The Best Mariachi in the World*. McHenry, IL: Raven Tree Press.

Squires, Janet. 2006. *The Gingerbread Cowboy*. New York: HarperCollins.

Stanley, Diane. 2007. *Goldie and the Three Bears*. New York: HarperCollins.

Starbright Foundation. 2001. *Once Upon a Fairy Tale*. Los Angeles: Viking.

Steig, William. 1990. *Spinky Sulks*. New York: Trumpet Clubs.

————. 1996. *The Toy Brother*. New York: HarperCollins.

Sturges, Philemon. 2002. *The Little Red Hen (Makes a Pizza)*. New York: Puffin.

Swope, Sam. 2001. *The Araboolies of Liberty Street*. New York: Farrar, Straus & Giroux.

Thomas, Joyce Carol. 2008. *The Blacker the Berry*. New York: Amistad.

Tolhurst, Marilyn. 1994. *Somebody and the Three Blairs*. New York: Scholastic.

Trivizas, Eugene. 1997. *The Three Little Wolves and the Big Bad Pig*. New York: McElderry.

Turner, Ann. 1986. *Street Talk*. Boston: Houghton Mifflin.

Urbanovic, Jackie. 2007. *Duck at the Door*. New York: HarperCollins.

Van Allsburg, Chris. 1979. *The Garden of Abdul Gasazi*. Boston: Houghton Mifflin.

————. 1987. *The Z Was Zapped*. Boston: Houghton Mifflin.

————. 1988. *Two Bad Ants*. Boston: Houghton Mifflin.

————. 1991. *The Wretched Stone*. Boston: Houghton Mifflin.

————. 1992. *The Widow's Broom*. Boston: Houghton Mifflin.

————. 1996. *The Mysteries of Harris Burdick*. Boston: Houghton Mifflin.

————. 2006. *Probuditi!* Boston: Houghton Mifflin.

Waber, Bernard. 2002. *Courage*. Boston: Houghton Mifflin.

————. 2005. *Fast Food! Gulp! Gulp!* Boston: Walter Lorraine Books.

Waddell, Martin. 2007. *Bee Frog*. Cambridge, MA: Candlewick.

Wick, Walter. 1997. *A Drop of Water*. New York: Scholastic.

Wiles, Deborah. 2001. *Freedom Summer*. New York: Atheneum.

Willis, Jeanne. 2005. *Tadpole's Promise*. New York: Antheneum.

Wong, Janet. 2000. *The Trip Back Home*. San Diego, CA: Harcourt.

Yashima, Taro. 1976. *Crow Boy*. New York: Puffin.

Yolen, Jane. 1997. *Nocturne*. New York: Harcourt.

Young, Ed. 2009. *Hook*. New York: Roaring Brook.

Young, Judy. 2009. *Minnow and Rose*. Chelsea, MI: Sleeping Bear Press.

Ziefert, Harriet. 2003. *31 Uses for a Mom*. Kirkwood, NY: Putnam.

Professional Resources

Allen, Janet. 2002. *On the Same Page: Shared Reading Beyond the Primary Grades*. Portland, ME: Stenhouse.

Allen, Jennifer. 2009. *A Sense of Belonging: Sustaining and Retaining New Teachers*. Portland, ME: Stenhouse.

Allington, Richard. 2005. *What Really Matters for Struggling Readers: Designing Research-Based Programs.* 2nd ed. New York: Longman.

Allington, Richard, and Anne McGill-Franzen. 2008. "Got Books?" *Educational Leadership* 65(7): 20–23.

Anderson, Carl. 2000. *How's It Going? A Practical Guide to Conferring with Student Writers.* Portsmouth, NH: Heinemann.

———. 2005. *Assessing Writers.* Portsmouth, NH: Heinemann.

Beaver, Joetta, and Mark A. Carter. 2006. *Developmental Reading Assessment 2.* Lebanon, IN: Pearson Learning.

Berk, Laura E., and Adam Winsler. 1995. *Scaffolding Children's Learning: Vygotsky and Early Childhood Education.* Washington, DC: National Association for the Education of Young Children.

Berliner, David C., and Bruce J. Biddle. 1996. *The Manufactured Crisis: Myths, Fraud, and the Attack on America's Public Schools.* Basic Books.

Boushey, Gail, and Joan Moser. 2006. *The Daily Five: Fostering Literacy Independence in the Elementary Grades.* Portland, ME: Stenhouse.

———. 2009. *The CAFE Book: Engaging All Students in Daily Literacy Assessment and Instruction.* Portland, ME. Stenhouse.

Calkins, Lucy. 1994. *The Art of Teaching Writing.* Portsmouth, NH: Heinemann.

———. 2005. Keynote address at Reading Recovery conference, Columbus, OH.

Calkins, Lucy, and colleagues. 2007. *Units of Study for Primary Writing: A Yearlong Curriculum (Grades K–2).* Portsmouth, NH: Heinemann.

Cambourne, Brian. 1988. *The Whole Story: Natural Learning and the Acquisition of Literacy in the Classroom.* New York: Scholastic.

Charney, Ruth. 2002. *Teaching Children to Care: Classroom Management for Ethical and Academic Growth, K–8.* Northeast Foundation for Children.

Clay, Marie M. 1991. *Becoming Literate: The Construction of Inner Control.* Portsmouth, NH: Heinemann.

———. 1998. *By Different Paths to Common Outcomes.* Portland, ME: Stenhouse.

———. 2000. *Running Records for Classroom Teachers.* Portsmouth, NH: Heinemann.

———. 2001. *Change Over Time in Children's Literacy Development.* Portsmouth, NH: Heinemann.

———. 2005a. *Literacy Lessons: Designed for Individuals, Part I: Why? When? and How?* Portsmouth, NH: Heinemann.

———. 2005b. *Literacy Lessons: Designed for Individuals, Part II: Teaching Procedures.* Portsmouth, NH: Heinemann.

———. 2007. *An Observation Survey of Early Literacy Achievement.* Portsmouth, NH: Heinemann.

Clayton, Marlynn K., and Mary Beth Forton. 2001. *Classroom Spaces That Work.* Greenfield, MA: Northeast Foundation for Children.

Cole, Ardith Davis. 2003. *Knee to Knee, Eye to Eye: Circling in on Comprehension.* Portsmouth, NH: Heinemann.

Collins, Kathy. 2004. *Growing Readers: Units of Study in the Primary Classroom.* Portland, ME: Stenhouse.

———. 2008. *Reading for Real: Teach Students to Read with Power, Intention, and Joy in K–3.* Portland, ME: Stenhouse.

Corgill, Ann Marie. 2008. *Of Primary Importance: What's Essential in Teaching Young Writers.* Portland, ME: Stenhouse.

Cullinan, Bernice. 1992. *Invitation to Read: More Children's Literature in the Reading Program.* Newark, DE: International Reading Association.

Curtis, Deb, and Margie Carter. 2003. *Designs for Living and Learning: Transforming Early Childhood Environments.* St. Paul, MN: Redleaf Press.

Daunis, Sarah, and Maria Cassiani Iams. 2007. *Text Savvy: Using a Shared Reading Framework to Build Comprehension, Grades 3–6.* Portsmouth, NH: Heinemann.

Diller, Debbie. 2003. *Literacy Work Stations: Making Centers Work.* Portland, ME: Stenhouse.

———. 2008. *Spaces and Places: Designing Classrooms for Literacy.* Portland, ME: Stenhouse.

Dorn, Linda, and Carla Soffos. 2001. *Shaping Literate Minds: Developing Self-Regulated Learners.* Portland, ME: Stenhouse.

———. 2005. *Teaching for Deep Comprehension: A Reading Workshop Approach.* Portland, ME: Stenhouse.

Fairfax County Public Schools. 1998. "Sound Teaching." Resource Kit. Fairfax County, VA: Fairfax County Public Schools.

Fay, Kathleen, and Suzanne Whaley. 2004. *Becoming One Community: Reading and Writing with English Language Learners.* Portland, ME: Stenhouse.

Fisher, Bobbi, and Emily Fisher Medvic. 2000. *Perspectives on Shared Reading: Planning and Practice.* Portsmouth, NH: Heinemann.

Fletcher, Ralph. 2006. *Boy Writers: Reclaiming Their Voices.* Portland, ME: Stenhouse.

Fletcher, Ralph, and JoAnn Portalupi. 2001. *Writing Workshop: The Essential Guide.* Portsmouth, NH: Heinemann.

Fountas, Irene, and Gay Su Pinnell. 1996. *Guided Reading: Good First Teaching for All Children.* Portsmouth, NH: Heinemann.

———. 1998. *Voices on Word Matters: Learning About Phonics and Spelling in the Literacy Classroom.* Portsmouth, NH: Heinemann.

———. 2001. *Guiding Readers & Writers, Grades 3–6.* Portsmouth, NH: Heinemann.

———. 2006. *Teaching for Comprehending and Fluency: Thinking, Talking, and Writing About Reading, K–8.* Portsmouth, NH: Heinemann.

———. 2007. *Fountas and Pinnell Benchmark Assessment System.* Portsmouth, NH: Heinemann.

———. 2009. *When Readers Struggle: Teaching That Works.* Portsmouth, NH: Heinemann.

Freire, Paulo. 2005. *Teachers as Cultural Workers: Letters to Those Who Dare to Teach*. Boulder, CO: Westview Press.

Frost, Shari. 2009. "Towards Thoughtful Strategy Instruction." Choice Literacy. http://www.choiceliteracy.com/public/853.cfm.

Fullerton, Susan K. 1997. "What's in a Name?: Teaching Print Conventions Using Children's Names." Paper presented at the Virginia State Reading Association Annual Conference, Arlington, VA.

Gandini, Lella. 1998. "Educational and Caring Spaces." In *The Hundred Languages of Children: The Reggio Emilia Approach to Early Childhood Education—Advanced Reflections*, ed. C. Edwards, L. Gandini, & G. Forman. Norwood, NJ: Ablex.

Garan, Elaine. 2007. *Smart Answers to Tough Questions: What to Say When You're Asked About Fluency, Phonics, Grammar, Vocabulary, SSR, Tests, Support for ELLs, and More*. New York: Scholastic.

Gilles, Carol. 1992. "How Can Whole Language Help the 'Labeled' Learner?" In *Questions and Answers About Whole Language*, ed. O. Cochrane. New York: Richard C. Owen.

Glover, Matt. 2009. *Engaging Young Writers, Preschool–Grade 1*. Portsmouth, NH: Heinemann.

Graves, Donald. 1994. *A Fresh Look at Writing*. Portsmouth, NH: Heinemann.

Greene, Amy H., and Glennon D. Melton. 2007. *Test Talk: Integrating Test Preparation into Reading Workshop*. Portland, ME: Stenhouse.

Gruen, Sara. 2007. *Water for Elephants*. Chapel Hill, NC: Algonquin Books.

Harste, Jerome. 1992. "We Seem to Have Everyone Now Claiming to Use Whole Language. Just What Exactly Is and What Is Not Whole Language?" In *Questions and Answers About Whole Language*, ed. O. Cochrane. New York: Richard C. Owen.

Harvey, Stephanie, and Anne Goudvis. 2000. *Strategies That Work: Teaching Comprehension to Enhance Understanding*. Portland, ME: Stenhouse.

———. 2007. *Strategies That Work: Teaching Comprehension for Understanding and Engagement*. 2nd ed. Portland, ME: Stenhouse.

———. 2008. *The Comprehension Toolkit: Language and Lessons for Active Literacy (Grades 3–6)*. Portsmouth, NH: Heinemann.

———. 2008. *The Primary Comprehension Toolkit: Language and Lessons for Active Literacy (Grades K–2)*. Portsmouth, NH: Heinemann.

Harwayne, Shelley. 2000. *Lifetime Guarantees: Toward Ambitious Literacy Teaching*. Portsmouth, NH: Heinemann.

Heard, Georgia, and Jennifer McDonough. 2009. *A Place for Wonder: Reading and Writing Nonfiction in the Primary Grades*. Portland, ME: Stenhouse.

Holdaway, Don. 1979. *The Foundations of Literacy*. New York: Scholastic.

Horan, Nancy. 2008. *Loving Frank*. New York: Ballantine.

Horn, Martha, and Mary Ellen Giacobbe. 2007. *Talking, Drawing, Writing: Lessons for Our Youngest Writers*. Portland, ME: Stenhouse.

Johnson, Pat. 2006. *One Child at a Time: Making the Most of Your Time with Struggling Readers, K–6*. Portland, ME: Stenhouse.

Johnston, Peter. 2000. *Running Records: A Self-Tutoring Guide*. Book and audio cassette. Portland, ME: Stenhouse.

———. 2004. *Choice Words: How Our Language Affects Children's Learning*. Portland, ME: Stenhouse.

———. 2007. "Revolutionary Contributions." *The Journal of Reading Recovery* 7 (1): 67–68.

Keene, Ellin Oliver. 2008. *To Understand: New Horizons in Reading Comprehension*. Portsmouth, NH: Heinemann.

Keene, Ellin Oliver, and Susan Zimmermann. 1997. *Mosaic of Thought: Teaching Comprehension in a Reader's Workshop*. Portsmouth, NH: Heinemann.

———. 2007. *Mosaic of Thought: The Power of Comprehension Strategy Instruction*. 2nd ed. Portsmouth, NH: Heinemann.

Kohn, Alfie. 1994. *The Risks of Rewards*. ERIC/EECE Clearinghouse on Elementary and Early Childhood Education. Available online at http://www.alfiekohn.org/teaching/pdf/The%20Risks%20of%20Rewards.pdf.

Krashen, Stephen. 2004. *The Power of Reading: Insights from the Research*. 2nd ed. Portsmouth, NH: Heinemann.

Kriete, Roxanne, and Lynn Bechtel. 2002. *The Morning Meeting Book*. Turners Falls, MA: Northeast Foundation for Children.

Kucer, Stephen B. 2005. *Dimensions of Literacy: A Conceptual Base for Teaching Reading and Writing in School Settings*. Mahwah, NJ: Lawrence Erlbaum.

Lyons, Carol. 2003. *Teaching Struggling Readers: How to Use Brain-Based Research to Maximize Learning*. Portsmouth, NH: Heinemann.

Martel, Yann. 2001. *Life of Pi*. San Diego, CA: Harcourt.

McBride, Maryann. 2009. "Meaning: The Glue and the Grease." Presentation at the National Reading Recovery and K–6 Classroom Literacy Conference, Columbus, OH.

McCarrier, Andrea. 2008. "Engaging Children in a Writing Process Through Community Writing." In *Guiding K–3 Writers to Independence: The New Essentials* by Patricia L. Scharer and Gay Su Pinnell. New York: Scholastic.

McCarrier, Andrea, Gay Su Pinnell, and Irene Fountas. 2000. *Interactive Writing: How Language & Literacy Come Together, K–2*. Portsmouth, NH: Heinemann.

Mere, Cathy. 2005. *More Than Guided Reading: Finding the Right Instructional Mix*. Portland, ME: Stenhouse.

Miller, Debbie. 2002. *Reading with Meaning: Teaching Comprehension in the Primary Grades*. Portland, ME: Stenhouse.

———. 2008. *Teaching with Intention: Defining Beliefs, Aligning Practice, Taking Action*. Portland, ME: Stenhouse.

Miller, Donalyn. The Book Whisperer. http://blogs.edweek.org/teachers/book_whisperer/.

Mooney, Margaret E. 1990. *Reading To, With, and By Children*. Katonah, NY: Richard C. Owen.

Nichols, Maria. 2006. *Comprehension Through Conversation: The Power of Purposeful Talk in the Reading Workshop*. Portsmouth, NH: Heinemann.

Owocki, Gretchen. 2003. *Comprehension: Strategic Instruction for K–3 Students*. Portsmouth, NH: Heinemann.

Parker, Emelie, and Tess Pardini. 2006. *"The Words Came Down!": English Language Learners Read, Write, and Talk Across the Curriculum, K–2*. Portland, ME: Stenhouse.

Parkes, Brenda. 2000. *Read It Again! Revisiting Shared Reading*. Portland, ME: Stenhouse.

Partners in Print. http://www.pacificlearning.com/p-3862-partners-in-print-englishspanish-combo-package-primary.aspx.

Payne, Carleen daCruz. 2005. *Shared Reading for Today's Classroom: Lessons and Strategies for Explicit Instruction in Comprehension, Fluency, Word Study, and Genre*. New York: Scholastic.

Payne, Carleen daCruz, and Mary Browning Schulman. 1998. *Getting the Most Out of Morning Message and Other Shared Writing Lessons*. New York: Scholastic.

Pearson, P. David. 2000. Address at the Ohio Reading Recovery Conference.

Pearson, P. David, and M. C. Gallagher. 1983. "The Instruction of Reading Comprehension." *Contemporary Educational Psychology* 8: 317–344.

Ranger Rick. 2008. "Iguanas." *Ranger Rick*. July: 24–27

———. 2008. "Masked Bandits." *Ranger Rick*. May: 16–19.

Ray, Katie Wood. 2006. *Study Driven: A Framework for Planning Units of Study in the Writing Workshop*. Portsmouth, NH: Heinemann.

Ray, Katie Wood, with Lisa Cleaveland. 2004. *About the Authors: Writing Workshop with Our Youngest Writers*. Portsmouth, NH: Heinemann.

Ray, Katie Wood, and Matt Glover. 2008. *Already Ready: Nurturing Writers in Preschool and Kindergarten*. Portsmouth, NH: Heinemann.

Ray, Katie Wood, with Lester Laminack. 2001. *The Writing Workshop: Working Through the Hard Parts (And They're All Hard Parts)*. Urbana, IL: National Council of Teachers of English.

Rosenblatt, Louise. 1994. *The Reader, the Text, the Poem: The Transactional Theory of the Literary Work*. Rev. ed. Carbondale: Southern Illinois University Press.

Routman, Regie. 2003. *Reading Essentials: The Specifics You Need to Teach Reading Well*. Portsmouth, NH: Heinemann.

———. 2007. *Teaching Essentials: Expecting the Most and Getting the Best from Every Learner, K–8*. Portsmouth, NH: Heinemann.

Scharer, Patricia, and Gay Su Pinnell. 2008. *Guiding K–3 Writers to Independence*. New York: Scholastic.

Schulman, Mary Browning. 2006. *Guided Reading in Grades 3–6: Everything You Need to Make Small-Group Reading Instruction Work in Your Classroom*. New York: Scholastic.

Schulman, Mary Browning, and Carleen daCruz Payne. 2000. *Guided Reading: Making It Work*. New York: Scholastic.

Sibberson, Franki, and Karen Szymusiak. 2003. *Still Learning to Read: Teaching Students in Grades 3–6*. Portland, ME: Stenhouse.

Smith, Frank. 1994. *Understanding Reading: A Psycholinguistic Analysis of Reading and Learning to Read*. Hillsdale, NJ: Lawrence Erlbaum.

———. 1998. *The Book of Learning and Forgetting*. New York: Teachers College Press.

———. 2005. *Reading Without Nonsense*. New York: Teachers College Press.

Squire, Larry. 1996. *Your Brain*. The Dana Foundation. Video.

Stead, Tony. 2008. *Good Choice! Supporting Independent Reading and Response, K–6*. Portland, ME: Stenhouse.

Strachota, Bob. 1996. *On Their Side: Helping Children Take Charge of Their Learning*. Turners Falls, MA: Northeast Foundation for Children.

Szymusiak, Karen, Franki Sibberson, and Lisa Koch. 2008. *Beyond Leveled Books: Supporting Early and Transitional Readers in Grades K–5*. 2nd ed. Portland, ME: Stenhouse.

Taberski, Sharon. 2000. *On Solid Ground: Strategies for Teaching Reading, K–3*. Portsmouth, NH: Heinemann.

Tharp, Roland G., and Ronald Gallimore. 1988. *Rousing Minds to Life*. New York: Cambridge University Press.

Thompson, Terry. 2008. *Adventures in Graphica: Using Comics and Graphic Novels to Teach Comprehension, 2–6*. Portland, ME: Stenhouse.

Tovani, Cris. 2000. I *Read It, but I Don't Get It: Comprehension Strategies for Adolescent Readers*. Portland, ME: Stenhouse.

———. 2004. *Do I Really Have to Teach Reading? Content Comprehension, Grades 6–12*. Portland, ME: Stenhouse.

Vygotsky, Lev. 1978. *Mind in Society: The Development of Higher Psychological Processes*. Ed. and Trans. M. Cole, V. John-Steiner, S. Scribner, and E. Souberman. Cambridge, MA: Harvard University Press.

———.1986. *Thought and Language*. Rev. ed. Cambridge, MA: MIT Press.

Watson, Marilyn, and Laura Ecken. 2003. *Learning to Trust: Transforming Difficult Elementary Classrooms Through Developmental Discipline*. San Franciso, CA: Jossey-Bass.

What Works Clearinghouse. 2008. "Intervention: Reading Recovery." U.S. Department of Education. http://ies.ed.gov/ncee/wwc/reports/beginning_reading/reading_recovery/.

Wood, David J. 1998. *How Children Think and Learn*. Oxford, United Kingdom: Wiley-Blackwell.

Yokota, Junko. 2002. Quoted on Web site "Windows and Mirrors: Exploring the World of Children's Books Through Genres." http://webinstituteforteachers.org/~anitajhill/2003/main.htm.

INDEX